The Transformation *of the* Christian Right in the 1980s

Matthew C. Moen

The Transformation of the Christian Right in the 1980s

Matthew C. Moen

The University of Alabama Press
Tuscaloosa

Manufactured in the United States of America

Paperback printing 2008

designed by Paula C. Dennis

∞
The paper on which this book is printed meets the minimum requirements of American National Standard for Information Science—Permanence of Paper for Printed Library Materials, ANSI Z39.48-1984.

Library of Congress Cataloging-in-Publication Data

Moen, Matthew C., 1958-
The transformation of the Christian Right in the 1980s / Matthew C. Moen.
p. cm.
Includes bibliographical references and index.
ISBN 978-0-8173-5532-6 (pbk. : alk. paper)
1. Christianity and politics—History—20th century. 2. Christians—United States—Political activity. 3. Fundamentalism—History—20th century. 4. Conservatism—United States—History—20th century. 5. United States—Politics and government—1977-1981. 6. United States—Politics and government—1981-1989. I. Title.
BR115.P7M5444 1992
322'.i'097309048—dc20 91-31447

To my wife Donna
with love

Contents

Tables and Figures

Preface

This study is part of a continuing interest in conservative religious "pressure groups" that began while I was an undergraduate student at Augustana College in Sioux Falls, South Dakota, observing the Christian Right's 1980 campaign to unseat liberal Senator George McGovern. The vitriolic nature of that campaign on both sides sparked an interest that was fed by subsequent journalistic and scholarly assessments of the Christian Right's prospects.

In 1984 I had an opportunity to spend time on Capitol Hill, and I interviewed people who were either advancing or combatting the Christian Right's agenda there. The culmination of that research was *The Christian Right and Congress* (1989), which examined the tactics and successes of conservative religious interest groups on Capitol Hill. This study draws from that book but is not simply a continuation; its principal objective is to chronicle and assess the panoply of changes that occurred in the Christian Right during the 1980s. Until recently, the movement's infancy precluded meaningful discussion of changes over time.

This book provides a political scientist's best assessment of the transformation of the Christian Right in the 1980s; it is not intended as a statement about either the relative merits of conservative Christianity or the desirability of religious conservatives' influence in American politics. Its principal audience is the scholar who is interested in the Christian Right's persistence and evolution; however, its normative, historical nature puts its contents within the reach of a wide readership.

The most pleasant part of an author's task is thanking those people who contributed to the book. In that regard, each of the individuals interviewed for this volume donated time and shared incisive thoughts. The Faculty Research Funds Committee of the University of Maine provided financial support to conduct personal interviews; the dean of the College of Social and Behavioral Sciences, Julia Watkins, provided release time to work on the manuscript. June Kittridge efficiently typed the chapters. Mary Alice Johnson, an exceptionally talented undergraduate student, provided valuable research assistance over many months.

The manuscript benefited from the careful scrutiny of two perspicacious reviewers, Anson Shupe and Paul Gardner, whose thoughtful comments enhanced the quality of the final product. Naturally, they are absolved for the book's interpretations or any shortcomings. The manuscript also benefited from the wider community of scholars, whose research over the years has contributed so much to my own understanding of the Christian Right.

For its part, The University of Alabama Press did another first-rate job. This is my second book published by the press, and I have been fortunate to work with and learn from its people. Special thanks go to Press Director Malcolm MacDonald, who expressed interest in the project when it was only a six-page outline.

On a personal note, my wife Donna and my parents, Kenneth and Verona Moen, provide the constant support and encouragement that make such projects possible. In a different vein, about the time that this manuscript was sent to the Press for review, my office neighbor and friend, Barrie E. Blunt, was diagnosed with an illness that shortly thereafter took his life. He loved scholarship and life, and North Stevens Hall is not the same without him. Barrie never had the chance to read this book, but he knew about it, and he will be in my thoughts whenever I pick it up.

The Transformation of the Christian Right

1

The Metamorphosis

The primary objective of this book is to chronicle and evaluate the transformation of the Christian Right. The basic parameters of the inquiry are the years 1979 through 1989, a period that constitutes the first decade of the contemporary Christian Right's existence.

Implicit in this objective is the assumption that the Christian Right has indeed evolved and changed. A leading figure in the movement believed so, saying in an interview conducted in 1989: "I am still analyzing the changes which have occurred."[1] This volume offers the same assessment, arguing that the Christian Right has changed in salient and significant ways related to its structure, strategy, rhetoric, and leadership. Ensuing chapters will document those changes. In due course, distinctions will be drawn among the individuals and organizations composing the Christian Right, so that precision is added to discussions of how the movement has changed.

The central thesis underpinning this volume is that the Christian Right has gradually become more politically sophisticated. An auxiliary theme is that the movement has grown more secular in character. Because both of those themes will surface throughout the book, some explication is necessary at the outset.[2]

Circa 1979, the Christian Right became a recognizable political player, with the incorporation of several organizations, the most conspicuous of which was the Moral Majority. Shortly after their formal incorporation, those organizations began promoting a philosophy of traditional morality, free enterprise, and "peace through strength." Those philosophic roots translated into support for such policies as abortion restrictions, the budget and tax cuts of the Reagan administration, and aid to the Contra rebels fighting in Nicaragua.

Almost from the outset, it was evident that the leaders of the Christian Right generally lacked strong political skills. Their lack of political adroitness was symbolized by the elevation of a recent college graduate to head the Washington, D.C., office of the Moral Majority, and it was manifested in the course of battles over school prayer and abortion on Capitol Hill, during which the Christian Right often failed to present its case effectively or efficiently. The lack of sophistication was apparent to some of the more astute leaders of the Christian Right, reflected in this 1984 interviewee comment: "There is no question that in time the level of political sophistication will increase, but in the meantime, let me say there is still room for improvement."[3]

The dearth of political skill, which was so apparent in the Christian Right's early years, stemmed from a lack of political experience. Scholars have documented the political abstinence of evangelical and fundamentalist Christians for much of the twentieth century, noting that beliefs in dispensational theology (that people should focus on their spiritual afterlife rather than attempt to redeem human institutions) retarded an active political role.[4] Then too, the famous Scopes trial of 1925, which pitched conservative Christian beliefs in creationism against scientific evidence of evolution, caused evangelicals and fundamentalists to seek refuge in their spirituality. According to John H. Simpson, it was not the inability of conservative Christians to compete on a theological playing field that made them eschew politics for decades: "Rather it was the denouement of the so-called 'monkey trial' in 1925 that fixed an image of fundamentalism as unbending, irrational, and uncivil in doctrine and practice, a movement fit only to be cast aside in the name of science, progress, and civilization."[5] The political abstinence of religious conservatives, in the wake of the Scopes trial, made their awakening in the late 1970s all the more compelling. As Kenneth D. Wald noted: "Of all the shifts and surprises in contemporary political life, perhaps none was so wholly unexpected as the political resurgence of evangelical Protestantism in the 1970s."[6]

The infusion of conservative Christians into politics en masse gave the movement's early leaders the opportunity to sharpen their political skills over time and provided a large pool of interested people, out of which a small cadre of politically adroit leaders could emerge. Eventually, the leadership of the Christian Right would become more sophisticated, an assessment that was confirmed in interviews conducted in the post-Reagan era. Gary Jarmin, one of the movement's prominent figures during the 1980s, flatly stated in 1989: "The sophistication in the Christian Right has clearly increased," an assertion he supported with an example: "I participated in a meeting at the White House the other day on a child care bill [the "ABC" bill]. As I looked around, there were twenty to twenty-five quality people with talent and experience there who are part of the [conservative Christian] movement. That was not the case even four or five years ago."[7] Laurie Tryfiates, field director of Concerned Women for America, a major Christian-Right group, echoed Jarmin's comments: "The conservative Christian movement is far more sophisticated [in 1989] than it was in the 1970s."[8] Even a representative of the "loyal opposition" to the Christian Right provided a similar assessment. Joseph Conn, director of communications for Americans United for the Separation of Church and State, explained: "The Christian Right went through a rather inarticulate phase of existence in its early days. . . . Over time [though], the old guard of the movement has mostly disappeared from the scene. Those early people were strongly motivated by fundamentalist religion, but were not particularly sophisticated in politics. . . . They gradually dropped out or were moved to the sidelines, leaving the political arena to the somewhat less narrowly sectarian, but more sophisticated people."[9]

One of the recurring themes of this volume is that the Christian Right gradually became a more sophisticated political player. It did so by virtue of its early leaders gaining some experience in politics, and by the infusion of politically adept newcomers to supplement (or supplant) the "old guard." Evidence supporting the proposition of increased sophistication will be presented in subsequent chapters. Before leaving this theme, though, two refinements to it are in order. First, the growth of political sophistication proceeded imperfectly. To use a pedestrian metaphor, for every two steps the Christian Right's leaders took forward toward sophistication, they took one step backward. Second, the increase in political adroitness occurred among the elite leadership rather than among the mass followers. Gary Bauer, president of the Family Research Council, a relatively recent Christian-Right organization, drew such an elite/mass distinction in an interview, noting that certain skills "present at the leadership level" were imperfectly expressed "in the rank and file."[10] Both of those refinements to the sophistication thesis will receive attention in subsequent chapters.

The auxiliary theme of this book is that the Christian Right has become more secular in character. The word "secular," of course, connotes nonreligious, or worldly. The argument here is not that the people composing the Christian Right, either at the elite or mass level, personally became secularized. There is no evidence available to support that proposition, and even if there were, it would be inappropriate to speculate on individual religious commitment. Christian Voice's "moral report cards" used to say that "only God can judge what is truly in the heart of a man." Accepting that premise, there will be no attempt to assess individuals' spirituality in this volume.

The argument regarding secularization is twofold. First, as part of their growing political sophistication, Christian-Right leaders began incorporating the *trappings* of secularism, dropping religious references from their organizational titles and promotional literature, and soliciting the support of secular organizations sharing their political agenda. Second, the movement's leaders began deliberately sacrificing their religious principles from time to time, in pursuit of secular political objectives. Put another way, they periodically put temporal political affairs ahead of religious beliefs; by doing so, they mimicked the unethical behavior often exhibited in the secular political world and more commonly associated with the secular than the religious realm. Their moral lapses did not make them secular people, only imperfect people, like everyone else. Their ethical lapses were de facto evidence of secularization, though, in the sense that religious people conveniently overlooked their beliefs when doing so helped achieve secular political goals.

The argument that the Christian Right's leaders became secularized in the manner described assumes the existence of strong religious motivations and principles from the outset, which were then temporarily sacrificed. Was that the case? Was the Christian Right anchored in religious values at the outset? Available evidence suggests so. Recall the perspicacious comment of Joseph Conn, cited earlier, that the early leaders were low on sophistication but "strongly motivated by fundamentalist religion." Along the same lines, a legislative director of one of the Christian-Right groups stated in a 1984 interview that his group had always been "a Christian organization, with a key spiritual component and a primary motivation that is Christian oriented." The fact that representatives of both the opposition and the Christian Right agreed on the point lends credence to it. Archival evidence drawn from such early groups as Christian Voice and Moral Majority offers further proof of strong religious roots; one scholar even organized an early book on the Christian Right around the theme of religious moralism.[11] Further evidence is discussed in the next chapter, which covers the early Christian-Right groups.

In short, the argument is that the Christian Right's leaders incorporated the trappings of secularism as a political ploy and deliberately downplayed their religious principles when doing so advanced secular political goals. These twin propositions will be revisited in subsequent chapters.

The nature of the social scientific enterprise is such that hypotheses fit reality only imperfectly. After they are offered and tested, in the words of empiricists, there is still "unexplained variation." Although the sophistication/secularization themes offered in this volume explain much of what has occurred with the Christian Right over time, they do not capture the totality of what has transpired. As these themes are revisited throughout this book, it will be necessary to draw distinctions among the individuals and the organizations composing the Christian Right, since some exhibited more sophistication and/or secularization than others. It would be inappropriate to advance either of these themes sans such distinctions.

Sources

The information for this book is derived from secondary and original sources. The secondary sources include studies done by scholars, public opinion polls, data from statistical abstracts, data from the 1988 Republican primary contests, and journalistic descriptions of the activities of the Christian Right. Another source, somewhat more original in character, is the materials of such organizations as the American Freedom Coalition, the Family Research Council, and Concerned Women for America. They were gathered during visits to the Washington, D.C., offices of those groups in the summer of 1989.

The original data for the book comes from personal interviews with people who have been involved with the Christian Right and its political agenda. Two separate sets of interviews were done in Washington, D.C., about five years apart. The first set, consisting of thirty-three interviews, was done in 1984 with the legislative directors of the National Christian Action Coalition, the Moral Majority, and Christian Voice; the White House liaison to the conservative religious community; the legislative counsel of the American Civil Liberties Union; lobbyists for People for the

American Way, the Lutheran Church, and the Baptist Joint Committee on Public Affairs; members of Congress, such as Senator David Boren, Representative Philip Crane, Representative Henry Hyde, and Representative Bob Edgar; and, congressional staff members in the offices of Senator Jesse Helms and Senator Don Nickles, as well as on the subcommittees of the House and Senate judiciary committees. Together, those interviews yielded about two hundred single-spaced pages of transcripts. Those interviews already have been and will continue to be cited in this volume, but the interviewees' comments are reported anonymously, in deference to the fact that a number of years have passed. It is unfair to attribute comments made in 1984 in a book focused on change over the course of the 1980s. Attribution in that context reduces interviewees to seers and soothsayers, whose measure of accomplishment then rests upon their ability for prognostication.

The second set, consisting of eight interviews, was completed in 1989. Included in that set were the following people: Gary Bauer, president, Family Research Council; John Buchanan, chairman of the board, People for the American Way; Joseph Conn, communications director, Americans United for the Separation of Church and State; Gary Jarmin, legislative director, American Freedom Coalition; Colleen Kiko, minority counsel, House Judiciary Subcommittee on Civil and Constitutional Rights; Howard Phillips, chairman, Conservative Caucus; Laurie Tryfiates, field director, Concerned Women for America; Michael Schwartz, social policy specialist, Free Congress Foundation. Together, those interviews comprised about forty single-spaced pages of typed transcripts. Since they were completed in the post-Reagan era, and focused on the theme of this book, their specific citation is far more appropriate. Hence, the comments of those interviewees are attributed, except in the few instances where they specifically requested that material be kept "off the record."

The disparity in size between the two sets of interviews was driven by two factors. First, the 1984 interviews were conducted while this author was working on Capitol Hill and able to leave work to complete them at the interviewee's convenience. In contrast, all of the 1989 interviews (except one) were done in ten days. Second, the 1984 interviews were broader in scope, covering variously the rise of the Christian Right, its attempts to gain access to the congressional agenda, and its role in specific legislative fights in Reagan's first term. In contrast, the 1989 interviews were focused specifically on the ways in which the Christian Right was transformed over time. The more narrowly drawn topic reduced the need for voluminousness.

Taken together, the two sets of interviews provide a reasonable means of assessing and interpreting changes in the Christian Right over time. Accordingly, the remarks of interviewees are incorporated freely throughout the remainder of the book.

Why Study the Transformation?

The Christian Right was a prominent performer on the political stage of the 1980s. One of its major accomplishments was to register hundreds of thousands, perhaps millions, of new voters. The estimated number of registrants varies widely. The Reverend Jerry Falwell asserted that the Moral Majority alone, registered about two million voters in 1980.[12] Kenneth D. Wald gathered materials from journalistic sources, including the Associated Press, which placed the number of new registrants somewhere between 200,000 and 3,000,000 as of 1984.[13] Gary Jarmin stated in a 1989 interview: "According to estimates by others, we have registered about 8.2 million voters since 1980."[14] That estimate translates into a continuation of Falwell's claim about the 1980 effort, with roughly 2,000,000 being registered in each two-year election cycle. Most observers would consider it inflated.

The variance in the estimates of new registrants testifies to the real difficulty of assessing voter registration campaigns. Scholars are not well positioned to provide assessments of such campaigns; indeed, they find it problematic to measure the more verifiable activity of evangelical and fundamentalist voting behavior, due to operationalizations employing both doctrinal and denominational definitions *of evangelical* and *fundamentalist.*[15] Journalists are better positioned to provide assessments of voter registration drives, but as the figures collected by Wald reveal, there is little consensus among them, with estimates ranging from 200,000 to a figure fully fifteen times higher.[16] The figures are conjecture; journalists essentially relate the inflated claims of Christian-Right leaders, mixed with a healthy dose of skepticism.

Whatever the ultimate results, one thing is certain: the Christian Right worked assiduously in the 1980s to register new voters. A 1984 interviewee, once linked to Moral Majority, echoed Falwell's claim about the importance of the registration effort in 1980: "The only real substantive accomplishment of Moral Majority in 1980 was Jerry Falwell's registration of new voters, accomplished in large part through the [I Love America] rallies held at state capitals." Along similar lines, Christian Voice created a subdivision, entitled "Christians for Reagan," which focused on voter registration in 1980.[17] The American Coalition for Traditional Values performed a voter registration role for the Reagan campaign in 1984.[18] Thus, the combined voter registration efforts of the Christian Right groups were quite impressive in their scope, regardless of whether they resulted in registration of only hundreds of thousands of voters, rather than millions.

A second accomplishment of the Christian Right was to infiltrate the Republican Party. In 1984, a legislative director of one of the Christian-Right groups lamented the lack of attention to the Republicans: "Prominent wealthy Christians keep giving money to Falwell and Robertson rather than the Republican party, and they should realize they will not get appointments for people [to the Reagan administration] by doing that. In order to exert real influence, we need to get involved in the political process from the precinct to the presidency." In the years following that comment, the Christian Right began systematically penetrating the Republican party, though not in any conspiratorial sense. Rather, it simply began recruiting people at the local level to participate in Republican party politics.

The efforts to infiltrate the Republican party paid off. By 1986, the Christian Right had established a strong presence in a host of especially southern and midwestern states.[19] All of those inroads were realized by what Gurwitt described as "an increasingly organized and politically sophisticated network of conservative evangelical Christians."[20]

By the time that Pat Robertson launched his 1988 presidential campaign, a network of activists was already in place. As Joseph Conn aptly noted in a 1989 interview: "The big story [of recent years] is Pat Robertson being able to place people in state and local posts in the Republican Party."[21] The grass-roots activities of the Robertson campaign, and of the Christian Right generally, will be covered in greater detail in subsequent chapters. Here, it is sufficient to note that those activities were ample enough to make the Christian Right a prominent political player.

A third accomplishment of the Christian Right was to shape the political agenda. This author's earlier book (*The Christian Right and Congress*) focused on the legislative influence of the Christian Right and presented its agenda-setting successes during the Reagan years.[22] It argued that the

Christian Right took "numerous issues that were lying virtually dormant on the agenda, redefined and enlarged their appeal, and then placed them on both the systematic and the congressional agendas."[23] Daniel Hofrenning implicitly confirmed that finding, when he discovered that virtually all religious lobbyists (including those of the Christian Right) focused their attention and resources on shaping the political agenda. Marshaling both qualitative and quantitative evidence, he asserted: "The broader picture that emerges [from this study] is that religious groups are more oriented toward changing the scope and bias of the pressure system. In doing this, they are seeking to change the political agenda."[24]

A narrowly drawn but good example of altering the political agenda, according to Gary Jarmin, was the increased focus on ethics in politics. In response to a question about whether the Christian Right had injected morality back into politics, Jarmin replied: "I think so. Other groups like Common Cause are pushing for personal morality/ethics for members of Congress at this point. We helped begin that focus, though [by focusing on the immorality of certain public officials]."[25] Whether the Christian Right actually initiated the focus on ethics, or merely contributed to it, might be disputed. Regardless, ethics were "front and center" in the late 1980s, causing resignations and investigations, in the House of Representatives alone, of Speaker Jim Wright, Majority Whip Tony Coelho, and Representatives Barney Frank, Newt Gingrich, Gus Savage, and Donald Lukens. Quite clearly, ethics rose to prominence on the public and legislative agendas; without question, the Christian Right played some part in that rise.

The ability of the Christian Right to register voters, to penetrate the grass roots, and to shape the narrower congressional and broader public agendas all show that it has been an important force in American politics, worth studying both generally and in terms of its transformation over time. After all, the study of change permits a number of intriguing questions to be addressed: How have changes in the movement altered its organizational and leadership structures? Has the Christian Right lost its ability to set the political agenda? What new strategies, if any, have leaders pursued over time? Have they framed issues in the same terms at the end of the 1980s as they did at the beginning of the decade? On balance, is the Christian Right better positioned in American politics today than it was when it first arose in the late 1970s? Those questions are indicative of the type that this volume addresses.

A second reason for studying the transformation of the Christian Right, more utilitarian in nature, is that scholars have not done so. Scholars have carefully documented the manner in which the Christian Right has influenced politics, through studies of its clout in the 1980, 1984, and 1988 elections, its lobbying efforts on Capitol Hill, its use of political action committees, its influence with the Reagan administration, and its attempts to recruit candidates to run for public office.[26] They have not yet examined the manner in which the Christian Right itself has been transformed by a full decade of political activism. That neglect is unfortunate, because it results in a skewed understanding of the relationship between the Christian Right and the political world. Scholars have fleshed out answers to this question: How has the Christian Right affected politics? They have not provided answers to the question this volume addresses: how has politics changed the Christian Right? Surely it deserves an answer.

A third reason for studying the transformation of the Christian Right is that it is a propitious time to do so, in the wake of the Reverend Pat Robertson's unsuccessful bid for the 1988 Republican presidential nomination and of the Reverend Jerry Falwell's decision, in June 1989, to close the Moral Majority.[27] According to Walter Barbee, chairman of Virginians for Family Values, a group which focuses on sex-education programs in local schools and on governmental roles in child care: "The Falwell-Robertson phenomenon was the first wave [of Christian Right activism]. The second wave is forming."[28] That assessment suggests that this book's focus on change and transformation has merit. More important, it points out the need to document such change, before a "second wave" of activism obscures understanding of the first wave.

Outline of This Book

The remainder of this volume focuses on changes in the Christian Right over time, with an eye toward increased sophistication and secularization. Chapters 2 through 4, which comprise Part I, focus primarily on issues of organizational change. Specifically, chapter 2 concentrates on the national, direct-mail lobbies launched in the late 1970s. It examines the nature of those organizations and the reasons behind their eventual stagnation. It also draws lessons from the pattern of decline that they collectively exhibited. An integral part of that discussion is the lack of political skill that was manifested in the early organizations and contributed to their demise.

Chapter 3 is a continuation of the discussion, tackling the organizations that were launched in the 1980s and suggesting that their mission differed from that of the earlier groups. This chapter is heavily descriptive, containing brief discussions of the groups that arose and folded during the decade and more extensive discussions of those that arose then and remained active into the 1990s. Many of the key leaders of the contemporary Christian Right are discussed en route.

Chapter 4 focuses on the impact of rapid organizational change on the political power of the Christian Right. It opens with a discussion of the reasons that a relatively large number of groups were launched, proceeds with a treatment of overlapping elite membership in them, and then documents the importance of free publicity to organizational turnover. From there, it examines the downside of rapid organizational change, particularly as it relates to maintenance of an active political agenda. The chapter closes with a retrospective look at periods of Christian-Right activism in the 1980s.

Part II of the book focuses on strategic changes. Chapter 5 documents how the Christian Right switched its strategic focal point over time. It opens with a chronicling of the reasons why the Christian Right initially channeled its resources into legislative struggles, before moving to a discussion of how the movement fared on Capitol Hill over the course of the Reagan presidency. This chapter also provides an extensive treatment of the Christian Right's efforts "off the Hill"—namely its attempts to infiltrate the bureaucracy, exploit the courts, and organize followers at the grass roots. Data on turnover in the executive and judicial branches is presented, as well as a look at the Robertson campaign, the most striking manifestation of grass-roots activism.

Chapter 6 focuses on the use of rhetoric in the movement. It begins with a discussion of the strong moral overtones present in the movement initially and explains how those overtones were injurious to its political goals. The chapter then examines the incorporation of liberal rhetoric, showing how issues were recast and reformulated in an attempt to build a broader base of support for them. The chapter closes with a discussion of whether the apparent moderation of the Christian Right will be self-fulfilling.

Part III of the book examines the consequences of the transformation of the Christian Right. Chapter 7 focuses on the relationship of distinctiveness to political influence, opening with a discussion of the Christian Right's successes, in conjunction with its distinctive character; it then examines the erosion of that unique character, arguing it undermines one of the Christian Right's primary sources of political power. Chapter 8 revisits the sophistication and secularization themes, projecting the path the Christian Right will follow in the years ahead.

Part I.

Organizational Change

2

The Kaleidoscopic Structure

Throughout 1979, a collection of conservative groups tried to besmirch the reputation of Senator George McGovern by purchasing ads in the electronic and print media in his home state with the theme, "George McGovern doesn't represent South Dakota." The ads were designed to drive up his "negatives" in public opinion polls heading into 1980, when the senator would be running for a fourth term. The ads produced the desired effect. A poll conducted in the fall of 1979 encouraged incumbent House Republican Jim Abdnor to challenge the senior senator because of his vulnerability.[1]

In an effort to breathe life back into a flagging campaign, the campaign staff of Senator McGovern produced and released a lengthy document in July 1980 that assailed conservative groups for "negative campaigning." The document was a compilation of local and national news stories, reprints of direct-mail letters of conservative groups, and copies of leaflets being distributed on Sunday mornings at church parking lots on the abortion issue. The strategy behind the issuance of the document was to make the conservative groups' tactics, rather than the senator, the issue in the campaign. It was an attempt to alter what William H. Riker has dubbed the "heresthetic," meaning the environment within which people form their opinions.[2]

An integral element of the campaign document issued was the chronicling of the "interlocking directorate" of conservative elite leaders, implying that a conservative conspiracy was afoot, as evidenced in the fact that the leaders "serve on one another's governing bodies, trade contributions of money and skill, and support each other's special interests in a variety of ways."[3] The web of relationships did not merely exist, but was a plot.

Over time, liberals became less likely to interpret the Christian Right conspiratorially, but their fundamental perception that it was driven by an "interlocking directorate" did not change. In 1984, a lobbyist who often opposed the Christian Right's agenda analogized that its organizational structure was like a child's kaleidoscope. He reasoned that in both the Christian Right's organizational structure and the kaleidoscope, the constituent elements were locked in place; it was simply a matter of rearranging them to obtain a new look. He remarked, somewhat contemptuously: "They [Christian-Right leaders] organize and reorganize their groups, but maintain the same individuals in the various organizations." It was the same sentiment expressed by the McGovern campaign, less the conspiratorial element.

The kaleidoscope analogy was apt during the Christian Right's first decade. The same people were often involved in the creation of new organizations, and they served on one another's leadership boards. As the liberal opposition eventually came to understand, however, those relationships were fairly natural. Indeed, it would have been perplexing for religiously motivated people, who shared very similar views about the challenges facing American society, not to work closely together. For liberals to discover the interlocking web of relationships, in a system where coalition politics is an integral part of success, must have struck conservative elites as having a firm grasp of the obvious, since one of their stated goals was the establishment of such a network.[4]

This chapter focuses on the four major Christian-Right groups launched in the late-1970s, which opened offices in the nation's capital. They initiated the kaleidoscopic arrangement recognized later by liberals. The chapter is divided into three parts. The first part provides an overview of the early organizations, while the second identifies their common characteristics and explains their shared fortune. The third part draws some brief lessons from the experiences of the early groups, both for the Christian Right and for the larger universe of American interest groups.

The Early Players

The first four major organizations of the Christian Right were the National Christian Action Coalition, the Religious Roundtable, Christian

Voice, and Moral Majority. They converged on several key points. For one thing, they were all formally incorporated within twelve months of one another, beginning in December 1978. Then too, they all promptly opened Washington, D.C., offices, to lobby on Capitol Hill. As one interviewee remarked retrospectively in 1984: "The Christian Right here in Washington, D.C., consists of a set of well-funded political lobbying offices." Yet a third point of convergence was a shared agenda of traditional values, conventional morality, and "peace through strength." Finally, several of the groups were headed by prominent fundamentalists, who were making their initial forays into politics.

To point out that the early organizations of the Christian Right were closely affiliated is not the same as saying that they always worked in concert. The various groups sometimes even emphasized different political activities. Christian Voice, for instance, concentrated its resources on lobbying, because it had a proven and accomplished lobbyist in Gary Jarmin. In contrast, the Roundtable focused more on recruiting local ministers into politics, a task of salesmanship that was consistent with leader Ed McAteer's background over the past twenty years, as a salesman for the Colgate-Palmolive company. Even so, the origin, lobbying emphasis, and political objectives of the early organizations revealed a close affiliation. In metaphoric terms, they were all pieces of the same puzzle.

The first of the four groups organized was the National Christian Action Coalition (NCAC), in December 1978. It was launched by Bob Billings, in response to the Internal Revenue Service's attempts to revoke the tax-exempt status of schools it believed were racially discriminatory. That causative agent was summarized by Gary Jarmin in an interview: "What set the movement off was the attempt of the IRS to institute quotas for private Christian schools, which if they were not met, would result in the loss of tax-exempt status."[5] Whether quotas were involved is a matter of dispute, but what is indisputable was the importance of the issue to the Christian Right.

The National Christian Action Coalition was led by Billings for about one year (though he had run its predecessor as well, formed in 1977, called Christian School Action.) In 1980, he quit to conduct a fundamentalist outreach program for the Reagan campaign, bequeathing the NCAC to his son Bill. Throughout its existence, the NCAC produced a newsletter on a subscription basis for fundamentalist churches, which apprised them of any pending congressional legislation that might affect their private-school operations. Lacking a "big name" minister, though, the NCAC soon receded from the limelight. Bill Billings noted, as far back as 1980, that once Falwell became involved in the movement: "they [Moral Majority] went up front and we kind of went into the background."[6] By 1984, the NCAC consisted only of Bill and one part-time assistant; according to an interviewee at the time, it was on a "missionary budget." Unable to keep it alive, Billings shut down the organization in 1985 and returned to his former occupation as a school administrator.

The Religious Roundtable was the brainchild of New-Right operatives, plus Ed McAteer. It was formed primarily to recruit fundamentalist ministers into politics, with the expectation that they would bring their congregations with them. McAteer had deep roots in the Southern Baptist Convention and made it his primary recruiting ground. To facilitate his work, he wooed and promptly appointed the Reverend James Robison of Fort Worth, Texas, as the Roundtable's vice-president; Robison was amenable, having recently clashed with the Federal Communications Commission over his right to broadcast an anti–gay-rights program.

In the summer and early fall of 1980, McAteer personally conducted a series of consciousness-raising and training sessions for conservative religious leaders. Those sessions attracted an estimated twenty thousand ministers.[7] Concurrently, the Reverend Robison began organizing a mass rally in Dallas, called the National Affairs Briefing. It vaulted the Roundtable specifically, and the Christian Right generally, into the public eye, when some sixty speakers (including Republican presidential nominee Ronald Reagan) addressed some fifteen thousand assembled conservatives. The rather strident language used by some of the speakers, though, and the specter of anti-Semitism expressed at the rally, badly damaged the Roundtable's reputation.[8] McAteer was forced to close down his lobbying operation in Washington shortly after it was opened. Subsequently, he returned to his hometown of Memphis, where he kept the Roundtable alive as a platform for conservative political pronouncements. Following McAteer's unsuccessful bid for a U.S. Senate seat in 1984, however, the Roundtable lapsed into virtual oblivion.

Despite the diminished status of the Roundtable, McAteer has stayed active. Recently, he led opposition to the recasting of the social agenda in terms of "cultural conservatism," a phrase coined by New-Right operative Paul Weyrich.[9] It has distinctly secular connotations, which its progenitor clearly hopes will lend itself to alliances of secular and religious conservatives. The attempt to recast the concerns of the Christian Right in secular language did not sit well with McAteer. As Joseph Conn pointed out in a 1989 interview: "Paul Weyrich, a New-Right activist who played a key role in bringing fundamentalists into politics, has tried to recast the New-Right agenda and build broader support for it, by speaking about the concept of cultural conservatism. By that, he means conservative political principles that Christians, Jews, and even atheists can share without giving up their theological differences. Ed McAteer, the Baptist who helped organize the Christian Right, circulated a letter saying that he was not involved in this pursuit of cultural conservatism, and suggested that it was a sellout of sorts because it did not explicitly cite God and the Judeo-Christian ethic as its foundation."[10] McAteer is still around, then, but the Roundtable is essentially a letterhead organization that serves his need for a platform.

The third organization, of the initial set of groups, was Christian Voice. It was launched by the Reverend Robert Grant and the Reverend Richard Zone, who used it as a vehicle for opposing a gay-rights measure in California. Christian Voice leapt to national prominence when it released a "moral approval rating" of members of Congress, which was based on a small sampling of issues. The formation of a subsidiary division known as "Christians for Reagan," and an advertising campaign implying that President Carter approved of homosexual lifestyles, resulted in further notoriety.[11]

The controversy engendered by the 1980 electoral activities led to a plethora of changes at Christian Voice. A number of its congressional advisory members resigned. Zone dropped out, and the group retreated from its position on rating members of Congress, saying that it did not mean to imply that it was judging personal character. Following that shake-up, the organization stabilized and routinized its operations. Much of Christian Voice's attention was then focused on lobbying the Congress for a school-prayer constitutional amendment.[12] Its literature's claim to have "directed the 1983–1984 battle to return prayer to public schools" was not especially hyperbolic.[13] Its role in this battle encapsulated the activity of the organization in Reagan's first term.

As Reagan's second term began, in the wake of the defeat of a school-prayer amendment, Christian Voice's leaders mostly suspended active lobbying. In its place, they concentrated almost exclusively on printing campaign literature and distributing "report cards" (less the word "moral") at election time; they claimed distribution of thirty million report cards by the end of the 1986 election cycle.[14]

After the 1986 election, Christian Voice's top leaders decided to commission a poll that profiled their constituency, as a means of deciding what course of political action to pursue. Gary Jarmin explained in an interview:

> Following the 1986 election, Christian Voice had a poll conducted nationwide. We filtered out a group that was conservative, religious, and registered to vote. About 9% of that group was black. We asked them extensive questions about issues and politics. Once we did the crosstabs, we found that about 46% of our sample was Republican and about 54% was Democrat or Independents. About two-thirds of the group was Protestant and about another third Catholic or some more minor religions. In any case, we found that there was a good deal of agreement among these people without respect to party affiliation, religion, or color. What we concluded was that the party structure artificially divided people.[15]

Acting on that conclusion, the leadership of Christian Voice created a new organization the ensuing year (the American Freedom Coalition, discussed in the next chapter). The embarkment of the leadership to form a new group caused Christian Voice to lapse into moribundity. The changed atmosphere was evident in a visit to the headquarters of Christian Voice in 1989. Its space in the Heritage Foundation building was shared with Jar-Mon consultants, and its literature was of 1988 vintage, with no reference to any ongoing or future activity.[16] Jarmin acknowledged the diminished role for Christian Voice, saying simply that it would "still serve as a door opener to churches and continue to teach people how to participate in politics" but that the American Freedom Coalition would be the vehicle for Christian Voice's leadership outside the church.[17] Christian Voice, in the post-Reagan era, has been reduced to a "letterhead" organization that periodically issues campaign literature.

The fourth organization formed, which experienced its heyday in the first Reagan term, was the bellwether of the Christian Right—the Moral Majority. It was clearly the most salient, and therefore possibly the most important, organization of the movement in the Reagan era. Pollsters queried the public about the organization and its leader, Reverend Jerry Falwell; prominent politicians courted or disparaged it for electoral advantage; enterprising capitalists generated bumper stickers asserting that "the Moral Majority is neither." According to prominent theologian Richard John Neuhaus, the Moral Majority was "the single most visible institutional expression" of the claims of religious conservatives.[18]

The Moral Majority was originated by a variety of New-Right and religious conservatives, and cleverly named by Paul Weyrich. Its constituency grew out of Falwell's series of "I Love America" rallies, held primarily during 1979; it quickly mushroomed into a prominent national organization. By November 1980, in the wake of the presidential election, it had attained a name recognition rate of 40 percent, which it boosted to 55 percent the next year.[19] Reliable membership estimates to accompany the name recognition that Moral Majority achieved have proven difficult to obtain, evidenced by the fact that they have ranged from several hundred thousand to several million.[20]

Throughout Reagan's first term of office, the Moral Majority expended most of its political capital lobbying the Congress on the social issues. Those lobbying efforts, which culminated in 1984, when the Moral Majority raised and spent $11 million, met with decidedly mixed success: the social issues were placed on the congressional agenda and some victories were achieved, but the key roll-call votes on the major objectives were lost.[21] In the process, the Moral Majority undercut its position on Capitol Hill. Its success reduced the need to lobby Congress for further changes in public policy; its failures, abetted by a tendency to present its case inefficiently and ineffectively at times, left its reputation in tatters.[22] The combination of success and failure, when coupled with lobbying personnel who were exhausted and constituents who had been tapped out financially, contributed to the demise of the organization.

Sensing that the Moral Majority could not continue to exist by itself, in 1986 Falwell collapsed it into the Liberty Federation. The Federation was designed to engulf Moral Majority, adopting its platform of domestic social issues, but also going beyond that point, into international issues. As Falwell put it at the press conference announcing the reorganization: "We want to continue to be the standard bearer for traditional American values. But it's time to broaden our horizons as well."[23] The avowed outreach was perplexing, since for many years the Moral Majority had staked out positions on such international issues as South African sanctions, aid to the Contras, and military aid to Israel. In fact, an interviewee closely connected with Moral Majority remarked in 1984 that it addressed "an entire range of concerns in the social justice, defense, and economic realms . . . [handling] just as many issues as it is capable of handling." The reason for the structural reorganization professed by Falwell made little sense against that backdrop, leading one to surmise that it was a smokescreen to nix a dwindling organization.

In November 1987, following about a year of limbo for Moral Majority and a controversial stewardship of the "PTL Club" (for a defrocked Jim Bakker), Falwell took the further step of formally resigning the presidency of Moral Majority.[24] He bequeathed it to Jerry Nims, an Atlanta businessman who served on the board of directors for Falwell's "Old Time Gospel Hour," on the condition that he "wind it down and bury it."[25] According to Falwell, he resigned because he was "tired of being the lightening rod" for his opponents, was called "to be a preacher of the Gospel . . . [not] a politician or a businessman" and was anxious to return "back to the pulpit, back to preaching, back to winning souls."[26] Quite understandably, most observers interpreted that action and those words as the political obituary of the Moral Majority.

Falwell, however, saved the official announcement of the termination of Moral Majority for June 11, 1989, some nineteen months following his resignation as its president, and exactly one decade to the month after the group had been formally incorporated. In his announcement, Falwell asserted that the organization's mission had been realized in part, and in any case had been taken up by other Christian-Right groups: "The purpose of the Moral Majority was to activate the religious right. Our mission has been accomplished. . . . Other groups have been born to take our place. We no longer need to be the quarterback."[27] Accepting Falwell's revised and rather restrictive definition of purpose, that the Moral Majority was constructed to "activate the religious right," rather than to return America to "moral sanity" as its early literature proffered, then certainly its "mission was accomplished."[28] Then too, Falwell's remarks had validity inasmuch as other groups did arise to assume Moral Majority's tasks; indeed, the next chapter is mostly an exegesis of those replacement organizations. New-Right conservative Howard Phillips wryly confirmed both of Falwell's assertions, in an interview conducted five days after Falwell's announcement: "The disbanding of the Moral Majority, for about the fourth time, is evidence of a pluralized leadership in the movement. I have considerable respect for Reverend Falwell, who helped wake people up to what was going on in the country."[29]

Omitted from explanations by religious conservatives for the termination of the Moral Majority was that it had appropriated increasingly negative connotations over time. In the Gallup Poll conducted in the wake of the 1980 election (in which the Moral Majority achieved a 40 percent name-recognition rate), a contingency question revealed that only 8 percent approved of the Moral Majority, 13 percent disapproved, and 15 percent expressed no opinion.[30] In the next year's Gallup Poll (in which Moral Majority achieved a 55 percent name-recognition rate), a contingency question revealed that out of that 55 percent, only 12 percent approved of it, 28 percent disapproved, and 15 percent had no opinion.[31] Thus, the percentage of the sample that was familiar with the Moral Majority and approved of it rose only 4 percent, a statistically insignificant rise given polling error; by way of contrast, the percentage of the sample which disapproved more than doubled in one year, from 13 percent to 28 percent. The more people knew about Moral Majority, the less they liked it.

Once scholars gained access to the American National Election Study (NES) data, they started churning out very similar assessments. Emmett H. Buell, Jr., and Lee Sigelman profiled statistically "average" citizens from the 1980 NES data and concluded that "by our estimate, more than two-thirds of average Americans were hostile or critical toward the Moral Majority."[32] Clyde Wilcox analyzed the same data, using different operationalizations of variables, and found support for Buell and Sigelman's central conclusion "that the vast majority of the population does not support the Moral Majority."[33] A subsequent study of 1984 NES data by Sigelman, Wilcox, and Buell found that little changed over four years: "Popular support for the Moral Majority was as limited and restricted in 1984 as in 1980. . . . Moreover, the demographic and attitudinal sources of Moral Majority support and opposition changed little during these years. As in 1980, then, the Moral Majority in 1984 appealed to a small and unrepresentative segment of the U.S. public."[34] In a different vein, James L. Guth and John C. Green discovered through use of 1980 and 1984 NES data, as well as a supplementary mail survey, that "Moral Majority supporters are a distinct minority among both activists and voters."[35] All of those studies echoed the findings of Anson Shupe and William Stacey, based on their survey questionnaire distributed in the Dallas–Fort Worth area in 1981, that there was little evidence that even sympathetic citizens agreed with the issues stances of Moral Majority.[36]

The public's negative perception was not lost on Christian-Right leaders interviewed in the week surrounding the demise of the Moral Majority. In their view, the decline in affection was inevitable, caused by the fact that Moral Majority was both the acknowledged flagship of the Christian Right and the organization willing to jeopardize its long-term stability in order to spur religious conservatives into politics. Gary Bauer, president of the

Family Research Council, a fairly new Christian-Right group, diligently laid out that line of reasoning:

> The Moral Majority was one of the first groups of what has come to be called the Christian Right. Since it was one of the first groups, it suffered accordingly as people opposed to its agenda attacked it. It was not surprising to the Washington, D.C., community that the Moral Majority was laid to rest. In recent years, it had experienced retrenchment. . . . [Also,] one of the first people to alert conservative Christians to the problems of society was Jerry Falwell. He took the lead to sound the alarm. Having done so, he was the focus of considerable attack. To put it simply, Falwell became "damaged goods."[37]

Similar sentiment was expressed by Michael Schwartz, of the Free Congress Foundation, who said that "people like Jerry Falwell were lightening rods for criticism. . . . To his credit, Falwell was intelligent and humble enough to realize that the political playing field was better left to others at that point."[38]

Taken together, it is clear that the Moral Majority was closed down for a surfeit of somewhat contradictory reasons. To some extent, especially with regard to energizing a conservative Christian constituency, its objectives were realized. For those unfinished tasks, a variety of groups were in place and prepared to sally forth. Then too, Reverend Falwell and Moral Majority had developed strong negative connotations, and the percentage of the public that disapproved of both continued to rise over time. On the home front, Falwell sought to redirect his energy into his ministry, saying he wished to be remembered as a minister rather than as a political activist; he also sought to develop Liberty University into a nationally prominent educational institution. Those tasks required a reallocation of time and effort. The Moral Majority was as an artifact of earlier priorities, and Reverend Falwell put the best face on it when he closed down its operations.

The actual announcement of the closure of the Moral Majority engendered little interest. It was made in Las Vegas, Nevada, during the week of the annual meeting of the Southern Baptist Convention. The announcement was anticlimactic because of the reshuffling within the organization that had occurred two years earlier, the lack of public attention it had commanded since that time, and the fact that careful observers knew prior to the announcement that the Moral Majority had already closed its

Washington, D.C., office and leased its space near the Senate's Hart Building to a private political consultant.[39] In the words of one interviewee, the "closedown of the Moral Majority was testimony to the passage of an era when there was a focus on one or two leaders by the media."[40] The quiet passage of the Moral Majority belied its role in the politics of the early 1980s.

The Common Denominators

By the time of Reagan's reelection in 1984, the four major Christian-Right organizations formed in the late-1970s suffered from stagnation. The National Christian Action Coalition had lapsed into a letterhead organization, located above a restaurant in northern Virginia and virtually without a staff to assist its director. It closed its door permanently the following year. The Religious Roundtable rallied conservative ministers for Reagan in 1980, but shortly thereafter closed down its newly opened lobbying office in Washington and by 1984 ceased to answer its phone.[41] Christian Voice and Moral Majority both survived Reagan's first term, and technically even continued beyond his second term into the Bush presidency. However, their heyday was clearly in the early 1980s. Gary Jarmin, chief lobbyist for Christian Voice, said as far back as 1984 that he was going to spend more time off the Hill in years to come;[42] thereafter, Christian Voice reduced its Washington lobbying operation, and eventually supplanted it with the American Freedom Coalition. Moral Majority peaked circa 1984, which led to its later merger with the Liberty Federation in 1986, its abandonment by the Reverend Falwell in 1987, and its termination in 1989.

The stagnation and termination of the early Christian Right groups is an intriguing, and interestingly enough, understudied phenomenon. Those organizations literally catapulted onto the national scene, taking their liberal opposition by surprise.[43] Moreover, they quickly and effectively placed their concerns on the public and congressional agendas, obtaining action on issues that had laid dormant for years. Presumably, they should have remained intact and vibrant, if not actually stronger in numbers and influence, given an early record of success which rivaled that of any new set of interest groups. Instead, they declined, in some cases gradually and in other cases precipitously.

Important elements of the explanation include those already discussed:

the inevitability of the early groups serving as foci for criticism and their inability to retain a constituency drawn from a generally hostile population. To some extent, though, both of those points still beg the fundamental questions. The fact that the early groups were attacked might have strengthened, not weakened, them, due both to their increased salience and to the tendency of sympathetic citizens to support institutions under attack. Scholars of the American presidency have recognized the proclivity of citizens to support a president in times of foreign-policy crisis, terming it the "rally-around-the-flag" variable.[44] The same phenomenon might easily have occurred with the Christian Right, with religious conservatives flocking to it, just because liberals were barraging it with very pointed public criticism. Likewise, while the inability to recruit a large constituency suggested that growth and expansion was problematic, it scarcely explained the defection of original supporters. It was not fated that the early organizations fade away, but they did so. What further factors explain their demise? What caused the stagnancy and demise of the early Christian-Right groups?

One part of the explanation, relevant to three of the four early organizations, is that they were religiously fundamentalist in character. It is unnecessary to belabor that point—a very quick look at the leadership illustrates it. The Reverend Falwell, of Moral Majority, was a well-known fundamentalist minister; Bill Billings, of the National Christian Action Coalition (NCAC), was a graduate of fundamentalist Bob Jones University, and his "Alert" newsletter was supported heavily by fundamentalist churches; Ed McAteer, of the Religious Roundtable, was a prominent layman within the heavily fundamentalist Southern Baptist Convention, whose own pastor was once the president of that denomination. Only Christian Voice considered itself in the evangelical camp, evidenced by early brochures that called upon "evangelical Christians of all denominations" to join the battle against secular society.[45]

The fundamentalist nature of the organizations beset them with problems, emanating from the openly separative strain in fundamentalist theology. It is widely recognized that such a strain of thought exists, encouraging people to focus on their spiritual lives rather than their civic responsibilities; it is also well-documented that historically it has translated into low rates of political participation.[46] The early fundamentalist groups were in an impossible situation. How could they sustain enthusiasm for political activity, in the face of theological cross-pressures? Would shrill rhetoric energize those people who had committed themselves to politics, or would it discourage others from ever becoming involved? How prevalent should religious references be in organizational literature? That constant balancing act, on a fulcrum of theology and politics, was an onerous burden for the early organizations. It was particularly tough on the leaders of the NCAC and the Roundtable, whose constituencies lacked the satisfaction of tangible attention to their work in the popular press, as happened with Moral Majority.

Quite apart from balancing spiritual and temporal concerns, organizational leaders faced the problem of their constituencies succumbing to symbolic assuagement. Murray Edelman has posited that the unorganized and the politically inexperienced are easily the most susceptible to symbolic manipulation;[47] the recently organized and inexperienced fundamentalists were prime targets. Thus, when President Reagan devoted 7 percent to 15 percent of his State of the Union addresses to the social issues in his first term, fundamentalists were partially mollified, just as they had been agitated by the use of rhetoric in the late-1970s.[48] Many fundamentalists were new to politics, brought into it reluctantly out of concern that their spirituality would be tarnished. Once shifts in public discourse suggested that desirable changes were afoot, it was all too easy for those people not enrolled in the movement to keep their distance and for those who had become active to fall back into their apolitical habits. That lapse contributed to the decline of the early organizations.

A second part of the explanation for the demise of the early groups, offered by conservative leaders themselves, is that they tried to build a social movement of locally minded people around national issues. They built their organizations by direct-mail solicitation, on nationally prominent issues such as abortion and Contra aid. In the short run, that tactic proved effective and lucrative; over the long term, it became impossible to sustain people's interest through direct mail on national issues, because of the constant appeals.[49] People in "middle America" simply grew tired of contributing to seemingly endless and psychologically remote struggles, fought out in the nation's capital. One observer who was sympathetic to the Christian Right nonetheless confessed in a 1984 interview that the earliest organizations were "paper tigers" in the sense that they were built on direct mail. It was a problem that Christian-Right leaders perceived, one of whom remarked in a 1984 interview: "I believe that the real future of the movement is grass-roots organizing and coalition building. . . . As the grass-roots work succeeds, then we will have an effect on national politics." As far back as the end of Reagan's first term, then, some leaders were cognizant of the problem of sustaining membership rolls. It was simply too late for them to salvage their organizations by that time, which were soon abandoned or reduced to platforms for issuing political edicts.

Several people were very forthright about the problem when they were interviewed for this volume. Howard Phillips, for instance, remarked: "The Christian Right groups located almost completely in Washington, D.C., have never been as successful as those with a grass-roots structure. . . . [They] were not always wary enough of the 'Washington syndrome' or, if you prefer, the 'Potomac trap.' They failed to see that most people out in the country did not wake up and go about their day on the basis of what was on the front page of *The Washington Post*."[50] Similar sentiments were expressed thoughtfully by Gary Jarmin:

> One of our weaknesses has been that it was hard to sustain grass-roots coalitions around national issues. In other words, we suffered from trying to keep local people focused on national issues. . . . What used to happen with the Christian Right is that when a particular issue was settled, the coalition in support of it scattered. Groups like the American Conservative Union and the Conservative Caucus had some success in trying to build a network of people in congressional districts on national issues [compared to Christian Right groups], but quite frankly, did not have that great of success—they have little staying power. It simply does not work very well to try to motivate local people on an ongoing basis on national issues. What the movement had to do, it has begun to do: build local coalitions around local issues.[51]

Again, the problem was discerned, but only after several of the early organizations had atrophied.

The final part of the explanation for the demise of the earliest groups is that their leaders simply lacked prescience. The point just discussed—an inability to foresee the inevitable degeneration of organizations built too heavily on direct mail—is one example. There are other examples too. Both the NCAC and the Roundtable, for instance, were victims of the same mistake: their mission was defined too narrowly for them to survive. The NCAC was set up to monitor federal regulations affecting private religious schools. At first, it was a reasonable modus operandi, but inevitably it put the NCAC in the position of "crying wolf." After all, the organization's financial base consisted of subscriptions to its newsletter; if it did not portray the federal government as constantly threatening private religious schools, then subscribers were irrational to pay for its product. The NCAC was compelled to constantly step up its rhetoric to stay afloat. Eventually, interest among subscribers waned, when the ballyhooed disasters did not occur.

A similar fate befell the Roundtable. As one interviewee remarked in 1984: "The Roundtable was begun to organize preachers to support the [1980] Reagan candidacy, after which it was interested in pursuing the legislative goals of the religious right." Toward that end, McAteer conducted his series of consciousness-raising sessions for ministers and launched the mass rally in Dallas.[52] Having defined the organizational mission mostly in terms of electing Reagan, he was hard-pressed to retool the Roundtable in order to keep it afloat. As with the NCAC, the mission was too narrowly drawn for the organization to survive.

Interestingly enough, both Christian Voice and Moral Majority suffered some of the opposite problem: their leaders defined the organizational missions too broadly. Christian Voice's literature called for wholesale "spiritual warfare" against secular society, while Moral Majority's literature expressed the desire to "return America to moral sanity."[53] Within that context, those two groups focused on an array of issues: gay rights, abortion, pornography, school prayer, and the Equal Rights Amendment. Staking out such broad claims upon the polity was an exceedingly effective means of gaining access to the public agenda; however, it also undercut the possibility of still further success, since "the probability of success [for interest groups] appears to vary inversely with the scope of the demand."[54] With Moral Majority and Christian Voice, the mission was defined so broadly that absolute, ultimate success was elusive. How and when could successful "spiritual warfare" or a return to "moral sanity" be claimed? Those mandates invited and fostered discontent among newly mobilized supporters, who eventually realized that such goals could not and would not be achieved. Other successes were less satisfying in light of the broadly stated objectives.

The mistake surrounding the circumscription of mission was not the only one committed by the leaders of the two most salient early groups. Christian Voice's leaders erred with regard to the "moral report cards." Admittedly, those cards spawned widespread publicity for the organization when they were released, but most of that coverage soon turned negative. Perhaps Christian Voice's leaders figured that the popular press would overlook the ratings system, and that only interested voters would be privy to it; after all, interest-group scorecards on members of Congress was hardly a novel idea. However, the leadership might have foreseen the perils of a ratings system by which a Catholic priest and a Protestant clergyman received, respectively, 0% and 29% "moral approval ratings" while a self-admitted alcoholic homosexual who later lost a reelection bid, received a 100% rating.[55] As one interviewee suggested retrospectively and anonymously in 1989: "The [early] groups often made mistakes, such as Christian Voice issuing its famous report cards rating members of Congress. Those report cards gave almost uniformly low scores to Jewish, black, and female members of Congress . . . [and] made for an easy target." After the barrage of criticism, Christian Voice added the disclaimer mentioned previously, about the report cards not constituting judgment of a member's personal relationship with God; recall too, that it also dropped "moral" from the title of its "report cards." By that time, however, the negative publicity generated had besmirched Christian Voice's reputation. The report cards were a poor way to retain the allegiance of already skittish religious conservatives.

Elsewhere, this author has chronicled some of the mistakes committed by the Moral Majority in its early years: the decision to take part in the imbroglio concerning anti-Semitic remarks, the bullying of members of Congress, the squandering of resources, the inattention to proper organization, and the lack of a full understanding of strategy and of issues.[56] It is pointless to recapitulate that discussion, especially in face of the criticism that Moral Majority received over the years. Suffice it to say that it too failed to anticipate political developments. In fact, in the case of Moral Majority, the problem was rather pervasive.

All of this explication is not intended as disparagement. Christian-Right groups are scarcely alone when it comes to exhibiting a lack of foresight. In a study of the defeat of the Equal Rights Amendment, Jane J. Mansbridge illustrated the lack of prescience exhibited by women's groups, which pushed the symbol of 59 cents to demonstrate the proportion of earnings that females enjoyed in comparison to their male counterparts, only to have that figure steadily erode in relevance over time.[57] In the case of the Christian Right, the misjudgments were particularly understandable, since many of its people—even at the elite level—were relative newcomers to politics.

Common to all of the aforementioned concerns—fundamentalist susceptibility to symbolic politics, the erroneous attempt to build a national constituency from locally minded people, and the lack of political prognostication—was a lack of political skill and sophistication. The mass constituency was too easily "bought off," while the elite leaders bungled attempts to recruit locally minded people, to properly define organizational missions, and to push their agenda so as not to alienate policymakers. The early groups folded, in short, mostly because of a dearth of political skills. The leadership's sophistication would gradually increase, but too late to salvage the early organizations.

Some Lessons

The preceding discussion offers an opportunity to make a few summary observations. Barney Glaser and Anselm Strauss have shown the benefits of theorizing after the presentation of qualitative data, arguing that such an inductive approach often produces useful maxims.[58] So far, this chapter has chronicled the rise and fall of a set of analogous interest groups; it properly closes by drawing several lessons from that discussion. The lessons apply centrally to the Christian Right, but they may also have some broader application, to the universe of interest groups in American politics.

One lesson for the Christian Right is that its organizations must be institutionalized in a relatively brief period. Based on the fate of the early organizations, which all experienced their heyday by 1985, leaders seem to have the equivalent of about one presidential term to place their fledgling organizations on firm footing. After that length of time, they seem to dissipate. The period for successful institutionalization is quite brief, given the difficulty of launching an organization and gaining access to a crowded political agenda.[59] Of course, the time constraints may have been particularly pronounced in the early years, when the organizations consisted primarily of Christian fundamentalists, whose religious beliefs cross-pressured them to eschew politics. The successful institutionalization of subsequent Christian-Right organizations may not be so time-sensitive, since fundamentalists have had time to adjust to the theological cross-pressures and have been joined more and more by evangelicals, pentecostals and charismatics, for whom the cross-pressures may not be quite as intense.[60]

A second lesson for the leaders of the Christian Right is that they must pay careful attention to the task of conveying success. The leaders of

Christian Voice and Moral Majority, in particular, staked out broad claims upon the polity that netted them broadly based forms of influence, such as agenda-setting. That type of influence was well and good, but it was difficult to communicate to politically inexperienced supporters, who were not attuned to the importance of agenda access and could not be regaled with tales of agenda-setting when they had been enjoined by leaders to "put God back in the schools" and "halt the murder of the unborn." The task was especially problematic through direct-mail letters, which were the primary means of communication of the early groups. Why waste time and effort trying to relay subtle forms of influence in that context? Why not simply paste your opponents? It was easier and probably more lucrative. As new organizations are spawned, Christian-Right leaders must position their organizations so that tangible successes can be conveyed easily and regularly, as well as at a level appropriate to their audience.

The same two principles apply to the universe of American interest groups: they must be placed on firm footing rapidly and be positioned so that their leaders can claim and convey success. Moreover, judging from the collapse of the early Christian-Right organizations, interest-groups leaders should be sensitive to the importance of a well-conceived organizational mission and avoid relying too much on either political newcomers or direct-mail solicitation. It is difficult to generalize beyond those points, because of the bewildering diversity of interest groups and the lack of solid information about their operations.[61]

The preceding lessons may have particular relevance in the years ahead. Barbara Sinclair has documented rapid changes in the congressional agenda since the New Deal, and Jeffrey K. Hadden and Charles E. Swann have shown how quickly social movements can be assembled in a technological age.[62] Those findings imply that interest groups and issues will rise and fall speedily in the future, and leaders will have to be attuned to proper strategy if their groups are to survive and prosper in that environment.

3

The Reconstitution Continues

Reverend Falwell's announcement of the encapsulation of the Moral Majority by the Liberty Federation in January 1986 was met with indifference in the popular press. It is difficult to say why. The announcement may have been viewed as Falwell simply "sounding off" again, as he had done so often in the 1980s, or it may have been perceived as a change in name only rather than in substance. *Washington Post* columnist Mary McGrory sounded the latter theme, remarking that if Falwell really sought to achieve his political agenda, it would "not be enough to change the name of Moral Majority to the Liberty Federation."[1] Most other commentators neglected the matter altogether, a reaction that Jeffrey K. Hadden and Anson Shupe found "a strange response considering the tens of thousands of column inches that had been printed about the Moral Majority over the previous six years."[2]

The public attention the Liberty Federation received in the course of its existence was similarly restricted. One reasonable index of its public profile was the number of stories written about it in the "newspaper of record," the *New York Times*. During 1986, the *Times* mentioned Falwell's impending press conference on January 3, covered the actual press conference where he announced the Liberty Federation on January 4, and then wrote an editorial about the newly formed organization on January 8.[3] That was the sum total of coverage that year. In 1987, the Liberty Federation garnered coverage on two days and then received no attention in 1988 or in the first six months of 1989 (at which point Falwell terminated its sister organization, the Moral Majority.)[4] To put the matter in perspective, the Liberty Federation gained coverage on only three of the ensuing 1,268 days following its birth, for an average of one article every 423 days. In contrast, the Moral Majority received coverage 154 times during its first three years, for an average of one article every seven days.[5] That some disparity existed in the amount of coverage is not surprising, since the Christian Right's ability to shape the public agenda had tapered off, and Falwell's political activities were no longer a novelty by the late 1980s; however, the sheer magnitude of the difference strongly suggested that the Liberty Federation was inert. It did not attract attention because it was not active.

The two days in 1987 when the Liberty Federation received substantive coverage were not particularly helpful. On August 23, the *Times* reprinted a story from Falwell's hometown newspaper in Lynchburg, Virginia, that he had transferred an estimated $6.7 million out of his political organizations into his religious ministries over a three-year period.[6] The transfer encapsulated Falwell's changed political priorities, confirming the point made in the preceding chapter that he shifted both resources and attention away from his political operations as Reagan's first term of office wound down. The transfer of funds was not illegal, since contributors were not intentionally misled. It was fairly unethical, though Falwell refused to concede even that point: "I think that most people are giving because I signed the [fundraising] letter. They could care less if the project was being administered by whatever arms of the Jerry Falwell ministry enterprise."[7] At best, that statement revealed a rather cavalier attitude toward other people's money; at worst, it rationalized almost fraudulent behavior. In either case, Falwell's actions constitute one piece of evidence in support of the proposition presented earlier, that the conduct of Christian-Right leaders was sometimes at odds with their espoused religious principles.

Less than a month later, on September 19, the *Times* reported Falwell's opposition to the broadcast of a film on jailed South African anti-apartheid activist Nelson Mandela, on the grounds that it was too sympathetic to Mandela and the African National Congress.[8] Using the Liberty Federation as his platform, Falwell called for a boycott of that cable television program. It turned out to be the Liberty Federation's sole political activity that made it into the newspaper of record over a three and one-half year span. By the end of the 1980s, the Liberty Federation was completely defunct. It did not even have a telephone listing in the Atlanta, Washington, or Lynchburg, Virginia directories by the fall of 1989—all homes to Moral Majority at one time or another.[9] Apparently, Falwell tacitly terminated the Liberty Federation when he disbanded the Moral Majority.

In retrospect, it appears that Reverend Falwell decided to wind down the Moral Majority and gradually suspend his political role after the 98th Congress (1983–1984) adjourned, and following President Reagan's re-election in November 1984. The next year, he quietly diverted funds from his political operations into his religious ministries; in the opening days of 1986, he launched the Liberty Federation to obfuscate the declining status of Moral Majority and to provide himself a means to shift away from leading a salient religious interest group to assuming an apolitical role. Since he constructed the Liberty Federation as a means to an end, he paid scant attention to it, which is why it received so little press coverage. Subsequently, he handed over a diminished Moral Majority to his friend Jerry Nims (November 1987), with the injunction noted previously, to "wind it down and bury it." Then, in June 1989, Falwell terminated Moral Majority, tacitly killing whatever existed of the Liberty Federation. Falwell's extended exit assisted his successors, by giving them the opportunity to recruit the people he had brought into politics. Gary Jarmin noted in an interview that Reverend James Dobson, one of the contemporary leaders of the movement, was "probably not attracting all that much new blood" but was getting "remnants of the folks that Jerry Falwell . . . [and others] attracted into the movement."[10]

Laying the Foundation

The Reverend Marion "Pat" Robertson's approach to politics in the 1980s was reminiscent of the navigator in Greek mythology, who was forced to steer a course between the sea monsters Scylla and Charybdis, both of which presented peril and neither of which could be evaded without risking the other. In Robertson's case, the two equally unacceptable alternatives were involvement and abstinence from Christian-Right coalition politics. Involvement entailed Robertson placing his carefully cultivated personal reputation in a collective situation, where the excesses of a few zealots might tarnish him; that prospect was not very attractive to the son of a former United States Senator, particularly when many of the ringleaders of the Christian Right were political novices. On the other hand, noninvolvement meant that a significant social movement might proceed without him, which was hardly acceptable to a leading television evangelist with political ambitions and a constituency to protect. Which was worse: the possibility of going down with an errant ship, or missing it as it set sail? Unable to decide, much like the Greek navigators before him, Reverend Robertson did his best to steer a zigzag course.

At first, Robertson voiced a willingness to work in tandem with other Christian-Right leaders. In January 1980, he publicly stated that he was proud to work alongside people like Jerry Falwell and Adrian Rogers: "We've never done anything like this before, all together. We feel the world is in bad shape and we want to show some unity. . . . We think it's time to put God back in government."[11] Substantive political action complemented his rhetoric. For instance, Robertson worked closely with Bill Bright (Campus Crusade for Christ), Adrian Rogers, and John Gimenez to organize "Washington for Jesus" in April 1980. That event attracted a crowd estimated at 200,000, making it the second largest rally ever held on the Mall.[12] The proceedings were carried both live and on tape by Robertson's Christian Broadcasting Network (CBN). According to a 1984 interviewee who attended it: "The rally brought together a diverse set of leaders ranging from Bill Bright to the very charismatic Pat Robertson. It had great symbolic importance. More than that, though, it also was of great spiritual importance to the Christian people who attended." The spiritual component revealed the omnipresent religiosity of the movement in its formative stages, an element that slowly abated as its leadership became entangled with the secular political world.

Following the highly successful "Washington for Jesus" rally, Robertson and other Christian-Right leaders turned their attention to mobilizing religious conservatives for Reagan's 1980 presidential candidacy. The zenith of their efforts was the National Affairs Briefing, which Howard Phillips called the "major achievement" of the Religious Roundtable.[13] Enough has been written about that event, in the preceding chapter and elsewhere, so that recapitulation in detail is unwarranted.[14] It is sufficient to reiterate that anti-Semitic remarks were delivered at the rally, which caused a prudent Robertson to resign from the Roundtable rather than fruitlessly attempt to recast the remarks, as did some of his less politically astute colleagues.[15] Robertson began steering a solo course in politics thereafter, eschewing coalition efforts out of concern for his reputation.

Robertson's unaccompanied foray into politics came the next year, when he launched the Freedom Council. It was designed as a nonpartisan, grass-roots organization, whose modus operandi was to "encourage, train, and equip Americans to exercise their civic responsibility to actively participate in politics."[16] According to Howard Phillips, the Freedom Council was primarily a grass-roots organization at the outset: "The Freedom Council of Dr. Pat Robertson, when it was first formed, was designed to provide some of that grass-roots emphasis. At the time it was lacking in some of the other [Christian-Right] groups. Certainly the Freedom Council had the grass roots in mind when it formed and began operation."[17] Sara Diamond disputes that conclusion, arguing that the Freedom Council was constructed to give the *illusion* of a grassroots organization. She cites two pieces of evidence to support her view: a California state coordinator who acknowledged that direction to precinct coordinators came from Freedom Council headquarters in Virginia Beach, Virginia; and the fact that precinct coordinators were instructed to avoid the press.[18] While those findings may prove that the grass-roots emphasis was a facade, they may also simply point to Robertson's personal involvement in constructing a low-key operation. That deceptively simple explanation would account both for direction from the "top down" and for avoiding the local media. One of the legislative directors of a Christian-Right organization buttressed that interpretation while tacitly criticizing Robertson in a 1984 interview: "The Freedom Council set up under Pat Robertson has a healthy annual budget, but . . . it has no lobbying presence in Washington, D.C. In fact, it has absolutely no lobbying presence at all." The lack of a lobbying arm betrayed its genuine grass-roots emphasis.

During Reagan's first term of office, the Freedom Council was a bastion of stability and continuity. Robertson served as its president, and its activities were mostly restricted to recruiting sympathetic people. According to Gary Jarmin, it was a period of mixed success: "The Freedom Council was somewhat better at grass-roots organization [than were other Christian-Right groups]. It had more grass-roots coordinators, for instance, although it was still quite deficient in local organization."[19] Thus, the group was engaged in grass-roots work; in Jarmin's view, it simply was not effective enough. During those years, Robertson plainly went his own way, refusing to join his fellow television evangelists in an "umbrella" organization (the American Coalition for Traditional Values) constructed to register voters for the 1984 election.

When Reagan's second term opened in 1985, the Freedom Council became embroiled in two matters that caused its demise. First, Robertson leased the donor list of his Christian Broadcasting Network to the Freedom Council and to Victory Communications, the latter being a campaign contractor, that raised $11 million for his presidential bid in just fourteen months.[20] In essence, he leased a list of religious contributors to a tax-exempt "educational" organization, and to a presidential campaign arm. Second, Robertson used tax-exempt donations to the Freedom Council to construct a delegate-selection apparatus in Michigan, one of the early presidential caucus states.[21] In so doing, he used a tax-exempt educational organization to marshal convention delegates. Related to both of those incidents, he propped up the Freedom Council with the Christian Broadcasting Network's moneys, to the tune of $200,000 monthly.[22] Just like Falwell's transfer of money, that act was not actually illegal, but it was unethical and a fairly low standard of conduct for a minister of the Gospel.

Perhaps as part of a long-range plan, or simply sensing that trouble lurked, Robertson resigned the presidency of the Freedom Council in the waning months of 1985.[23] He was replaced by Jerry Curry, who acknowledged the following year that Council officials had made "false statements" about its activities to the IRS.[24] Not surprisingly, Curry's reign was short-lived. In May 1986, he was replaced by Robertson's close confidant, former *New York Times* editor and CBN University president Bob Slosser.[25] With the Freedom Council in trusted hands, Robertson focused exclusively on the presidential race. He announced in September, via a carefully crafted system of satellite feeds reaching dozens of auditoriums nationwide filled with his supporters, that he would seek the presidency if he could gather the signatures of three million people pledging their support.[26] With considerable fanfare, he later announced the goal was exceeded by 300,000 signatures.[27]

The Freedom Council, meanwhile, was dissolved in October 1986 in the midst of an IRS audit focusing on abuse of its tax-exempt status.[28] Its demise went mostly unnoticed, until the early months of 1987, when former employees informed the press that they were offered $100 to sign confidentiality agreements, which barred them from disclosing "records, files, data and all information" about the Freedom Council.[29] That disclosure hastened changes in Robertson's operation and goals. Over the next six months, he laid off hundreds of employees in his CBN operation (due to television evangelist scandals, such as the one involving Jim Bakker and the PTL Club); revamped his "700 Club" television program, bequeathing it to son Tim, after a farewell appearance; resigned his ministerial affiliation; and then, on October 1, 1987, formally entered the 1988 presidential race.[30] Except for the legal residue, the Freedom Council had ceased to exist almost exactly one year earlier.

Tradition and Unification

The Reverend Tim LaHaye was one the earliest leaders of the Christian Right. He lacked the salience of some of the national television evangelists but was well-known in fundamentalist circles. His reputation stemmed from a San Diego ministry spanning several decades, authorship of about two dozen books on spirituality, and Family Life Seminars, a series of workshops on marriage and familial relationships, conducted jointly with his wife.

According to a 1984 interviewee, LaHaye plied his reputation within fundamentalist circles to "quickly link up with the Moral Majority." He served on its board of directors, though only for a brief time. A 1984 interviewee with very intimate knowledge of the situation said that LaHaye had "absolutely no time" for one of Moral Majority's executive officers, and "reservations" about Falwell's proclivity to make himself the centerpiece of the organization. The combination drove the highly energetic LaHaye away from Moral Majority, though his personal relationship with Falwell remained intact, made evident by an outstretched hand in 1983.

In that year, LaHaye launched the American Coalition for Traditional Values (ACTV, pronounced "active"). Its initial role was to register religious conservatives for Reagan's 1984 re-election bid, much as the Religious Roundtable did in 1980. According to Diamond, there was a quid pro quo for LaHaye's work: Reagan was expected to appoint religious conservatives drawn from a "talent bank" to administration positions.[31] Solid evidence for that relationship was missing, however, since the erection of a talent bank was scarcely underway by the time the 1984 election ended.[32] In any case, LaHaye's placement at the forefront of a voter registration drive was a judicious decision: he lacked the "negatives" of some of his peers, while simultaneously possessing strong organizational skills. Said one 1984 interviewee: "LaHaye has the organizational ability to head any sort of larger organization engulfing all the others."

ACTV was constructed precisely as such an umbrella organization. Its executive committee, chaired by LaHaye, included these notable figures: Ben Armstrong, president, National Religious Broadcasters; Colonel Doner, executive board, Christian Voice; Richard Hogue, Oklahoma City television evangelist; Jimmy Swaggart, prominent national evangelist. Its executive board included almost all of the remaining leaders of the Christian Right: Jerry Falwell, Adrian Rogers, John Gimenez, Rex Humbard, D. James Kennedy, James Dobson, James Robison, Paul Crouch, Kenneth Copeland, Robert Dugan, Charles Stanley, Bill Bright, Jack Van Impe, and Don Wildmon. Virtually all of those men were prominent television evangelists, executive officers of major religious denominations, or heads of major conservative organizations. Below that elite level, ACTV claimed a board of directors consisting of nearly three hundred ministers residing in the nation's largest cities.[33] Its self-defined mission was "to engage the largest possible number of Christians in the electoral process through an aggressive voter registration drive and election day get out the vote campaign."[34]

One 1984 interviewee familiar with ACTV's formation conveyed its genesis at some length:

> ACTV began after some discussions among many of the TV evangelists across the country, about the need to set up an organization that would register Christian voters. Of the thirty-two individuals who consented to their involvement in setting up an organization, ten of them actually contributed their mailing lists. On the basis of those mailing lists, a phone bank was set up which contacted 110,000 evangelical and fundamentalist churches. The phone contact had been preceded by a letter from Tim LaHaye to people, and from other leading evangelists like Falwell to his own constituency. To further pique their curiosity about the organization, postcards signed by Senator Laxalt were sent out, that described the formation of the new group. Through all of those contacts, we got a solid base of pastors to work with.

ACTV was seeded by contributions from the television evangelists on its executive board and initially financed through the work of a professional fundraiser tied to the Reagan/Bush campaign.[35] In July 1984, ACTV's leadership was invited to the White House to receive accolades from President Reagan, Vice-President Bush, and other top administration officials.[36] Energized by that meeting, ACTV's leaders organized a registration effort that delivered an estimated 200,000 new voters for Reagan.[37]

Just a few weeks after the 1984 election, LaHaye held a conference in Washington to chart out the future course for ACTV. That conference created a schism. LaHaye wanted ACTV to organize further and wage war over "whose values are going to dominate American society," not unlike its predecessors in the Christian Right; other leaders wanted ACTV to remain an electoral organization.[38] As Robert Dugan, executive board member and the director of the Washington office of the National Association of Evangelicals, put it: "ACTV began with two purposes, voter registration and nonpartisan voter education. My hope would be that after the election it would lie dormant awhile and then gear up again in 1986."[39] Perhaps Dugan anticipated the fate of other broadly defined organizations, such as Christian Voice and Moral Majority. In any case, a decision was made to keep ACTV afloat, but to use it primarily as a "clearinghouse" for conservative Christians to communicate with one another. A couple of weeks later, LaHaye announced the relocation of ACTV's national headquarters from San Diego to Washington, D.C. It proved a fateful decision.

When he announced the relocation in December 1984, LaHaye also added that ACTV would no longer draw its financial support from direct-mail solicitations, sent out to the constituencies of the television evangelists serving on its executive board. In lieu of that support, ACTV would seek grants from foundations.[40] ACTV seemingly was kept afloat in that manner throughout 1985, capping the year with a "How to Win an Election" conference, which drew several hundred pastors and prominent conservative congressmen.[41] The organization seemed well situated to play a significant role in the 1986 elections.

In January 1986, however, a free-lance writer named Carolyn Weaver reported that LaHaye received financial support throughout 1985 from the Reverend Sun Myung Moon's Unification Church.[42] Weaver was inadvertently given a cassette tape by a staff assistant of Beverly LaHaye, which contained a letter dictated by Tim LaHaye to Unification Church official Bo Hi Pak. LaHaye was heard on the tape to say to Pak: "Once again, my friend, I am in your debt for your generous help to our work. You don't know how timely it was! This move and reorganization of the whole ministry to free me for more time in Washington and ACTV activities has been extremely expensive, much more so than I originally thought. . . . As soon as I can afford it, I plan to hire a PR firm to give more coverage for ACTV, get our message to the people."[43] LaHaye acknowledged dictating the letter but denied that Pak had provided assistance beyond a modest cash contribution at the ACTV conference on "How to Win an Election." Moreover, he tried to alter the terms of the debate, saying the real issue was the unethical use of a "private tape recording of the unedited first draft dictation of a letter that never appeared in that form."[44] The revelation that ACTV was propped up by Unification Church officials apparently convinced LaHaye that it was best to dump the organization.[45] In December 1986, after the election season was over and less than a year after the Moon connection was revealed, ACTV was disbanded.[46]

Unbelievably, when Falwell conclusively terminated the Moral Majority in June 1989, partly on the grounds that its mission had been taken over by other organizations, he cited ACTV as an example.[47] That statement was inexplicable. ACTV had closed two and one-half years earlier. Either the media misreported matters, Falwell stretched ACTV's existence to cast a better light on the closure of Moral Majority, or LaHaye closed down ACTV so quietly that even its executive board members (including Falwell) were not informed. Assuming that the media's representatives correctly reported matters—a reasonable assumption given the forthright nature of the stories and a lack of evidence to the contrary—then either LaHaye or Falwell knowingly misdirected the public. Once again, the lack of a high set of standards, commensurate with religious principles, was in evidence.

The Organizations of the Post-Reagan Era

Although one organization supported by Reverend Moon expired in 1986 (ACTV), another surfaced in 1987 that has become one of the staples of the Christian Right in the post-Reagan era. It is the American Freedom Coalition, hatched by Christian Voice personnel with financial support from the Unification Church. The marriage of the two was driven by the Christian Right's disarray in the waning months of 1986.

The disorder in the Christian Right at that time was the product of rapid changes in its organizational structure. The National Christian Action Coalition inaugurated the changes by folding midway through 1985. Reverend Falwell continued the reconstitution of the movement by launching the Liberty Federation in January 1986 while concomitantly fudging the status of Moral Majority. On top of those changes, Pat Robertson dismantled the Freedom Council in October 1986 and Reverend LaHaye the American Coalition for Traditional Values in December. By the end of 1986, then, the Christian Right had been greatly revamped, and most of the changes had transpired in that single year. As Christian-Right leaders surveyed the political landscape, they saw that of the four initial organizations, the NCAC had been dissolved, the Roundtable relocated to Memphis, the Moral Majority placed in limbo, and Christian Voice permitted to atrophy; of the next "wave" of groups, the Freedom Council and ACTV had been terminated, and the Liberty Federation sat mostly inactive. Seven groups formed since the late 1970s were either quiescent or officially terminated by the end of 1986.

The 1986 election results further complicated a difficult and fluid situation. In the interregnum between the closures of the Freedom Council in October and ACTV in December, the Democrats recaptured control of the Senate, ending six years of Republican control. In the process, such reliable Republican supporters of the Christian Right as Alabama's Jeremiah Denton, Florida's Paula Hawkins, and Georgia's Mack Mattingly were defeated. The Republican loss of the Senate plummeted the legislative prospects of the Christian Right for the 100th Congress (1987–1988).[48] Its leadership was forced to contend simultaneously with rapid organizational shifts and declining legislative fortunes.

In the midst of that turmoil, Christian Voice's brain trust sagaciously commissioned a nationwide poll (mentioned in chapter 2), in order to profile its constituency and map out its future course. Recall that a group of respondents who were "conservative, religious, and registered to vote" was selected and then plied with questions about "issues and politics." The central conclusion that emerged from the poll was that "the party structure artificially divided people," because there was considerable agreement among respondents regardless of "party affiliation, religion or color."[49] The polling could not have been done at a better time, given the wholesale organizational changes occurring.

The perspicacity of Christian Voice's leadership in having the poll conducted did not extend to its interpretation, however, since stratifying the population according to three criteria virtually guaranteed widespread agreement among respondents. How could there be any result other than "groupthink,"[50] when the sample drawn was simultaneously conservative, religious, and registered to vote? Given the homogeneous subset of the population sampled, any other result would have been startling indeed. That Christian Voice's leadership drew a rather tendentious conclusion runs contrary to the theme of increased political sophistication. It does not refute it, since the preponderance of evidence still suggests improved skills; however, it does necessitate a reminder of the corollary that political sophistication progressed incrementally and imperfectly.

In any case, the poll convinced Christian Voice's leaders to construct a new organization. With financial assistance from the Unification Church, they launched the American Freedom Coalition (AFC). The Reverend Robert Grant, president of Christian Voice, assumed the same title and role in the new organization. Gary Jarmin became the AFC's political director, having served as Christian Voice's legislative director. Many of Christian Voice's state directors followed suit, serving in their same capacity in the AFC.

The extensive ties to the Unification Church were uncovered by investigative journalists. According to one account, the AFC was the outgrowth of meetings between Jarmin (a former member of the Unification Church) and Bo Hi Pak, the same Moon associate whom Reverend LaHaye thanked on tape for supporting the relocation of ACTV's headquarters.[51] Apparently, Jarmin and Pak pondered the formation of a "third party" composed of Christian conservatives, a rumination implicitly confirmed by Jarmin's comment that the "party structure artificially divided people," but explicitly denied later, when he remarked that the purpose of the AFC was "not to become a separate political party as some have suggested erroneously."[52] Regardless of their intent, Jarmin and Pak's collaboration bred the AFC.

The financial assistance the Unification Church provided the AFC was manifested in many ways. In response to a request from Grant, the AFC was given time on the agenda of CAUSA conferences—Reverend Moon's political organization run by Pak. Moreover, the AFC was given access to CAUSA mailing lists of conference participants.[53] The Unification Church also facilitated $5 million in loans for the AFC's first direct-mail solicitation, contributed sixty church members as full-time state organizers, and produced a videocassette chronicling the congressional testimony of former National Security Council official Oliver North, which the AFC subsequently sold for $25 to 100,000 contributors.[54] The videotape was the linchpin of an operation that raised an estimated $1 million in its first year, and thereafter existed on an annual budget in excess of $2 million.[55]

AFC officials have demonstrated trepidation and ambivalence about the Unification Church connection. There is no mention of such a link in any of the AFC's promotional materials, including its major recruitment booklet.[56] For that reason, several of its state directors, when they were recruited for that position, were probably unaware of the Moon connection.[57] Whenever possible, the issue has been sidestepped. When queried directly, the Reverend Grant has relayed conflicting messages. One tack has been that it is necessary to accept money from those who have it, in pursuit of a just cause, even if that means that conservative Christians "have to hold their noses."[58] It is a line of reasoning far removed from both the dogmatism and the moralism of the early Christian Right.[59] It reflects a moral relativism that is often criticized in contemporary conservative circles.[60]

A second argument has been that Moon's role is only that of a single partner in a major national enterprise; hence, "domination of the AFC by any particular religious interest group or individual is not a valid or even thinkable concern."[61] Conveniently overlooked, of course, is the degree of Moon's support for the AFC. His financial assistance was crucial to the genesis and the solvency of the organization.

The Nature of the AFC

The AFC's leadership has marketed it as a super-coalition that is more "than the sum total of its parts."[62] Its "umbrella" nature parallels the role that LaHaye envisioned for ACTV, prior to its dismantling. As with every Christian-Right organization spawned over the years, it is difficult to ascertain reliable membership estimates. *Christianity Today* suggested in September 1988 that membership hovered around 300,000 nationwide, but that figure seemingly was derived from Reverend Grant's own estimate released seven months earlier.[63] In light of the systematically inflated estimates of the television preachers who directed the Christian Right in its early years, it is probably a figure that should be treated with caution.[64]

In many respects, the AFC appears part and parcel of the early organizations that scholars collectively labeled the "Christian Right." Its leadership includes some of the stalwart players of the movement, and its legislative objectives are very similar. The Moral Majority composed a ten-point platform in the early 1980s, which included support for anti-abortion legislation, a strong national defense, the concept of church/state separation, and traditional morality; the major recruiting booklet of the AFC explicitly mentions those same goals.[65] Perhaps for that reason, a 1989 interviewee who sought anonymity said of the AFC: "Their printed material looks reasonable and moderate in tone. However, upon closer scrutiny, it is very similar in nature to the material put out [by other Christian Right groups]." Without a doubt, that interviewee and others perceive more continuities than differences between the AFC and its predecessors. Were that not the case, the AFC would not warrant mention here.

By the same token, the AFC possesses two characteristics that set it apart from most of its predecessors. Both characteristics are important to document, because they foretell the direction of the Christian Right in the post-Reagan era. First, unlike all of its predecessors, except Concerned Women for America and the Freedom Council, the AFC possesses a decidedly grass-roots emphasis. The literature of the organization confirms this emphasis: "At present, no great figure has risen to lead our country in new directions. This offers a tremendous opportunity for the individual American once again to make his presence felt."[66] Gary Jarmin—probably the most experienced and accomplished Christian-Right lobbyist of the 1980s—embodies the change, stating flatly in an interview: "Personally, I have refocused most of my attention away from the Hill and to the grass roots. . . . The grass roots provide the long-term solution."[67] More to the point, the actual structure of the AFC reveals its grass-roots emphasis. It is organized around a series of national "task forces," which are supposed to be linked to precincts all across America. At the outset of the 1990s, the AFC had five such task forces in place.

One task force focuses on "Economic Justice." Its tenets are fairly mainstream Republican views. It calls for "privatizing" unspecified government "industries and services," for reducing government intervention into private enterprise, and for ending social welfare programs, which create a cycle of poverty.[68] The only religious reference is a single statement of acknowledgment of "the blessings that ultimately flow from the Creator, who instilled in all humankind the desire to prosper and to serve, out of which flows prosperity."[69] A professor of public finance at Shippenburg University in Pennsylvania was appointed its head.

A second task force focuses on the "Environment." The rhetoric accompanying this task force is rather shrill, accusing environmental groups of distributing misleading information, jeopardizing national security and the free enterprise system, and pursuing a "radical agenda" with regard to industrial growth and regulation. It calls for a "Neo-Environmental" movement, which is composed of environmentalists and business interests, working in conjunction with local governments.[70] Its dual message of incorporating business interests and decentralizing formulation of environmental policy, betrays a strong prodevelopment emphasis.

A third task force is on education. It asserts that the public school system is currently failing, that parents should be given more choices about where they send their children to school, and that the education "establishment" offers curricula devoid of moral standards. In addition to those assertions, the task force specifically calls for the incorporation of constitutional studies, school prayer, and local control of school systems.[71] Compared to the environmental task force, its rhetoric is very restrained.

"Religious Freedom" is a fourth task force, focused on the protection of First Amendment freedoms. It calls for an interdenominational effort to resist the secularization of American life and then, somewhat ironically, calls for the creation of a "network of attorneys" to combat secularization at the same time that it asserts the existence of "a crisis in religious freedom as demonstrated by the estimated 10,000 instances of litigation against groups and individuals during this decade [the 1980s] alone."[72] It is headed by Donald Sills, a preacher involved at one time in the Coalition for Religious Freedom (CRF), a group constructed in the mid-1980s to rally clergy support for the Reverend Moon following his imprisonment on charges of income tax evasion.[73] The outreach to clergy was on the basis that the secular state was interfering in church affairs and subjecting churches to illegal taxation.

In July 1984, the CRF sponsored a "Pageant for Religious Freedom" in the nation's capital, designed to attract attention for Moon's case. One 1984 interviewee noted that the gist of it was that "the Christian Right held a worship service in Constitution Hall. Moon paid expenses for any preacher who wanted to attend, and most of the crowd was composed of his followers. Interestingly enough, though, the black clergy of the Southern Christian Leadership Conference also got involved, and a good number of them were in attendance as well." To accentuate the interviewee's later point, Dr. Joseph Lowery, then president of the SCLC, presided over the rally along with Tim LaHaye.[74] A number of prominent television evangelists, including Jerry Falwell, Jimmy Swaggart, James Robison, and Tim LaHaye, served on the executive board of CRF; most eventually withdrew over complaints that Moon's people exercised too much financial control.[75] The Religious Freedom task force, then, has strong ties back to the Unification Church.

The fifth and final task force focuses on "World Freedom." Its promotional literature is out of sync with that of the other task forces. Each of the others begins with a section on why it is necessary to have a task force on the issue and provides some description either of how it works or what it must accomplish. In contrast, the World Freedom literature contains a few platitudes and a description of some of its programs, juxtaposed among pictures of Thomas Jefferson, John Kennedy, a hammer and sickle, and African UNITA leader Jonas Savimbi.[76] It is led by Steven Trevino, whose vita states he was a senior Soviet specialist with the Defense Intelligence Agency in the mid-1980s.

Through those national task forces, the AFC hopes to recruit local citizens into "precinct councils," via the issues that interest them most. According to Jarmin: "The idea of the precinct councils is to build local coalitions around issues and chaired by a precinct 'captain' of sorts. Within each precinct, various task forces [corresponding to the national ones] will be developed. Sally Jones might focus on education issues or General Slaughter might focus on defense issues. Those local people will then track the issues of interest to them personally. They will get together every so often for both socialization and information purposes." According to Jarmin, the socialization function is a vital element of the recruitment process: "We envision the precinct councils serving a 'welcome wagon' function. People will join them to meet their friends and neighbors. After that, they might be persuaded to register to vote, then to support a particular candidate, then to participate in some issue struggle."[77]

The formation of precinct councils is not envisioned as their terminus. Once put in place, they would be tapped at election time. Again, Jarmin provided a description of how he hoped the process would work: "Prior to election time, precinct council members can then canvass their neighborhoods, asking people which issues are important to them. The task force leaders in the precincts can then do follow-up visits, after the issues which affect people have been identified by [them]. . . . Sally Jones will get her list of people involved and interested in education; General Slaughter will get his defense-oriented people. Although canvassing separate neighborhoods, each identifies supporters of the other's issues which they share."[78] The "electoral connection" (to borrow David Mayhew's phrase)[79] would be the natural outgrowth of a solid grassroots organization. It would also place the AFC in a strong position vis-à-vis political candidates. Jarmin stated hopefully: "If we can put issue-oriented precinct councils in place, political candidates will come running to us. After all, what else could a candidate want than an already developed network of interested citizens?"[80]

Both the relative infancy and the grass-roots emphasis of the AFC have bred a situation in which it is little noticed. Neither the *New York Times Index* nor the *Social Sciences Index,* for instance, had any citations to the AFC by the end of the 1980s; the *Reader's Guide to Periodical Literature* had just three over a two-year period, all of which were focused on the Moon connection.[81] Apart from collecting signatures calling for a presidential pardon of Oliver North, an effort initially spearheaded by Jerry Falwell rather than the AFC, its public profile has been almost nil.[82] In fact, the AFC's only appreciable public activity in the 1980s, in the tradition of Christian Voice's "moral report cards," was to distribute "scorecards" (in the 1988 presidential race) that compared George Bush and Michael Dukakis. John B. Judis reported that the AFC distributed some 25 million "scorecards" (favoring Bush) nationwide; the AFC's own post-election report stated only that 8,130,000 were distributed in twelve key states with 168 electoral votes.[83]

The second way in which the AFC differs from its predecessors—in this case rather markedly—is that it claims to possess a secular rather than a religious orientation. It seeks to attract religious people, but within a secular context. The impetus for reaching out to religious people in secular fashion was driven by some religious factionalism in the early years of the movement. One close observer of such matters, Joseph Conn of Americans United for the Separation of Church and State, explained the dilemma that Christian Right leaders faced: "The Christian Right has at least three divergent theological wings in it. In addition to the fundamentalists and pentecostals, there are also the evangelicals, exemplified by the National Association of Evangelicals. Putting theology aside is not easy for the activists within the Christian Right. The splits caused by theological differences are probably one of the major reasons the Christian Right has not been as successful as it might otherwise have been."[84] Gary Jarmin acknowledged the same fact, while simultaneously providing background on the decision to approach politics in a more secular context: "We realized that if we got all conservative Christians participating, we were still talking about a modest proportion of the population. The AFC is an attempt to branch out. The AFC [therefore] has a secular orientation. We found that it was easier to attract religious people to work together in a secular context than in a religious context. Groups like the Moral Majority and the Freedom Council suffered by trying to bring people together in a religious context. For that reason, the AFC has been structured to get religious people to cooperate in a secular context."[85]

The claims of forming a secular organization are odd in light of the fact that the Unification Church provided crucial monetary support. The only way reconciliation is possible (apart from denying that the Unification Church constitutes a religious organization), is if the long-term intent is to sever financial links with Moon's organization. In that way, the AFC would have been launched with the help of a religious organization but then left to fend for itself in a secular political world.

Jarmin's statement about the secular context of the AFC has obvious implications for the secularization thesis presented in several places thus far. In one respect, it is a frank admission that it has been difficult to recruit and retain people within a religious context, and that it is necessary to assume the trappings of secularism—ipso facto, an illustration of the veracity of the secularization theme. In another respect, Jarmin's statement demonstrates a wholly different frame of mind among some of the elite leaders of the Christian Right. It would have been simply unthinkable for them, in the early years of the movement, to erect an organization not expressly predicated on religious principles. In contrast, in the post-Reagan era, at least the leaders of one organization freely ascribe a secular orientation to their organization. Their statements not only demonstrate the trappings of secularism but probably go even further, revealing acceptance of the norms and standards of the secular political process.

Taken together, the grassroots and secular emphases of the AFC reveal a remarkable evolution. During the 1980s, the Reverend Grant and Gary Jarmin were the instrumental figures in Christian Voice. It was an organization that grew out of an anti–gay-rights campaign, was built on direct-mail solicitation, was avowedly spiritual in orientation, expended its resources primarily lobbying Capitol Hill on such social issues as abortion and school prayer, and was headquartered in Washington, just a couple of blocks from the Senate office buildings. In contrast, the AFC is an avowedly grass-roots, secular organization, financed heavily by Moon's enterprise, and composed of grass-roots task forces. Those changes are not simply incremental, but are rather fundamental. They suggest a wholesale reorientation for at least one Christian-Right organization in the post-Reagan era.

The prognosis for the AFC is uncertain. So long as the Reverend Moon is willing to finance it and AFC officials are willing to accept that funding source, it can continue indefinitely. Given Moon's financial empire, he can keep the AFC afloat even in the face of substantial monetary losses.[86]

Otherwise, the prognosis for the AFC is not particularly good. It has prospered from its Moon connection but also suffers from it, as that link is more widely known. New-Right leader Paul Weyrich, of the Free Congress Foundation, in refusing to join an anticommunist lobby financed by Moon, put the matter bluntly: "I believe this is going to be a serious problem. . . . Moon doesn't exactly have a great image in this country."[87] The lack of popular support for Moon, coupled with the lack of support in certain segments of the conservative community, portend problems for the AFC.

Its problems certainly do not stop there either. For instance, the AFC will have difficulty pitching its strong anticommunist message in the 1990s, in light of dramatic changes in the communist world in the late 1980s. It will also face problems pushing its "prodevelopment" stance, due to growing support for environmental issues.[88] Then too, the AFC inherits some of the "baggage" of its predecessors and may suffer from the lack of differentiation the mass media has exemplified all too often when covering the Christian Right, most notably with respect to the television ministry scandals.[89]

Beside those difficulties, there is another set of problems surrounding the religious/secular balance of the AFC. The AFC seeks to draw religious people into politics through a secular organization. Secularization, in the words of Joseph Conn, "may make it easier to recruit people initially. It may still not mask the theological differences, though."[90] Besides, while it is self-evident that people might be enticed to join an organization that serves a "welcome wagon" function, taking them further along, into very controversial and substantive political issues, is an extremely delicate task, particularly when the people being led sense that their "welcome wagon" organization is something other than what it was first portrayed. Assuming that local AFC precinct captains have both the time and skills to finesse people into the group, they will then face the problem of obfuscating the very real theological differences that are bound to surface. Again, the words of Joseph Conn are pertinent: "I doubt if the Christian Right will be much more successful under the guise of secular organizations than it has been to date. Religion runs deeper than politics for most of its people. Bringing them together via a secular organization will not undo those theological differences."[91] For the AFC to succeed, it will need very patient and skilled local leaders across America, capable of gradually recruiting religious people into politics while minimizing theological differences. That task will be difficult, particularly set upon an edifice erected by the Reverend Moon, whose followers are still perceived as flower- and candy-selling "Moonies" throughout much of religious America.

If the AFC remains afloat, the reason will probably be that Moon sees benefits in bankrolling a group that mobilizes and organizes religious conservatives. Otherwise, the AFC will probably be kept around for a respectable time (perhaps until the 1992 presidential election), when it will be collapsed into a new organization. That kaleidoscopic pattern has been a familiar one for the Christian Right. If the AFC manages to remain afloat, sans Moon, it will probably be a marginal political player at the national level, but it may have a significant presence in select states and locales.

LaHaye's Ladies

Concerned Women for America (CWA) has been described as the "ladies auxiliary" of the Christian Right. Although the label is intended to be facetious, it basically fits the reality of the situation, since CWA is the sole Christian-Right organization that is overwhelmingly female in membership and led by a woman. The leading woman is CWA's founder and president, Beverly LaHaye, the wife of Reverend Tim LaHaye. Headquarters for CWA is a suite of offices located just a short distance from the nation's capitol building. Adjacent offices are occupied by "Family Life Seminars," the marriage and family workshops conducted jointly by the LaHayes.

CWA was launched by Beverly LaHaye in 1979 expressly to combat "the stereotype of women brought by the [feminist] National Organization of Women."[92] According to its recruitment brochure, which relates "The CWA Story," Beverly LaHaye became politicized by televised comments of Betty Friedan, founder of NOW, who purported to speak for all women while staking out a feminist position. Believing that "the feminist's anti-God, anti-family rhetoric didn't represent her interests" nor those "of the vast majority of women," LaHaye organized a small circle of friends to discuss opposition to the feminist agenda, particularly the Equal Rights Amendment.[93] That small clique, in turn, organized an anti-ERA rally at a local theater in San Diego. The organizers drummed up a crowd by contacting local churches, trying to reach "Christian churchwomen." The rally drew twelve hundred participants, a turnout which LaHaye later said "shocked" her by its size.[94] The rally participants were incorporated into

Bible study groups, which served as the nucleus of CWA when LaHaye launched it several months later.

Because it was literally the outgrowth of women's Bible groups, CWA possessed a profound spiritual component from the outset, as Laurie Tryfiates, CWA's director for field development, emphasized in an interview: "It really began as a handful of women brought together in neighborhood meetings. Beverly LaHaye began prayer groups to pray about the direction of America. From there the organization mushroomed. People began to put their feet to their faith, becoming active in influencing public policy, both locally and nationally."[95] As we shall see, that spiritual element was evident throughout the 1980s. In fact, it was so salient within CWA that its leader became the target of sarcastic comments from a prominent liberal, secular organization. Anthony Podesta, of People for the American Way (PAW), remarked that the difference between New-Right activist Phyllis Schlafly and Beverly LaHaye was that "Phyllis dissects an issue legally, while Beverly prays that it will be defeated."[96] Unlike the American Freedom Coalition, which has purposely reached out to a secular constituency, the CWA remains deeply rooted in religion. Thus, an important caveat is necessary with regard to the secularization theme proffered in this volume. The general drift toward secularization over the course of the 1980s was not manifested in CWA; it emerges as a key Christian-Right organization of the post-Reagan era, which unashamedly and unambiguously retains religious underpinnings.

The scriptural foundation for the political activism of CWA's women is Ephesians 5:11, a verse that commands the righteous to "take no part in the unfruitful works of darkness, but instead expose them." This verse is cited prominently in CWA's recruitment brochure.[97] In some ways, it is a rather odd verse to cite, since it does not mention politics at all, and it justifies activism only generally and indirectly. Then too, the verse is a form of rhetorical overkill, because it implies that CWA's opposition actually engages in "works of darkness" rather than possesses poor judgment. The verse is conspicuous evidence of the "religious crusade" of CWA, emphasizing as it does the struggle between good and evil, the righteous and unrighteous, in the temporal world.

The context of the verse also merits attention. Chapter five of Ephesians focuses on familial relationships, extolling the virtues of patriarchy, when accompanied by love and respect. That sentiment, of course, is anathema to contemporary feminists, who view women who subscribe to the New

Testament's ordering of the family as ignorant and oppressed sisters, in dire need of consciousness-raising. The feminist position is tinged with irony, as Allen D. Hertzke has pointed out, since "in its call for religious women to become politically active to protect the family and community, the organization [CWA] echoes one aspect of earlier suffragette arguments at the turn of the century."[98] The fissure between feminists and religiously conservative women is interesting because both camps share certain points of agreement: disdain for the depiction of women in pornography; the need for child-care assistance; the view that women collectively exhibit certain desirable attributes not fully expressed in men, be it the feminists' emphasis on compassion in the domestic and international arenas or the religious conservatives' emphasis on nurturing and prayer.[99] Although her position is not a particularly popular one in contemporary America, LaHaye voices it consistently and vigorously. The problem with preaching to the faithful, of course, is that it restricts opportunities for growth and expansion. Michael Schwartz, of the Free Congress Foundation, ably summarized the situation in a single sentence: "Beverly LaHaye, for instance, is very good with her own followers, but she does not have the stature and skills to reach out to a broader constituency."[100] She also does not have the message to do so.

To some extent, CWA faces a problem exactly opposite to that of the AFC in the post-Reagan era. Because it overtly combines religion and conservative politics, CWA attracts a narrow clientele. Its problem is summarized by Jarmin's comment cited earlier that even "if we got all conservative Christians participating, we were still talking about a modest proportion of the population." The virtue of tapping a narrowly drawn constituency, of course, is that it remains relatively easy to retain organizational coherence and intensity. When people are like-minded, it is easy to retain coherence; when they are both religiously and politically motivated, it is easy to maintain a level of intensity. On the other hand, an organization like the AFC has far greater potential to branch out (so long as the Moon connection is unnoticed) because of its secular approach.

The inherent trade-off between focus and growth is faced by all interest groups on a continual basis. However, this Hobson's choice was not an especially acute problem for the Christian Right for much of the 1980s, for in its heady days, groups demonstrated both intensity of commitment and growth in membership. In the 1990s, after a decade of activism and assimilation into a pluralistic political process, the same combination of traits is unlikely to be found in the organizations of the Christian Right.

CWA has opted for organizational coherence; the AFC has chosen to go for growth. Whether the CWA or the AFC prospers more in the 1990s ought to provide an inkling of which strategy is superior. In any case, the combination of strategies should serve the movement well in the years ahead.

Just as CWA retained its spiritual component throughout the 1980s, it also kept a grass-roots emphasis. From 1979 through 1984, in fact, CWA was not even located in the nation's capital; rather, it was headquartered in San Diego, the site of Tim and Beverly LaHaye's successful ministry. CWA was primarily a California-based composite of women's prayer groups, not part and parcel of the early lobbying efforts by organizations based in Washington and sustained by direct-mail, such as Moral Majority. For that reason, CWA was omitted from an earlier volume on the lobbying activities of the Christian Right, which was based on interviews before CWA even arrived in the nation's capital.[101] In 1985, the LaHayes moved to Washington to exert greater influence in national politics, taking with them both Tim's ACTV and Beverly's CWA organization. It was a courageous decision in many ways, because they left behind what the *Los Angeles Times* characterized as a "thriving complex of ministries."[102]

Despite the move, and some concomitant nationalization (discussed shortly), CWA has remained a heavily grass-roots organization. The evidence is pervasive. Hertzke pointed out that CWA broadcast a daily program through forty Christian radio stations nationwide, as well as organized a "535 Program," which assigned women to track the relevant activities of all 535 offices on Capitol Hill and transmit that information to district representatives and local CWA chapters. Hertzke correctly perceived that the program emphasized the "constituency connection."[103] Four years after Hertzke discovered the program through interviews, it was still very much alive, reflected in this comment of CWA's Laurie Tryfiates: "Our 535 Program is designed to keep our representative form of government responsible to the people. A person is assigned to monitor the voting records of one of the 535 members of Congress. They can then keep their community informed about their representation in Washington, D.C."[104]

More recently, Diamond noted the cooperation of major corporations in keeping CWA afloat and entrenched in the grass-roots. She pointed out that Pepsico, Avon, Levi Strauss, Subaru, and American Express arranged a tax-deductible program, whereby the companies match employee contributions to CWA.[105] The corporation reduces its tax burden, receives accolades for its philanthropy, and bolsters a generally conservative, probusiness organization. In turn, CWA receives employee and corporate gifts from all around the country, involving local people psychologically and monetarily.

Perhaps even more striking than the local prayer groups, the radio broadcasts, the 535 Program, or the corporate sponsorship, though, is the way that CWA's director for field development, Laurie Tryfiates, characterized the fundamental problem facing America: "The problem with society today is that it encourages people to shirk individual responsibility. It is insufficient to lay the problems of today solely on the Congress or the bureaucracy. The problems stem from a citizenry that has retracted itself from individual responsibility."[106] That comment is very revealing. It defines the problems of America in terms of a lack of individual citizen responsibility, as well as implies CWA's commitment to change society "from the bottom up." In that respect, CWA is very different from early direct-mail organizations led by prominent television evangelists, and mostly committed to altering the public dialogue. The emphasis may also be a reason for CWA's apparent success. A strong message of individual citizen responsibility and accountability resonates in the ears of citizens who are tired of drugs, crime, and violence, as well as of societal-level explanations for those problems—that society has not done enough to address the "root causes" of those problems. Reflecting the view that the problems and solutions for America's ills are not at the societal level, Tryfiates cautioned: "The answer to the problems facing America are not all solved here in Washington, D.C. For that reason, there is little to be gained by every group flocking to the capital city. Indeed, we mimic the liberals if we think only of Washington, D.C., for answers."[107]

The people at CWA are proud of their initial and continual focus on the grass roots. Their recruitment brochure prominently notes that CWA did not move to Washington until 1985, and affirms that it remains "nurtured by families" and grounded in "chapters in all 50 states."[108] Once again, the remarks of Tryfiates are pertinent: "There is a greater emphasis [now] on the grass roots in the conservative movement. CWA was a leader in that regard. Early on it focused on grass-roots organization in order to influence public policy. In fact, CWA only came to Washington, D.C., in 1985."[109] Those comments are not only factually correct but also a fair characterization of CWA's leadership role vis-à-vis the grass roots. Lest CWA's cognitive skills be too highly rated, though, poor timing also played a role in its grass-roots focus.

To put the matter bluntly, the LaHayes' courageous decision to walk away from a successful San Diego ministry was ill-timed. CWA opened shop in the nation's capital at the outset of the 99th Congress (1985–1986), which in retrospect was precisely one congressional session past the peak of lobbying activity.[110] Any visions of launching a major lobbying effort to supplement the grass-roots effort were soon dashed, since it became clear that the major scuffles over the social issues were already over. In fact, as noted earlier, it was during the 99th Congress that virtually all of the early Christian-Right groups reorganized, retrenched, or dissolved. Thus, CWA remained heavily focused on the grass roots by default. It had no other choice. It arrived on Capitol Hill to provide reinforcements, just as the troops surrendered.

Beverly LaHaye found herself in an awkward position during that time. Her followers expected at least *some* nationally focused activity to supplement the grass-roots work. Why else relocate to Washington? Yet LaHaye personally did not want to squander CWA's precious resources on fruitless struggles on Capitol Hill. How could she "nationalize" CWA, affirming the wisdom of the relocation to her constituency, while at the same time marshaling resources in light of an expensive relocation and an unreceptive Congress? The answer was to construct a heavily symbolic Legislative Affairs division, rooted mostly in the successful grass-roots work of the constituency-oriented 535 Program. The existence of such a division was the signal of a national policy commitment, but the structure put in place ensured that the division would mostly prop up and tie back to the grass-roots work. One indication of the restricted role of Legislative Affairs was that it employed only one part-time lobbyist in the 100th Congress (1987–1988).[111] Another indication, of more recent vintage, is that some of its "position reports" issued on congressional legislation in the 101st Congress (1989–1990) were the work of another division.[112] Finally, although purely circumstantial, the CWA public affairs office demurely rejected a request for an interview with anyone from the Legislative division.[113] There is no irrefutable evidence, but very strong reason to suspect, that Legislative Affairs does little above and beyond coordinating the grass-roots–oriented 535 Program. As a lobbying office, it seems to be mostly symbolic.

Another way that LaHaye coped with the dilemma she faced was to organize an Education and Legal Defense Foundation, which brought top-flight Washington legal talent to bear on local court cases. A collection of lawyers, operating out of a newly opened Washington office and litigating on local issues, bridged the gap between constituency expectations to "nationalize" CWA and LaHaye's personal interest in expending resources on realistic objectives. It had the additional benefit of further propping up the grass-roots work. It was probably not happenstance that Hertzke spoke with CWA's General Legal Counsel when he conducted his 1985 interviews; by 1986, the legal affairs division had five full-time lawyers litigating a dozen local cases with precedent-setting potential.[114] The following year, two full-time litigation positions were dropped, but several part-time lawyers were added, two additional cases were taken, and discussions were held about the need for a national network of legal offices, similar to those of the ACLU, to be called the American Justice League.[115]

According to its literature, CWA's legal affairs division takes approximately ten new cases each year. It weighs four criteria when deciding which cases to accept: the precedent-setting potential; the centrality of the issues to CWA's agenda; the ability of individuals to litigate in the absence of assistance; the organization's existing caseload.[116] Those criteria suggest that CWA is reasonably selective, opting only for cases that broach new legal territory or have high visibility. Its track record attests to the same. CWA has been embroiled in three particularly salient cases, two involving the content of school textbooks and a third involving special education benefits for a blind man to attend Bible college.[117] Those cases received fairly extensive coverage, particularly the school-textbook decisions.[118]

The salience of CWA's legal affairs division placed Beverly LaHaye in the thick of the 1987 confirmation fight over Robert Bork's nomination to the Supreme Court. President Reagan used CWA's annual convention to deliver a major speech in support of his nominee; LaHaye reciprocated for the attention by collecting 76,000 pro-Bork signatures, staging a "Women For Bork" rally on Capitol Hill, and testifying before the Senate Judiciary Committee on behalf of the beleaguered nominee.[119] The range and depth of legal activities demonstrates the privileged position of the legal affairs division within CWA. It is the division that worries liberal opposition, a fact noted by Nadine Brozan: "But it is in the legal arena that Concerned Women has had the most impact, and where it provokes the most worry among its opponents."[120] Indeed, despite his sarcastic comments about LaHaye "praying on issues" rather than legally dissecting them, Anthony Podesta of People for the American Way sees the litigation efforts as "sophisticated and well-financed."[121] Given LaHaye's past resource distribution and personal proclivity, the legal affairs division will probably remain the linchpin of CWA's efforts to enact its vision for America.

In addition to the various divisions discussed thus far, CWA has been involved with one special Central America project since 1987. The project is known as "Amor a la Libertad" (For the Love of Freedom), a pet interest of former President Reagan, that is designed to shuffle financial and humanitarian aid to Costa Rica to assist Nicaraguan refugees. Every three months, CWA has shipped food, clothing, and medical supplies to Central America; it has also established a school to teach both adults and children living in Costa Rica.[122] Demonstrating the religiosity undergirding CWA, when LaHaye traveled to Costa Rica to dedicate the school she invoked Psalm 103, which chronicles the obligations of Christians to assist the oppressed.[123] The future of "Amor A La Libertad" is uncertain at best, particularly in light of the February 1990 elections in Nicaragua, which may have rearranged policy alliances and preferences in the United States vis-à-vis Nicaragua for years to come. Even if the project folds, however, it should be considered a domestic political coup. One criticism leveled at the Christian Right during the 1980s was that it was too indifferent to the underprivileged for a movement with spiritual foundations. Christian-Right leaders, in the words of a 1984 interviewee, lacked "a strong social conscience." The Costa Rica program provided a basis to deflect such criticism, just as Falwell's "save-a-baby" adoption program had some years prior.

The CWA edifice rests heavily upon individual $15 annual membership contributions. For that amount, a contributor receives a CWA lapel pin and a monthly periodical, *CWA News,* which contains feature stories on locally active women, updates on litigation and field activities, and solicited articles from leading conservatives on such issues as abortion and the Strategic Defense Initiative. The periodical is fairly substantial and presumably costly—some twenty-four pages, with full-color graphics and pictures. Its dissemination must consume a sizable portion of the modest $15 membership fee. CWA has tried to supplement membership contributions with grant moneys, albeit with little success.[124] It has relied on contributions, as well as on the matching corporate donations mentioned previously, to raise its budget above the cumulative membership dues.

The $15 annual membership fee is one point of convergence between CWA and the early direct-mail lobbies, such as Christian Voice and Moral Majority. Hertzke aptly recognized the common characteristic, arguing that all three organizations were "distinct from the older denominational institutions in that they are not assured of ongoing, stable funding."[125]

There are a couple of points that probably should be added, though, that differentiate CWA somewhat from the other organizations in terms of financial support. For one thing, CWA has corporate sponsors, which the other organizations did not. For another, the $15 membership fee is an annual one to support a national office and local infrastructure, which is remanded to contributors in the form of a substantial periodical, and of solidary incentives related to participation in local prayer groups. The latter concerns are admittedly a matter of degree, rather than of kind, since organizations like Moral Majority also provided a monthly newsletter and solidary benefits through direct-mail. However, they did not do so as well or as often as CWA.

Just how large an organization is CWA? It is difficult to say with any degree of confidence, because CWA's membership count is cumulative rather than current. It counts all individuals who were ever involved with the organization at one time or another as members; that additive procedure, resulting in 565,000 members, allows CWA to claim that it is larger than the three major feminist organizations combined.[126] In 1986, Russell Chandler deduced that CWA's active membership was around 266,000, which he calculated by dividing its $4-million annual budget by $15 membership contributions.[127] By the same logic, CWA's active membership was about 413,000 the following year, when its budget was $6.2 million.[128] The problem with such logic is that it overlooks contributions above and beyond dues. The $4-million 1986 budget, for instance, could be the result of 266,000 active members pledging $15 apiece, or 160,000 members giving $10 above and beyond their $15 membership contribution. It is surely safe to conclude that its membership is under 500,000; it may be less than half that size.

Looking ahead, CWA is safely ensconced in the nation's capital, and well-situated to play a role in the politics of the 1990s. It is firmly rooted in an estimated eighteen hundred local prayer chapters across America,[129] and solidly supported by thousands of modest annual contributions. It has a salient and aggressive Legal Department, which provides it the symbolic and substantive successes so crucial to organizational maintenance. CWA also has another asset: a virtually unblemished public reputation. At various times in the 1980s, most of the leading personages and organizations of the Christian Right fell into disrepute, sometimes falling so far that they were unable to resurface. Flak directed at CWA has not been especially damaging, because it has been aimed at the substance and policy of the organization rather than on the conduct of its leaders. The criticism CWA has received has looked like "sour grapes" on the part of liberals opposed to its conservative agenda.

One visible manifestation of CWA's Board of Directors' confidence in the longevity of the organization is that in 1987 it granted Beverly LaHaye lifetime tenure as president. That act was more than a vote of confidence; it was a signal of LaHaye's long-term commitment. Because it is a conservative, religious, and primarily women's organization, it is unlikely that CWA will grow much in the 1990s. As Gary Jarmin lamented when speaking about organizational maintenance and growth: "Americans move from location to location with considerable regularity anymore. . . . One is always in the business of recruiting new members."[130] The fact that CWA appeals to a narrow band of the population suggests it will probably remain stagnant in membership size. In all likelihood, it will continue at about the same level doing exactly what it has been doing for over a decade: providing religious, conservative women the inspiration and the means to participate in civic life.

Focusing on the Family

The final Christian-Right organization of the post-Reagan era that warrants discussion is the Family Research Council (FRC). It is headquartered midway between the White House and Capitol Hill, and directed by Gary Bauer, formerly a top aide to Education Secretary William Bennett and later the domestic policy advisor of President Reagan. As the Reagan era closed, Bauer moved several blocks down Pennsylvania Avenue to run the FRC. He promptly gained attention in conservative circles in his new role when he publicly challenged Republican National Committee Chairman Lee Atwater to a debate over the party's position on abortion after Atwater's statement that the party was broad enough to accommodate "pro-choice" candidates.[131]

The FRC is the Washington political arm of the Reverend James Dobson, whose Colorado Springs ministry employs dozens of people. His radio program, "Focus on the Family," is broadcast daily over 1,450 stations nationwide, giving it the second largest audience in the country, after commentator Paul Harvey.[132] Howard Phillips, chairman of the Conservative Caucus, noted the importance of Dobson to the Christian Right in the 1990s: "Of the people out there working, Dr. Dobson probably has the largest following, budget, and staff. . . . He is less known than some of the major television ministers of the early 1980s, but his work is very important."[133] The Reverend Falwell similarly noted the centrality of Dobson to the movement, saying that he was its "rising star."[134] Dobson certainly shone brightly on the public horizon of the late 1980s, but it was mostly through his contact with celebrities and criminals. In January 1988, he eulogized basketball star Pete Maravich; in 1989, he conducted a radio interview with serial killer Theodore Bundy two days before his execution, and he later interviewed Dr. Elizabeth Morgan, the woman imprisoned on contempt charges for refusing to disclose the location of her daughter in a custody/sexual abuse case.[135]

Although he has attracted national attention and accolades from religious conservatives, Dobson has strongly resisted incorporation into the Christian Right. At the end of the 1980s, following Falwell's praise, Dobson flatly declared: "When headlines say I'm the new leader [of the Christian Right] . . . that implies a whole lot that I wouldn't touch with a ten-foot pole."[136] The same sentiment was expressed by FRC President Gary Bauer in an interview: "The term Christian Right is not one which Dr. Dobson would be comfortable with, as he would prefer not to be lumped together with a variety of groups."[137] Why the reluctance? Part of it is the realization that inheriting the mantle of the Christian Right brings with it the "baggage" of the earlier groups and their leaders. Another part of the explanation is Dobson's caution about political involvement at all. According to Michael Schwartz, of the Free Congress Foundation, "Jim Dobson has the stature to lead the Christian Right, but he is very nervous about his present role."[138] That nervousness has caused Dobson to distance himself rhetorically from the Christian Right.

Gary Bauer has similarly distanced the FRC from the movement. When this author wrote a short article on the Christian Right that mentioned the FRC, which was picked up by the *Washington Times,* Bauer's press secretary called the newspaper, objecting to the excerption of the story and a picture of Bauer.[139] The *Times* reported the conversation, noting that "Mr. Bauer and his outfit are striving for a middle-of-the-road image, and our excerpt from an article characterizing Mr. Bauer as a member of the Christian Right didn't help. So it goes."[140] In an interview, Bauer laid out the bases for distinguishing "the Family Research Council and some of the other conservative Christian groups. First, we will be engaged in more research than they are, trying to provide the in-depth study that is needed to make sound public policy. Second, we will not endorse any political candidates, as have many other groups."[141] He also implied a third distinguishing feature, the absence of a foreign-policy agenda, saying the FRC "will not take positions on a range of issues that the Moral Majority took an interest in, such as aid to the Contras or support for the Strategic Defense Initiative."[142]

Despite persistent attempts at distancing, Dobson and the FRC are clearly an integral part of the Christian Right in the 1990s. Liberal and conservative interviewees alike agreed on that point, with Jarmin pointing out that Dobson "has been trying to build local coalitions on issues of interest to the family."[143] Dobson himself made an interesting statement in the midst of denying an affiliation with the Christian Right, saying: "We are limited in our charter and in our desire, really, to the pro-family movement and the foundations of the Judeo-Christian heritage of the Western world."[144] Those exceedingly expansive limits provide for inclusion of the entire domestic political agenda of the Christian Right and even employ the same "family" and "Judeo-Christian" language that the early leaders often used. Coupled with the fact that he is a fundamentalist minister, politically conservative, and intent on organizing people to advance a conservative social agenda, it is evident that Dobson is one of the players of the contemporary Christian Right, despite his protestations to the contrary. The same can be said for the FRC. Bauer stated in an interview that the FRC "handles only issues somehow touching upon the family," but added that "we interpret the family somewhat broadly, leading us to concern ourselves with issues like the tax code's impact on the family, in addition to traditional concerns like abortion and pornography."[145] That agenda is virtually indistinguishable from the one that Moral Majority advanced in the 1980s.

By the same token, it is clear that the FRC is more research-oriented than previous Christian-Right groups, just as Bauer suggested. That emphasis was manifested in the release of a major report in December 1989, on the "state of the American family." The report suggested the 1990s will be a "devastating decade" for families, unless specific legislative actions—the repeal of no-fault divorce laws; the extension of tax breaks to families with preschool children; the elimination of welfare policies that pay in situations without marriage—are taken to reverse trends of divorce and single parenthood.[146] According to Bauer: "Barring a reversal of these trends, more and more children will be denied the opportunity to grow up in an intact, two-parent family."[147] The study not only documented single-parent families and births out of wedlock, on the basis of Census Bureau data, but went further, calling for tax relief for low- and middle-income parents in order to reverse the alarming trends.[148] Allen D. Hertzke and Mary K. Scribner's treatment of the fight over child-care policy captured the thrust of the FRC's agenda and its research emphasis. In an interview, an FRC lobbyist said that day-care approaches providing direct assistance, rather than tax breaks for families with children, penalized parents who stayed home to care for their children.[149] That policy stance was the product of the FRC's research efforts.

What role does Bauer envision for the FRC over the long term? He remarked in an interview: "Our hope is to become known as the premier experts on the family and family issues in the Washington, D.C., area. At that point, policymakers can come to us for advice and assistance as to how their decisions will affect American families."[150] That goal is an ambitious one but is fairly tangible compared to the Christian Right's early goal of "putting God back in government."[151] It reflects a far more subtle and realistic understanding of the American political system, and to that extent, feeds into the sophistication theme enunciated here. The anger of the early fundamentalist leaders is not found in Bauer or the FRC, though the deep concern about the direction of American society remains intact.

It is too early to speculate on the long-term prospects of the FRC. Bauer implies an extended role for the organization and himself, with his talk of becoming the "premier experts" on the family. It is certainly within the financial means of the Reverend Dobson to keep the FRC afloat. In fact, there is some reason to believe it will prosper during the 1990s. Unlike such early groups as the Roundtable or the NCAC, the FRC has identified issues with genuine staying power; it is ably led; it produces a product (research) greedily consumed in the nation's capital; it conveys a more moderate image. Perhaps for those reasons, People for the American Way's chairman, John Buchanan, said that Dobson could prove the most troublesome Christian-Right leader of all.[152] If Dobson overcomes his skittishness about political involvement, and Gary Bauer remains at the helm, the FRC could emerge as the leading organization in the 1990s. Perhaps that is why President George Bush telephoned a hospitalized Reverend Dobson in August 1990, right after delivering a televised foreign policy address.[153]

4

Continuity and Change

One of the most striking aspects of the Christian Right's structure in the 1980s was the multitude of organizations. On average, a new national organization was launched about every other year, following the close promulgation of several groups in the late 1970s. Table 4-1 documents that regularity, showing that new groups were added in 1981, 1983, 1986, 1987, and 1988.

Little explication is required. The National Christian Action Coalition was the first group spawned, back in 1978. It was closely followed by the Religious Roundtable, Christian Voice, Moral Majority, and Concerned Women for America, all launched in 1979. In the 1980s, groups were then added about every other year or so. More specifically, two were added during Reagan's first term, and three in his second term.

At the outset of chapter 2, it was analogized that the Christian Right was much like a kaleidoscope, containing certain constituent elements that could be rearranged to obtain a new look. In Biblical imagery, the movement had "old wine that could be poured into new skins." Now that the organizations composing the Christian Right have been identified and discussed, it is appropriate to analyze the reasons for all of the groups, as well as to gauge the benefits and costs of kaleidoscopic change.

Why All the Groups?

Part of the explanation for a multitude of groups in the 1980s involves the rivalries that existed between elite leaders. Some of those rivalries were

Table 4-1 The Construction of Christian-Right Organizations, 1978–1989

	Organization(s) Founded
1978	National Christian Action Coalition
1979	Religious Roundtable
	Christian Voice
	Moral Majority
	Concerned Women for America
1980	—
1981	Freedom Council
1982	—
1983	American Coalition for Traditional Values
1984	—
1985	—
	(ACTV and CWA relocated to Washington, D.C.)
1986	Liberty Federation
1987	American Freedom Coalition
1988	Family Research Council
1989	—

well publicized and deeply rooted in theological differences. The legislative director of a Christian-Right group explained in a 1984 interview the most notable rivalry between Pat Robertson and Jerry Falwell: "Robertson is a charismatic [Christian] who has been apprehensive about getting involved with fundamentalist Jerry Falwell, just as Falwell has been about getting involved with him." Still other rivalries were grounded in the avarice and ambition of prominent television evangelists, jockeying for the titular leadership of the Christian Right. Many lesser-known rivalries were uncovered in 1984 interviews: that the Reverend Tim LaHaye had disliked certain Moral Majority executive officers and had "reservations" about the direction Falwell was taking the organization; that Robertson began the Freedom Council out of "apprehension" about being involved with fundamentalist, political neophytes; that Ed McAteer began the Roundtable because he "felt slighted" that he was not tapped as Moral Majority's first executive director; that Bob Billings, of the National Christian Action

Coalition, rebuffed Falwell's plea to collapse his group into a Moral Majority "superorganization." Joseph Conn, of Americans United for the Separation of Church and State, alluded to the rivalries that spawned numerous groups in the 1980s: "The reasons underlying the creation of new groups are complicated. The new groups may have stemmed from the large egos of successful television ministers or from diversity within the conservative Christian community over theology."[1]

An equally pertinent explanation for the multitude of groups, though, is actually the antithesis of rivalry: elite leaders acted together to create them.[2] Their prototype for creating a variety of overlapping organizations was the proliferation of liberal interest groups in the 1960s and 1970s. The federal government's expenditures more than quadrupled during those two decades, and as Jack L. Walker noted: "The creation of massive new government programs in social welfare, education, health care, housing, and transportation . . . began to foster voluntary associations among the service providers and consumers of the new programs."[3] The veracity of Walker's assertion was evidenced by the 30 percent rise in the number of interest groups during that time, many of which had a distinctively liberal bent; in fact, the clientelage that existed during this period was so apparent that it led one scholar to produce a noted critique of "interest group liberalism."[4]

Even as liberal interest groups proliferated and liberalism itself grew ascendant, conservative forces were hit with the resignation of President Nixon. Left with a Republican party that had been eviscerated, and with the lesson that it was necessary to rebuild a conservative movement within that party from the "bottom up," since misfeasance at the top had wreaked havoc, conservative leaders set about the business of copying the liberals' formula for success. New-Right leaders Richard Viguerie, Paul Weyrich, and Howard Phillips, in particular, actively spawned a host of overlapping organizations in the mid-1970s, a tactic that those political mentors both realized vis-à-vis the Christian Right and passed on to its politically inexperienced leaders.[5] Both New-Right and Christian-Right conservatives sought to imitate and eventually surpass the liberals.

Journalists Jack Germond and Jules Witcover recognized the imitative strategy of conservative leaders: "By following such an approach, the conservatives are essentially following the same strategy that made the liberal coalition in the Democratic Party the dominant force in our politics over the last several decades."[6] New-Right conservatives were certainly forthright about their intentions. Viguerie wrote a book about the emerging conservative movement, which asserted that "all the New Right has done is copy the success of the old Left . . . [employing] single-issue groups, multi-issue conservative groups, coalition politics, and direct mail."[7] He added that conservative leaders were "constantly looking" for groups to add to the coalition and noted that his colleague Paul Weyrich put great stock in the potential of religious groups and "family oriented issues" in the 1980s.[8] Christian-Right leaders were similarly forthcoming, though by the time they entered the scene, the strategy of adding groups was well-developed (and they were a part of it). Bill Billings, of the National Christian Action Coalition, for instance, produced a volume that extolled the virtues of coalition-building and cooperation among closely affiliated organizations.[9]

Liberals and conservatives alike who were interviewed for this volume confirmed the imitative nature of Christian-Right leaders and attested to the strategy of launching overlapping groups. One person sympathetic to the Christian Right stated in a 1984 interview: "What these guys did was to imitate the liberals, and they are perfectly willing to say that." In point of fact, in another 1984 interview, the legislative director of one of the major organizations did say it: "The fundamental point to understand about the various organizations is that they are the products of conscious design. . . . The Left has had a multiplicity of groups [for a long time], and a decision was made to try and follow that example, creating as many groups as possible. The Left invaded the consciousness of people with that strategy, and the Right wants to do the same." Yet another legislative director, also interviewed in 1984, went one step further, contending: "Many of the groups organized *were expressly designed* to counter similar groups on the Left [emphasis added]."

In the interviews completed five years later, people echoed those earlier assessments. They focused particularly on how Christian-Right leaders added groups, as they were needed, so the movement would prosper. Longtime activist Gary Jarmin stated:

> As I have thought about the key to success over the years, I have come to the conclusion that social movements can sustain themselves in one of two ways. First, they can be built around a single charismatic personality, who can keep people motivated and involved. Second, they can develop a variety of organizations, each with its own niche. The National Rifle Association succeeds, for instance, because it is focused solely on keeping the right to bear arms. The American Civil Liberties Union prospers over time because it keeps

> a focus on First Amendment issues. . . . The Christian Right has gone the way of creating multiple organizations, each with their own niche.[10]

Joseph Conn, of Americans United, said virtually the same thing in a different way: "Over time, what the Christian Right has done is to create a group when there was not a group in place to meet its needs."[11] New-Right leader Howard Phillips concurred, though as a ringleader of such efforts, he found nothing surprising about it: "There have been a number of groups in the Christian Right, each of which has contributed in its own way. The major achievement of the [Religious] Roundtable, for instance, was the 1980 meeting in Dallas; the main achievement of Christian Voice was the promulgation of report cards rating members of Congress according to their votes. It should not be surprising that a number of groups would exist. Nor should it be surprising that different groups contributed in different ways. That is not uncommon for political movements."[12]

The commingling of Christian-Right leaders further confirmed the deliberate attempt to launch overlapping organizations. They acted in concert with one another, at least if creating multiple groups and then serving in them is a fair measure of collusion. Wald recognized that tendency in the earliest Christian-Right groups, and, in an analogy reminiscent of the 1980 McGovern campaign document, suggested that the groups resembled an "interlocking directorate."[13] Table 4-2 provides data on that point, not only for the early groups, but for all ten of the national organizations of the Christian Right active in the 1980s.

The information in the table suggests that an "interlocking directorate" existed, but it also shows that there was widespread variation by person, organization, and time. There were a total of nine leaders with multiple memberships, roughly defined as serving on executive boards or advisory councils (not simply being members of a group). The most active "conspirators" were Bob Billings, Jerry Falwell, Robert Grant, Gary Jarmin, and Tim LaHaye, all of whom had three major organizational affiliations in the 1980s. They were followed by several people with two affiliations; both Beverly LaHaye, of Concerned Women for America, and Ed McAteer were content to restrict their involvement to their own progeny. Looking vertically down the columns, the table shows that the American Coalition for Traditional Values and Christian Voice were the most inclusive organizations, with seven and five members respectively. The Religious Roundtable and the Moral Majority came next, with three members apiece. Pat

Table 4-2 Elite Membership in Multiple Christian-Right Organizations, 1978–1989

	NCAC	RR	CV	MM	CWA	FC	ACTV	LF	AFC	FRC
Robert Billings	x		x	x						
James Dobson							x			x
Colonel Doner			x				x			
Jerry Falwell				x			x	x		
Robert Grant			x				x		x	
Gary Jarmin			x				x		x	
Beverly LaHaye					x					
Tim LaHaye			x	x			x			
Ed McAteer		x								
Pat Robertson		x				x				
James Robison		x					x			

Abbreviations: NCAC = National Christian Action Coalition
RR = Religious Roundtable
CV = Christian Voice
MM = Moral Majority
CWA = Concerned Women for America
FC = Freedom Council
ACTV = American Coalition for Traditional Values
LF = Liberty Federation
AFC = American Freedom Coalition
FRC = Family Research Council

Robertson's desire to "go his own way" is revealed by the lack of overlapping membership in his once-active Freedom Council.

Finally, there is a time dimension to the "interlocking directorate" notion, although it is evident from the table only in conjunction with the information presented in table 4-1 about the genesis and duration of particular organizations. In essence, there was much more of an interlocking directorate initially than there was in later years, calling into question Robert Zwier's characterization of a "loosely knit" set of groups.[14] The most heavily involved people (Robert Billings, Jerry Falwell, Tim LaHaye) and the most serviced organizations (American Coalition for Traditional Values, Christian Voice) were products of an earlier era. The people and organizations still active in the 1990s—such as Concerned Women for America, the American Freedom Coalition, and the Family Research

Council—are far less linked together than their predecessors. That fact lends credence to Gary Jarmin's observation in a 1989 interview: "Most of the groups of the movement today have found a particular niche. . . . The niche of Concerned Women for America, for instance, is in getting women involved at the grass-roots level through prayer clubs and meetings. . . . The development of multiple groups with their own places in the Christian Right is a positive thing."[15]

Whether deliberate strategy or rivalry provides more of the explanation for the sheer number of organizations during the 1980s is unclear. It is interesting, though, that Jarmin stressed the deliberateness of it all in his comment about multiple groups having "their own niches," while a representative of the opposition mostly emphasized the rivalry. According to Joseph Conn of Americans United: "The continual revamping of groups is not generally a deliberate tactic. Instead, the constant reorganizing of groups is the product of changing personalities in the movement."[16] A person might easily have expected the opposite, with the "opposition" claiming that the formation of new groups by the same people was evidence of a conspiracy, and the Christian Right's leaders downplaying deliberateness for the same reason.

The absence of such expected outcomes implies wholesale change in attitudes on both sides from the early 1980s. At that time, liberals were almost paranoid about the collusion of Christian-Right elites, claiming they were a menace to the democratic process.[17] For their part, movement leaders stressed the fact that they were merely doing what their liberal religious brethren had been doing for years, namely making their presence felt in the public arena.[18] That the "opposition" no longer stresses collusive behavior of Christian-Right leaders suggests that it no longer fears the movement as a political force to the same degree and has accepted its legitimate public role to a greater degree. Of course, those concessions have been driven by the empirical reality that there is less collusion. For their part, Christian-Right leaders not merely conceding, but actually stressing the development of multiple groups as a deliberate ploy, suggests that the "moral outrage" that drove the formation of early organizations has dissipated. They no longer rely on pure moral indignation to spur their movement but instead rely on the deliberate addition of organizations filling particular niches.

The existence of both deliberate strategy and rivalry as explanatory factors for the sheer number of groups created a fascinating mix of mutualism and conflict in the 1980s. Virtually all Christian-Right leaders agreed that the secular state needed a thorough thrashing, and they were in a position to assist one another. However, they were also rivals, divided by personal interest, theological differences, and organizational and ministerial imperatives. During the 1980s Christian-Right leaders had incentives to cooperate and to backbite. During the 1990s those same tensions will exist, but to a far lesser degree, since the sheer number of players has decreased. As leaders and followers alike have left the movement or found a "home" in a particular organization, and as the organizations themselves have carved out particular niches, the extent of cooperation and conflict both will decrease. The only area where it may remain intense is over the titular leadership of the Christian Right. That position was held by Jerry Falwell through the mid-1980s and by Pat Robertson in the late 1980s, but it is open to any one of several figures in the 1990s. Whomever takes it will enjoy some ability to shape the public dialogue, but will also serve as a linchpin for criticism, as did Falwell and Robertson.

The Benefits of Proliferation

Putting aside the question of whether the restructuring of the Christian Right is *best* explained by strategy or rivalry, proliferation nonetheless provided certain benefits. A major one was the opportunity to shift the movement incrementally to accommodate changing needs. Scholars have shown that it is tremendously difficult for organizations to change their mission,[19] as suggested here in our discussion of the inability of the National Christian Action Coalition and the Religious Roundtable to redefine their narrowly construed missions. A solution to that problem is to add organizations with different essences, as a means of shifting to meet new circumstances. Essentially, that tactic was followed by Christian-Right leaders, who continuously added organizations when and where they needed them, in order to redefine the movement as its needs changed. For example, when a grass-roots presence was needed, because the earliest organizations were direct-mail lobbies, Pat Robertson created the Freedom Council. When the lobbies fell short of what they sought in the 98th Congress (1983–1984), Tim and Beverly LaHaye relocated their operations to the nation's capital. When the Freedom Council disbanded, leaving somewhat of a void in the grass roots, Robert Grant and Gary Jarmin launched the American Freedom Coalition, with its focus on precinct councils. There were other factors at work in those decisions, of course, and surely there was no great "master plan" at the outset of the 1980s to redefine the movement over the course of the decade. Instead, it was a case of elite leaders surveying the situation and then adding groups whose orientation fit the movement's needs at the time.

A second benefit of continually launching new groups was to protect the Christian Right from the demise of any single organization. A particular organization could collapse, or its leader fall, and there would still be a viable movement. A 1984 interviewee made the point lightheartedly: "If Falwell ran away with his secretary [for example], then the entire movement does not fall as well." He continued, more philosophically: "Each group does its own thing and appeals to its own constituency. It makes the movement very fragmented, but in a sense it aids it because it means the entire movement will not rise or fall with any one group or any one person. . . . The numerous groups and leaders keep the movement strong by diversifying it." That deceptively simple point is easily overlooked in the rush to interpret a multitude of groups as evidence of deep divisions and transience.[20] It helped the Christian Right survive exposure of the "Moon connection" and the fall of the American Coalition for Traditional Values, the withdrawal of Jerry Falwell from politics, and the collapse of several early organizations.

A third benefit of adding new groups was to garner free publicity. Table 4-3 shows the publicity that Christian-Right organizations received in the *New York Times Index* and *The Reader's Guide to Periodical Literature,* two reasonable indices of print media attention. The columns present the ten major organizations of the Christian Right, the year they were spawned, the number of references to them in the *Times* and the *Reader's Guide* in the first three years after they were launched, and the number of references to them in the 1980s (in parentheses).[21] The groups are ordered as they were covered in previous chapters.

Two major findings may be culled from this table. First, the Moral Majority clearly received the most publicity. The figures in parentheses tell the story. In the *Times,* Moral Majority commanded 210 out of 243 (86%) citations to Christian-Right groups in the 1980s. Its dominance was less impressive but equally evident in the *Reader's Guide,* with 62 out of 93 (67%) citations. Interestingly, Moral Majority so dominated column space in the print media that the previous point about multiple groups insulating

Table 4-3 Publicity Received by Christian-Right Organizations in the 1980s

Organization	Year Launched	Number of Citations: NYT		Number of Citations: Reader's Guide	
National Christian Action Coalition	1978	0*	(0)**	1	(1)
Religious Roundtable	1979	8	(9)	1	(1)
Christian Voice	1979	10	(12)	5	(6)
Moral Majority	1979	161	(210)	44	(62)
Liberty Federation	1986	5	(5)	11	(11)
Freedom Council	1981	0	(6)	0	(0)
American Coalition for Traditional Values	1984	1	(1)	2	(5)
Concerned Women for America	1979	0	(0)	1	(2)
American Freedom Coalition	1987	0	(0)	4	(4)
Family Research Council	1988	0	(0)	1	(1)
Total		185	(243)	69	(93)

* Citations received in first three years after organization was launched.
** Total citations received for the organization through December 31, 1989.

the movement is less useful. The media virtually equated Moral Majority with the Christian Right, a fact that engendered hostility among other Christian-Right leaders who were interviewed in 1984. One of them said, with obvious displeasure: "The media has focused on Falwell and continues to run to him whenever he makes some pronouncement. However, there are many other groups of a large size that are still growing and that are effective in their own right." Another leader implied that Moral Majority's high public profile was ill-conceived, if not actually irrelevant to success: "Although money and media attention are necessary to achieve some measure of success, it does not follow that legislative and electoral success will follow. . . . Winning and losing legislative and electoral struggles is more important [than] . . . whether I had 7,000 newspaper articles written about me this year compared to 5,000 last year." Five years later such enmity had disappeared, with Gary Jarmin reflecting: "The contribution of people like Jerry Falwell was really to wake people up, to tell the Christian community that it had to become involved."[22] Howard Phillips, in a quotation partly excerpted earlier, added that he had "respect" for Falwell for waking "people up to what was going on in the country."[23]

The other organizations listed in table 4-3 were arrayed somewhat differently in the two indexes in terms of coverage. In general, the Liberty Federation probably fared second best, with 5 out of 243 (2%) citations in the *Times* and 11 out of 93 (12%) in the *Reader's Guide.* (Those figures provide yet more evidence of Falwell's imposing presence in the 1980s.) Christian Voice probably came next, with 12 out of 243 (5%) citations in the *Times* and 6 out of 93 (6%) in the *Reader's Guide*. After that point, the picture is muddled. About all that can be said is that the National Christian Action Coalition and Concerned Women for America were the least covered among the early organizations, while the American Freedom Coalition and the Family Research Council are new enough that the dearth of attention is understandable.

Second, and more pertinent to this discussion, is the relative congruence of the column figures and their companion figures in parentheses. The congruence indicates that most of the Christian-Right's organizations received the bulk of their coverage within the first three years after they were formed. Setting aside those groups that by definition received all of their publicity within three years, either because they lasted only that long (American Coalition for Traditional Values), or because they were formed during or after 1987 (American Freedom Coalition, Family Research

Council), the data from the *Times* shows that coverage came early. For instance, 8 of the 9 (89%) citations to the Roundtable and 10 of the 12 (83%) to Christian Voice came within their first three years. In fact, simply using the total figures (disregarding the previously disqualified groups), some 76% (184 out of 242) of all citations were logged in that time frame. The aggregate figure is heavily influenced by Moral Majority's experience, of course, but not really skewed by it. The only exception to this general pattern is exhibited by the Freedom Council, which obtained coverage late in its existence, in the midst of financial irregularities and the Reverend Robertson's positioning for the 1988 presidential race.

The *Reader's Guide* tells a similar story. Every group except the Freedom Council received coverage; as the congruence of the two columns of numbers reveal, most of that coverage came early. Specifically, 62 out of 83 (75%) citations came within three years (again excluding the American Freedom Coalition and Family Research Council). With respect to particular groups, the National Christian Action Coalition, the Religious Roundtable, and the Liberty Federation received all of their citations within three years; Christian Voice had 83% (5 of 6) and Moral Majority had 71% (44 of 62) of their citations in the same time frame.

It would be imprudent to read much into the specific numbers. The same basic pattern holds across organizations, though, which is a significant finding. While Christian-Right leaders surely did not calculate the precise amount of coverage received when new groups were launched, they sensed that launching organizations in kaleidoscopic fashion was a means of gaining free publicity. Although publicity might not win legislative struggles, it was a linchpin for many successful interest groups, and a helpful by-product for preachers whose ministries profited from increased exposure.

The benefit of adding new groups to garner publicity was accentuated by the fact that the print media ignored the demise of organizations. Recall that the National Christian Action Coalition, the Religious Roundtable, the Freedom Council, and the American Coalition for Traditional Values were all terminated or moribund by the end of 1986. Of those terminations, only that of the Freedom Council was covered, and it only because of financial irregularities at the time that Pat Robertson was recruiting Republican delegates in Michigan. The others passed unnoticed. That fact was impressed upon Christian-Right leaders, who saw that the media liked to cover new groups but not the death of old ones. Since no one looked back, why not simply add new organizations? Why not create an uncontested illusion of vigor and vitality in the movement? Why not make the most out of slanted media coverage?

On the flip side of matters, the benefits of kaleidoscopic change were partly offset by accompanying costs. Restructuring had deleterious effects, particularly on the Christian Right's political agenda. Its leaders failed to discern that problem, however, until it was too late to salvage the situation.

Whither the Agenda?

The central problem of kaleidoscopic change was that it abetted the diminution of a full political agenda. In its early years, the Christian Right had an abundant agenda. It was locked in a struggle with the government over the tax-exempt status of its schools, giving it a cause célèbre.[24] It was embroiled in substantive national issues, working to defeat the Equal Rights Amendment and to restrict the availability of pornography and abortion services. The Christian Right was even on the cutting edge of certain matters, vocally questioning the quality and content of the educational product delivered by the public schools, and the use of the tax structure to drive familial arrangements.[25] Its centrality, if not its leadership, on a subset of national issues belied its image as a "backward-looking," reactionary movement.[26] More significantly, the far-reaching interests of the Christian Right demonstrated its full agenda.

Over the course of the 1980s, though, the Christian Right's agenda withered. The movement's leaders ceased identifying, cultivating, and springing new issues, losing much of the entrepreneurial spirit that they exhibited when they first became politically active. Put another way, the Christian Right slowly edged toward an almost purely reactive posture, content to advance the agenda of others rather than setting out its own agenda. Such cooptation is common fare in politics,[27] but it was exceedingly costly to the Christian Right. Its relatively large number of groups made the problem worse by creating a fluid operating situation, and, perhaps even more importantly, the continuous promulgation of groups in the 1980s simply obfuscated an eroding agenda until the damage was already done. Leaders kept forming, reforming, and launching groups. In the process, they let their own political agenda atrophy and took up someone else's causes as their own.

For whom did the Christian Right subordinate its agenda? In a nutshell, the answer is President Reagan. In a previous volume, this author demonstrated just how intricately and intimately the Christian Right was tied to Reagan.[28] Its leaders found it difficult even to criticize him, let alone distance themselves from his administration, because Reagan "mainstreamed" them into politics, providing them political credentials and a mantle of secular legitimacy. Reagan also publicly supported their social issues and demonstrated affection for their religious beliefs.[29] A conservative member of Congress noted in a 1984 interview: "Reagan presently is, and likely will remain, the closest the Religious Right will get to anyone in the Oval Office as sympathetic to their goals for the rest of the century.... Those who are in the Religious Right would do well to direct their prayers toward the President's continued good health."

How could the Christian Right's leaders resist Reagan's entreaties to subordinate their agenda to his, when the popular president was providing them substantive and symbolic support? The answer is that they could not. They were "captured" in that sense, unable to extricate themselves from a subordinate position, reflected in the comment of a legislative director of a Christian-Right organization, who was interviewed in 1984: "I think that the [Reagan] administration has done as much as it can, given the climate we have created for it." Unable to elevate or extricate itself, coupled with obliviousness to a withering agenda, the Christian Right was reduced to advancing the president's agenda, making his causes its own. Howard Phillips summarized the situation in an interview:

> My own view is that following the election of Reagan in 1980, much of the Christian Right subordinated its agenda to the Reagan agenda. All too many leaders were content to let the Reagan administration take the lead and then subsume their own concerns within the concerns of the administration. In the 1970s, the Christian Right was involved in ground-breaking work on issues; in the 1980s, it ceased to be ground-breaking in nature as it increasingly subordinated itself to the Reagan Administration.[30]

The extent to which the Christian Right subordinated itself was also apparent in a statement by Moral Majority's Cal Thomas that Jerry Falwell was content with the Reagan administration's efforts.[31] It was even more evident in the actions of Christian-Right leaders. A case in point was "Amor a la Libertad," Beverly LaHaye's project to assist Nicaraguan refugees.

LaHaye launched the project in July 1987, knowing that it vitally interested Reagan; the president showed his interest just two months later, appearing at the annual convention of Concerned Women for America and saying that "nothing we have done in the last six and one-half years has been more important than the survival of freedom in Central America. Believe me, I know how much your organization has done in that cause: setting up schools, medical clinics, and farms to help refugees fleeing oppression; $4 million worth of clothes in one shipment alone. And over the last few years, you've been vital in getting the message out to the American people."[32] Leaving aside CWA's political credentials vis-à-vis Central America for the moment, the mere existence of "Amor a la Libertad" revealed how CWA willingly became involved in advancing Reagan's agenda. Reagan's assertion that CWA was "vital in getting the message out" is particularly interesting. It shows that CWA was a mouthpiece for Reagan's controversial Central America policy. CWA gleefully echoed the "party line," which may have served White House interests but not necessarily CWA's own interests, apart from showing its "human face."

A similar pattern was exhibited with Falwell and South Africa. In the mid-1980s, the Reagan administration was locked in a struggle with Congress over the use of economic sanctions to force changes in the apartheid system of South Africa. The administration repeatedly argued against sanctions, saying that they would only harm the black people of South Africa while doing precious little to change the white government's policy toward apartheid.[33] In the midst of that controversy, Falwell traveled to South Africa in 1985, touring select parts of the country and meeting with leaders of the government. He returned to the United States, claiming that many black leaders opposed imposition of sanctions, and implying that apartheid was less nefarious than it was usually portrayed, because of the black tribal structure.[34] Months later, he followed up the trip with the announced boycott of a television program on black South African leader Nelson Mandela.[35] By attacking sanctions and the portrayal of apartheid, Falwell echoed the Reagan administration's "go slow" policy. As with LaHaye and Central America, Falwell served as a mouthpiece for a controversial administration policy. Falwell then became an easy target for the poisonous pen of rival groups, such as People for the American Way.[36] More to the point, both LaHaye and Falwell seemed to be lackeys for the administration.

The common denominator of LaHaye's actions in Central America and

Falwell's excursion to South Africa was that a Christian-Right leader became embroiled in an exceedingly complex and controversial issue, into which he or she had no special insight, nor any political credentials. Moreover, LaHaye and Falwell became involved in issues lacking clear religious bases, or even worse, mandating a position at odds with their own. Was there a religious basis for Central American or South African involvement? If so, were the Scriptural imperatives assisting the anti-Sandinista forces and opposing economic sanctions? Christian-Right leaders found themselves parroting the Reagan Administration's positions on complicated foreign policy issues; in doing so, they sounded off about issues over which they had limited expertise and experience, as well as suspect religious bases. It might not have been so serious had those been isolated examples, but at various times in the 1980s, Christian-Right leaders ambled into debates over aid to Israel, tax cuts, budget cuts, the B-1 bomber, the MX missile, aid to Afghan rebels, and support for the Strategic Defense Initiative. In all of those cases, the Christian Right had no special role to play, except to echo the Reagan Administration's positions.

So far, scholars have centered the debate over Reagan's support for the Christian Right on the issue of congruence between rhetoric and results, mostly claiming that Reagan promised much and delivered little.[37] That conclusion may or may not be accurate, but it is surely incomplete. To the extent that Reagan "used" the Christian Right, it was not solely, nor perhaps primarily, by promising results and not delivering; rather, it was by convincing Christian-Right leaders to stake *their* prestige and *their* reputations on a wide range of issues that they had no business addressing, because they had no particular credentials. When they pledged fealty to the Administration's entire political agenda, Christian-Right leaders undermined their own credibility and undercut development of their own agenda.

Just as significant as the loss of credibility of certain leaders was the loss of initiative of the Christian Right as a whole. By frequently reducing themselves to mouthpieces for the Reagan Administration, Christian-Right leaders let their attention be diverted from those types of issues where they had experience and expertise, as well as legitimate concerns: the government's investigations of the financial operations of religious ministries; the government's attempts to dictate policies of private, religious schools; the use of public funds to support projects mocking traditional morality and Christian beliefs, such as in the arts; and the negative impact of existing tax policies on the traditional nuclear family. Those broad agenda items were permitted to atrophy during much of the 1980s, while leaders flitted off to distant places and sounded off about matters beyond their purview. Those items would arise again in the early-1990s, in the form of such controversies as the reauthorization of the National Endowment for the Arts and child-care legislation, but by then the Christian Right was more of a marginal rather than a central player, carping about details but riding rather than driving events.[38] Given its early agenda, the Christian Right should have structured the debate, or at least been a principal player on such issues.

Along similar lines, the Christian Right never located and developed replacements for key social issues that were disposed of in the 1980s. Michael Schwartz, of the Free Congress Foundation, stated the problem nicely: "In the early 1980s, its agenda was focused on the Equal Rights Amendment, abortion, and school prayer. Today, the ERA is a dead issue, which was a victory for the movement. The school prayer issue is a dead issue also, which is a loss for the movement. With a couple of its major issues gone, the Christian Right has a pretty thin agenda."[39] As Schwartz so perceptively implies, the Christian Right ceased to develop, redefine, and recombine issues, a process that scholars argue is crucial to success and longevity, because the political agenda is dominated by revamped ideas and issues.[40] Its leaders awoke one day to find an astronomical black hole into which their issues had disappeared, forcing them to set their sights on creating and articulating a new agenda.[41]

The vacuity of the Christian Right's agenda should have been recognized by 1987. Having neglected to develop new issues, and suffering from the disposition of others, Christian-Right leaders were left that year with staging a campaign on behalf of a Marine lieutenant colonel, Oliver North, who was made the new cause célèbre. Jerry Falwell gathered petitions on North's behalf calling for a presidential pardon and invited him to speak at Liberty University's graduation exercises.[42] Beverly LaHaye's CWA had North address its national convention.[43] The American Freedom Coalition similarly sought a presidential pardon and was visited by North during its first annual national convention.[44] North was potentially useful to the Christian Right, serving as a conduit for raising money and as a force for reinvigorating the movement. Still, the fact that the Christian Right was reduced to creating a brouhaha over the plight of a single lieutenant colonel, rather than avidly working to define the direction of American public life, suggested intellectual and agenda emptiness. Having paid insufficient attention to such matters in the early 1980s, by the latter part of the decade leaders could only saddle themselves to a transitory figure and ride him for all he was worth.

Inattention to maintaining a full political agenda was partly a function of being part of a governing coalition, but it was also a product of kaleidoscopic change. The legislative director of a Christian-Right organization sensed the problem in 1984, in a quotation partly excerpted earlier: "Many of the groups organized were expressly designed to counter similar groups on the Left. That strategy has created a fundamental problem, though, from which we are just beginning to extricate ourselves: it resulted in a mentality designed more to counter liberal groups than to fulfill a leadership role ourselves." The proliferation of organizations, in other words, while beneficial to the movement in key respects, created a situation and a state of mind wherein Christian-Right leaders focused on defeating the opposition, rather than developing their own full political agenda. Rapid organizational change kept the movement going and in the public eye but proved costly in terms of political initiative.

The problem of an eroding agenda was abetted by a low level of political sophistication among early elite leaders. The very same interviewee who sensed the problem caused by kaleidoscopic change continued on to say that the 98th Congress (1983–1984) was notable for the "defensive posture" the Christian Right had to assume—a comment made about the very time period that the Christian Right pressed its claims most vigorously, and enjoyed its greatest successes on the Hill.[45] Even more revealing, the interviewee went on to assert that "we have now developed . . . our own agenda of concerns" and then proceeded to define that *agenda* in terms of placing people "in the federal bureaucracy to write regulations." That work may have qualified as a strategy of sorts but scarcely as a political agenda.

Happily for the Christian Right, and consistent with one of the themes of this volume, the level of sophistication has risen with regard to developing and maintaining an agenda. The Family Research Council best exemplifies that fact. Its leaders have carefully restricted its focus to issues somehow touching upon the family structure, purposely avoiding the array of defense and foreign-policy issues that other groups eagerly and amateurishly tackled. They have also latched on to an enduring set of issues, particularly meaningful as the American family structure continues to deteriorate.[46] The FRC has not staked its success or its longevity on popular figures and passing issues. The same tendencies are true to a lesser extent with the remaining Christian-Right organizations. The American Freedom Coalition continues to press a variety of issues, but toward an end goal of erecting local, grass-roots precinct councils. Concerned Women for America is still involved in Central America but is primarily focused on identifying domestic issues and court cases with precedent-setting potential. Its Central America connection may wither completely, as the Reagan administration's policy toward the area recedes into the past. The Christian Right failed to maintain a full agenda in the 1980s and suffered accordingly. As the 1990s opened, leaders were addressing that problem, adding elements of focus and endurance to their agenda.

Consistent with the auxiliary theme of this volume, the push toward kaleidoscopic structural change betrayed the sacrifice of religious principles in pursuit of secular political objectives. Perhaps the most visible manifestation of that tendency was the attempt of Christian-Right leaders to manipulate mailing lists in order to "pick the pockets" of followers. While their efforts and goals may have been well-intentioned, the process of sharing lists for the express purpose of raising money was something more befitting secular charities than conservative religious interest groups. A number of examples have been mentioned previously: Robertson's donation of his CBN mailing list to his political operations; television ministers lending their lists to Tim LaHaye to build the American Coalition for Traditional Values; Christian Voice leaders trying to take their constituency along into the Moon-backed American Freedom Coalition. The practice was not pervasive by any means, just present. In some ways, it was not even especially serious. After all, it would be unfair to expect elites to build a separate constituency for each organization when they were involved in a common endeavor. What was rather sordid, though, was the somewhat new raison d'être of the movement that accompanied the manipulation of lists: leaders became preoccupied with organizational maintenance, losing sight not only of their social agenda but possibly even of the larger goal of injecting religious beliefs and values onto a "naked public square."[47] The point should not be overblown, because the altered purpose was simply a matter of degree. But, on balance, it seems accurate to assert that the Christian Right lost sight of the question, What is wrong with America and how can we change it? Over the course of the 1980s, the operative question became, How do we best stay afloat? Then, when staying afloat proved troublesome, some leaders turned to the bane of their theological heritage for funding, the Reverend Sun Myung Moon.

Looking Back and Ahead

The 1980s was a time of sweeping organizational change for the Christian Right. Most of the groups that inaugurated the decade did not finish it. Related to this change, leaders rose and fell, agenda items came and went, and bases of financial support shifted. Looking back, the changes in the Christian Right might be categorized into three fairly distinct and analytically useful periods. No classification scheme can capture all nuances, but it can accentuate and differentiate phenomena in ways that further understanding of the political world.

The first period, running from about 1979 through 1984, might be labeled the *expansionist period.* Its distinguishing characteristic was the rapid rise of numerous organizations that established a Washington presence, including the National Christian Action Coalition, the Religious Roundtable, Christian Voice, and Moral Majority. Most of those groups were headed by, and appealed to, fundamentalist Christians; most of them lacked sufficient grass-roots structures to carry them, and so were heavily dependent on direct-mail solicitation for solvency. The clear leader during this period was the Reverend Jerry Falwell, whose Moral Majority came to embody the entire Christian Right. The work of elite leaders resembled a "holy crusade," with its emphasis on "cleaning up America" and "putting God back in government." During the expansionist period, the Christian Right leapt to national prominence. Its leaders also exhibited amateurish political behavior, though, while they learned the ropes. That fact contributed to the unraveling of the early groups, and to stunted growth, even as Ronald Reagan won a second term of office.

The second period, running contiguously with the 99th Congress (1985–1986), can be viewed as the *transition period.* Its distinguishing feature was the stagnation and termination of most of the Christian-Right organizations. During that time, the NCAC, Freedom Council, and the American Coalition for Traditional Values were all disbanded; Moral Majority was collapsed into the Liberty Federation; the Roundtable and Christian Voice were permitted to atrophy, the former being relegated to Memphis and the latter being dropped in favor of the American Freedom

Coalition. Also during this time, Concerned Women for America moved from San Diego to Washington. Taken together, the organizational structure of the Christian Right underwent remarkable transformation. Accompanying that shuffling was the erosion of a direct-mail base. The conservative movement generally, including such highly successful direct-mail magnates as Richard Viguerie, suffered severe financial setbacks, which the Christian-Right groups shared.[48] Falwell still commanded the most public attention during this time, but his role as titular leader was far less pronounced, evidenced by the almost universal disregard of his announcement about the launching of the Liberty Federation. The Reverend Robertson began assuming an increasingly higher public profile. Finally, as the next chapter makes clearer, the transition period was marked by a shift in focus, away from Capitol Hill toward the grass roots.

The third period, beginning about 1987 and still under way in the early 1990s, could be classified as the *institutionalization period.* Its central characteristic is the presence of several financially stable organizations, headquartered in Washington but primarily interested in recruiting and organizing people out in the grass roots. Another feature is increased political sophistication among its elite leadership, caused by the incorporation of new people, such as Gary Bauer, and by increased experience for established players, such as Beverly LaHaye. Perhaps the most visible expression of the institutionalization of the Christian Right in the political system, was Pat Robertson's run for the presidency in 1988 and subsequent address to the Republican National Convention. A less visible expression, but equally pertinent, was the incorporation of conservative Christians into the Republican party apparatus in some states. During this time, Jerry Falwell essentially quit politics, stepping back into his role as a minister and as chancellor of Liberty University. Flowing out of his presidential bid, Robertson assumed the de facto leadership of the Christian Right. Whether he retains it in the 1990s is unclear.

Over the course of the 1980s, the Christian Right shook down to several organizations, each with its own niche. The American Freedom Coalition, supported by the Reverend Moon and led by Christian Voice's leaders, endeavors to organize evangelical Christians at the grass-roots level in a secular context. Concerned Women for America, led by Beverly LaHaye, remains steeped in religion, reaches out to fundamentalist women, and strives to marshal cases to take through the legal system. The Family Research Council, led by Gary Bauer, seeks to become the premier experts on family issues by engaging in research and eschewing overtly political practices. Having shaken "down and out," the Christian Right has been institutionalized and is in a position to inject itself routinely in the political process. Its adoption of new political strategies, which are the focus of the next part of this book, reinforces that situation.

Part II.

Strategic Change

5

Farewell to Capitol Hill

In August 1980, with an eye toward the upcoming elections, prominent New-Right activist Paul Weyrich remarked: "If you want to change America, you have to change the Congress."[1] His view was shared by leaders of the Christian Right, who erected several different organizations in 1979 and then contributed resources and registered voters in order to influence the 1980 elections. The purpose of this chapter is to relate the Christian Right's activities vis-à-vis Capitol Hill in the 1980s, chronicle its selection of other avenues for political activism, and analyze the consequences of those choices. The first part of the chapter draws from this author's earlier book on the Christian Right,[2] but it also brings new data to bear on the questions of why the Christian Right's leadership initially focused on Capitol Hill and how the movement fared during the Reagan presidency.

The decision of the Christian Right's leadership to focus on Congress at the outset of the 1980s was motivated partly by wholesale institutional change in the 1970s. Many of the changes resulted in a more accessible institution, such as the devolution of political power from the committees to the subcommittees, and the "sunshine reforms," permitting open committee sessions and television coverage of House floor proceedings. Likewise, the number of personal staff members and committee staff members virtually doubled during the 1970s.[3] All of those changes "opened up" the Congress, creating more access points for interest groups to lodge their demands. Congressional scholars noted accordingly that one major thrust of the reforms of the 1970s was to make the institution more responsive to external pressures.[4]

Another factor that played into the Christian Right's focus on Capitol Hill was the escalating cost of congressional campaigns. In 1974, House members spent a total of $44 million to win reelection; by 1980, they spent $115 million, a 161 percent increase, not adjusted for inflation.[5] The 1980 figure translated into a need for the average House member to raise over $350 every single day for two years. The Senate figures were equally striking, where total campaign expenditures rose from $28 million to $74 million over the same time period, a 164 percent increase.[6] Members of Congress constantly solicited money from interest groups; in return, interest groups gained access and influence with members. The relationship was more intricate and subtle than interest groups "purchasing" congressional support, as popular treatments alleged.[7] The fact of the matter, though, was that interest groups increased their contributions to congressional candidates through political action committees by an astounding 358 percent over six years, from $12 million in 1974 to $55 million in 1980.[8] The Christian Right never donated copious amounts of money to candidates in 1980 when it was established, let alone in the 1970s when it was coming together.[9] Despite that fact, the Christian Right's gravitation toward Capitol Hill must be understood in the context of the rising costs of congressional campaigns, which caused members to solicit resources from interest groups, be it money or the ability to register new voters. The Christian Right joined the parade of interest groups marching to Capitol Hill at the time.

There were other virtues in focusing on the Congress. One virtue was the complexity of the institution, which permitted the Christian Right's leaders to relate accounts of struggles to their best advantage. On an issue like school prayer, for example, they could lambaste the House Judiciary Committee for not proceeding with a bill, or emphasize progress in obtaining support for a "discharge petition" to extract the bill from the committee. The former tack was a tale of woe that could cause outrage and result in a financial contribution from one person, and the latter a tale of success that could create optimism and result in a contribution from a different person. People newly involved in politics and/or willing to rely on the organization they joined to keep them abreast of political developments (so that their personal investment in politics was minimized), both characteristics of the Christian Right's legions, were vulnerable to the way a story was told. The complexity of the Congress was therefore advantageous for the storytellers.

A second virtue was that the Congress provided an opportunity to place fledgling interest groups on firm financial footing. The legislative counsel of the American Civil Liberties Union stated in an interview: "The money is there for the legislative struggles where they [Christian-Right leaders] can whip up enthusiasm."[10] Why was money available for legislative tussles? It was easy to identify opponents and to evoke fear that the opposition would triumph in a powerful, complex institution. R. Kenneth Godwin has demonstrated that fear evocation is a prime tactic of successful direct-mail organizations.[11] The Christian Right's leaders recognized that using Congress as a "whipping boy" could be an effective means of raising money for their organizations. Their cognition was exemplified by the Reverend Falwell, who sent a letter along with Moral Majority membership cards that admonished members that "anti-morality legislation" might pass through Congress.[12]

The incentives for the Christian Right's leaders to focus on the Congress were even greater once the 1980 election ended. In addition to the elevation of a sympathetic Ronald Reagan to the presidency, Republicans gained thirty-three seats in the House of Representatives and took control of the Senate. The Christian Right's contribution to those results was disputed,[13] but the fact of the matter was that it partially assisted and certainly benefited from conservative gains at the national level. Those electoral results increased the likelihood of success at the national level, and reinforced the virtues of focusing on Capitol Hill.

Once Republicans reorganized the Senate committee structure, a prerogative of the majority party, the reasons to focus on the Congress were still more compelling. Virtually all of the Christian Right's social agenda came under the jurisdiction of the Judiciary Committee. In the 96th Congress (1979–1980), Senator Edward Kennedy had chaired that committee and used it to bottle up conservative social legislation, such as school prayer and anti-abortion constitutional amendments. He was assisted by Indiana Democrat Birch Bayh, who chaired the Constitution subcommittee, which possessed subcommittee jurisdiction over those same issues. When Republicans won control of the chamber, Kennedy was replaced as chairman by the bête noire of many liberals, South Carolina Republican Strom Thurmond; Bayh was replaced as subcommittee chairman by Utah's conservative Orrin Hatch. In addition to those dramatic personnel changes, Thurmond reorganized the subcommittee structure in ways that made it more amenable to the social issues. Specifically, he created a Separation of Powers subcommittee, with partial jurisdiction over the social issues, and "stacked it" with Republican senators John East, Jeremiah Denton, and Hatch. East and Denton were part of the New-Right "class of 1980" that swept into office with Reagan, and Hatch had established conservative credentials. Those three members, with East serving as subcommittee chair, were in a position to dominate Democratic members Joe Biden of Delaware and Patrick Leahy of Vermont. The Christian Right's leaders realized their issues would receive a sympathetic airing in that environment, and they were not disappointed, as East convened hearings on statutory avenues to restrict abortion as soon as the 97th Congress (1981–1982) was under way.[14] It was all the more reason to stay focused on Capitol Hill.

In a separate vein, the Christian Right's focus on Congress grew out of the fact that the other branches of government were not viable initial targets. The presidency was inaccessible on a regular basis, and in any case was occupied by a sympathetic Ronald Reagan after 1980. He could recommend measures to the Congress and lobby for them, but Congress had to enact them. The judiciary could be swamped with litigation, but that was costly and time-consuming. One of the central figures in creating the Christian Right remarked in an interview in 1984: "We did not have enough money to get involved in litigation [at the outset], and for that reason sought pursuit of our goals through the political process. We tried to get people interested and involved in politics, trying to influence those [members of Congress] who wrote the laws rather than those [judges] who interpreted them." As for the "fourth branch" of government, the bureaucracy, it could be shaped by the appointments process but only through the long and laborious process of infiltrating its lower levels. The Christian Right experienced the taste of success in the 1980 elections and was not especially interested at that time in the slow appointments process.

Given all of the virtues of focusing on Congress circa 1980, and a lack of viable alternatives at the time, the Christian Right's leaders understandably poured resources into legislative struggles. They erected lobbying divisions within their organizations and established contact with sympathetic members, such as Senators Thurmond and Hatch and Representatives George Hansen of Idaho and Albert Lee Smith of Alabama. The legislative directors of their lobbying offices established contacts with congressional staff members in personal offices, with one director claiming in a 1984 interview that by the end of Reagan's first term of office, he had "somewhere between 150 to 200 offices" that he was "in contact with on the Hill." The Christian Right's leaders also began establishing working relationships with other elements of the conservative community, through such informal gatherings as "Library Court" and the Kingston group.[15] Once Reagan and a Republican Senate formally took control in January 1981, the struggle on Capitol Hill began in earnest.

The Struggle on Capitol Hill

In the "lame duck" period between the 1980 election and the inauguration of a new administration, journalists conjectured that the Christian Right's social agenda would fare quite well in the 97th Congress (1981–1982). Richard Strout wrote an article for the *Christian Science Monitor* subtitled: "Congress braces for new grappling over tax credits, prayer, abortion."[16] A popular weekly magazine suggested that the Christian Right was positioned to launch "a massive overhaul of laws—from prayer to pornography."[17] The Christian Right's leaders were positively exuberant, exemplified in the comment of one leader that the movement was the "new wave in American politics."[18] A congressional staff member interviewed in 1984 summed up the situation: "Certainly the religious right had a cockiness to it when it came here [to Congress]. . . . No one really knew the extent of its power."

Two imposing elements stood in the way of the social issues. First, liberals and civil libertarians in Congress were uneasy, even hostile, to proposals to amend the Constitution to outlaw abortion or permit school prayer. Democratic leaders in the House of Representatives refigured the composition of the Judiciary Committee, where such proposals would be referred, in order to quash them. Four Democrats with liberal credentials were added to the committee to deflect the social agenda—Pat Schroeder of Colorado, Harold Washington of Illinois, Dan Glickman of Kansas, and Barney Frank of Massachusetts. Those four members did not disappoint the leadership, registering an average party unity score of 78 percent in the first session of the 97th Congress, meaning that they voted with a majority of their Democratic colleagues 78 percent of the time.[19] One 1984 interviewee connected with House Judiciary, when presented with the view that the Committee had been "stacked" in 1981, concurred: "Yes, it is accurate to say that Judiciary has been stacked, and proof can be found by simply looking at the people that have been put on the committee." The new personnel, coupled with full committee and subcommittee chairmen steadfastly opposed to the social issues, created what a Judiciary Committee member interviewed in 1984 called a "graveyard" for the social issues.

In the Senate, the structure was far more amenable to the social issues, but liberals and civil libertarians enjoyed the prerogative of the filibuster. They could head off substantive action on the social issues, by literally talking bills to death. Individual senators threw down the gauntlet early in the 97th Congress, challenging the tactics and the goals of the Christian Right.[20] In doing so, they demonstrated a willingness to contend over the social issues and altered the prognosis for those issues that journalists provided during the lame duck period.

The second major obstacle to the social agenda was the Reagan administration's early emphasis on the state of the economy and the nation's defense posture. Reagan addressed virtually only those two matters in his inaugural address, leaving out entirely discussions of the controversial social issues.[21] Subsequently, he dispatched top White House aides to Capitol Hill to convince supporters of the Christian Right's social agenda to defer action on it, until the economic and defense goals were achieved. Before long, journalists chronicled those attempts to defer action, an indication of the saliency and intensity of those efforts.[22] One 1984 interviewee analogized that people in the White House liaison office, where conservatives lodged their objections about inaction on the social issues, were akin to being "receptionists at a home for battered wives," because "people with grievances constantly aired their complaints about a lack of action."

The distinctly mixed environment on Capitol Hill for the social issues ultimately yielded distinctly mixed legislative results.[23] Notable failures in the 97th Congress (1981–1982) included opposition to the nomination of Sandra Day O'Connor to the Supreme Court, on the grounds that she was "pro-choice" on the abortion issue; an inability to leverage an omnibus measure, containing many items on the social agenda, out of the congressional committees to which it was referred; an inability to obtain floor votes in either chamber on constitutional amendments banning abortion and permitting school prayer; and defeat of a tuition tax-credit bill in the Senate.

On the other hand, the Christian Right assisted in two richly symbolic victories: prohibiting the Legal Services Corporation from taking any gay-rights cases and preventing the District of Columbia from lessening jail sentences for rapists, on the grounds that it sent a poor message to potential criminals that outweighed any perceived benefits in terms of higher rates of conviction for perpetrators. The Christian Right also helped kill a criminal-code reform bill that would have lessened the penalties for interstate transportation of obscene materials. Finally, though it did not obtain floor action on abortion and school-prayer constitutional amendments and did not win a floor vote on tuition tax-credit legislation, it did focus congressional attention on those issues—and merely contending over the social agenda provided valuable experience for the Christian Right's lobbyists and facilitated contacts on the Hill. On balance, the Christian Right fared quite well in the 97th Congress, considering that its agenda was contentious and its leaders were political neophytes.

In retrospect, though, the 97th Congress also constituted a "missed opportunity" for the Christian Right, in the sense that it would have achieved more if President Reagan had weighed in on the social issues. Reagan used his "honeymoon" period to lobby the Congress on a variety of economic and defense issues rather than on the social issues. One person interviewed in 1984, who was sympathetic to the administration, lamented that an excellent opportunity probably was missed in the early 1980s: "I would say the administration is committed to achieving success on the major non-economic issues like abortion, school prayer, and tuition tax credits. Further, I would say that President Reagan has the morally and politically correct position on those issues. Having said that, I would agree with those people who say the social issues have not been brought to a vote with enough frequency." If Reagan had expended political capital on the social issues, during the "honeymoon" period, the Christian Right might have fared even better.

The Peak Period

The 98th Congress (1983–1984) brought the Christian Right its greatest statutory and agenda-setting successes of the 1980s. An array of factors dovetailed during those two years, which allowed the Christian Right to achieve its notable legislative successes. Among other things, the groundwork had been laid for movement on the social issues during the preceeding Congress, in the form of congressional hearings and some minor skirmishes. Then, too, the Reagan administration's budget and rearmament goals were set in place, so that it was easier to interest the White House in what its people sometimes considered ancillary issues. Finally, Reagan faced reelection at the end of the 98th Congress and needed the "foot soldiers" of the Christian Right during the campaign season. The convergence of those factors provided an opportunity that the Christian Right's leadership plied to the fullest extent.

Perhaps the most notable success was passage of "equal access" legislation, which permitted voluntary student religious groups to use school facilities on the same basis as other voluntary student groups. It was both a substantive and symbolic victory, garnered by a coalition of religious interest groups but especially driven by the religiously fundamentalist leaders of the Christian Right.[24] It bred considerable litigation for the remainder of the 1980s, culminating in a Supreme Court decision upholding the constitutionality of the Equal Access Act in June 1990.[25] Hubert Morken has argued that even after the passage of the Equal Access Act, religion remained "on the margins, barely within the boundaries of public education."[26] That point is well taken and worth pondering, though it does not detract from the proposition that the Christian Right's leaders helped win passage of a major agenda item.

Other significant successes in the 98th Congress, partly achieved through the Christian Right's efforts, included defeat of the Equal Rights Amendment in the House of Representatives; passage of a heavily symbolic statute permitting "silent prayer" in schools; passage of several anti-abortion "riders," restricting the use of public moneys to pay for the abortion procedure; and passage of a statute allowing churches to voluntarily withdraw from the Social Security system, so that they would not be taxed by the government.[27] Complementing those successes were broad-based victories in the realm of agenda-setting. The Christian Right helped gain floor consideration of school-prayer and abortion constitutional amendments, measures that had not been voted on by members for years.[28]

The downside of the 98th Congress for the Christian Right was that it failed to win passage of the school prayer and abortion amendments, as well as a major tuition tax credit proposal. It also strove in vain to defeat the appointment of an ambassador to the Vatican.[29] Then, too, it inadvertently laid the groundwork for the demise of its own social agenda. Roger Cobb and Charles Elder have pointed out that issues receiving serious treatment from policymakers tend to fall off the political agenda.[30] The contentiousness of the social issues reinforced the proclivity of members of Congress to eschew further consideration of them in subsequent congresses. Who wanted to reconsider "no-win issues" like abortion, after an anti-abortion constitutional amendment had been the focus of hearings, floor debate, and a vote? Treatment of the social issues in the 98th Congress, in other words, lessened the chances of consideration of those issues in subsequent congresses.

The same principle cut another way, also to the Christian Right's disadvantage. Its victories in the 98th Congress shoved items off the congressional agenda, such as school prayer. Colleen Kiko, minority counsel of the Civil and Constitutional Rights subcommittee, of the House Judiciary Committee, said in an interview that school prayer was a moot issue by the end of the 1980s because of the passage of the Equal Access Act in the mid-1980s: "It is logical that a measure which permitted religious groups in schools would help defuse sentiment for state-sponsored prayer [in schools]." She went on to say, from her privileged position as an observer of the social issues: "The prayer issue is not completely dead. Some members of Congress, including Dannemeyer still raise the issue in the House. It is clear, though, that the issue has lost steam. . . . The public thinks it is not a good idea, and the Congress reflects that view. In short, there is not much action on school prayer on Capitol Hill anymore. In fact, the issue is not even taken very seriously around here, as it was at one time."[31] The Christian Right's failure to recombine ideas and revamp issues, as discussed in the previous chapter, proved fatal to its fortunes on the Hill after the 98th Congress adjourned. Its agenda was not redefined, and after it was disposed of, favorably or not, in 1983–1984, it was essentially moot thereafter.

The other problem the Christian Right faced in the post–98th Congress period was that its reputation on Capitol Hill was in tatters. Its leaders were factionalized, hyperbolic, and fairly unsophisticated in their efforts to enact legislation.[32] Their excesses sullied the Christian Right's reputation, making it more difficult to return to press any political agenda in Reagan's second term of office. Also, it became difficult for the leaders to relate the events on Capitol Hill to their best advantage, as their constituents, increasingly cognizant of the congressional process through repetition of direct-mail, grew weary of the emotional roller coaster they were asked to ride as the struggles over the social issues ensued.

The 1984 elections solidified the declining fortunes of the Christian

Right on Capitol Hill. Despite a landslide victory, President Reagan's coattails were exceedingly short, as Republicans lost two Senate seats and gained only fourteen House seats. In light of those results, the prognosis for the social issues was anything but favorable. The House of Representatives remained intractable, with 58 percent of the seats held by Democrats and the same triumvirate in control of the Judiciary Committee; the Senate was now less amenable, due to the loss of two Republican seats and the retirement of Senate Majority Leader Howard Baker, which spawned a Republican succession fight. The combination of the disposition of agenda items and the 1984 elections left the 98th Congress as the highwater mark for the Christian Right's fortunes on Capitol Hill.

The Transition

The previous chapter documented the rapid organizational change that occurred within the Christian Right during the 99th Congress (1985–1986), when the National Christian Action Coalition, Christian Voice, Moral Majority, the Freedom Council, and the American Coalition for Traditional Values were all terminated, revamped, or permitted to atrophy. At the same time, Concerned Women for America was moved to the nation's capital, the Liberty Federation was launched, and the American Freedom Coalition was on the drawing board. Those organizational changes were accompanied by a reduction in attention to the Christian Right's agenda on Capitol Hill. Table 5-1 summarizes one dimension of less attention to the social issues.

The table shows that the trio of top legislative priorities—abortion, school prayer, and tuition tax credits—received much less attention in the 99th Congress (1985–1986) than in the 98th Congress (1983–1984).[33] All in all, the 98th Congress had six hearings on the social issues, while the 99th Congress had only two. That decline in the number of hearings was less numerically significant than it was indicative of a changed environment on Capitol Hill.

A second indicator of decreased congressional interest in the social issues during the 99th Congress, which flowed out of the lack of hearings, was a lack of floor action. The Senate took up a "court-stripping" school-prayer bill in a perfunctory way but overwhelmingly defeated it in the first session (1985), out of concern over restricting the Supreme Court's jurisdiction.[34] Apart from some minor scuffles over intangible concerns, such as "secular

Table 5-1 Hearings on the Social Issues, 1983 – 1986*

	Abortion	School Prayer	Tuition Tax
98th Congress (1983–84)	1	4	1
99th Congress (1985—86)	0	2	0

*Hearings were held on the following bills in the 98th Congress: S.J. Res. 3 (abortion); S.J. Res. 73 (2 sets), H.R. 2723, and H.R. 1310 (school prayer); S. 528 (tuition tax credits). Hearings were held on the following bills in the 99th Congress: S.J. Res. 2 (2 sets, school prayer).

Source: Compiled from Congressional Information Service indexes.

humanism," there was no substantive floor action on the social issues.[35] Certainly there were no scuffles over proposed amendments to the Constitution comparable to those of the 98th Congress.

A third indicator of the drop-off in congressional attention to the social issues was Reagan's relative dismissal of them. He decreased the total attention he paid to the social issues in his State of the Union addresses by 42 percent from 1984 to 1985.[36] His relative inattention confirmed the fact that the social issues were no longer as salient, nor as important, on Capitol Hill.

The story was similar in the 100th Congress (1987–1988). As soon as Democrats recaptured control of the Senate in the 1986 elections, they reconfigured the Judiciary Committee, abolishing the Separation of Powers subcommittee that had served as a forum for the social issues. The new scheme eradicated a potential access point. With both chambers firmly controlled by the Democrats, and with unsympathetic Judiciary Committees in each, the social agenda was not welcome. The situation was only reinforced by the popular scandals that rocked television evangelism at the time, including the financial and sexual improprieties of the Reverend Jim Bakker of the PTL Club and the sexual voyeurism of the Reverend Jimmy Swaggart.[37]

Developments within the institution of Congress contributed still further to the demise of the social issues for the rest of the Reagan presidency. One such development was the formation of House and Senate select committees to investigate the sale of arms to Iran and the diversion of moneys from those sales to the Contra rebels fighting in Nicaragua. The investigation of the Iran-Contra affair preoccupied members of the 100th Congress, contributing to the demise of the social agenda. A second major development was the recentralization of power in Congress, which was lodged in its "money committees" because of the high budget deficits of the mid-1980s.[38] The nation's fiscal woes elevated the importance of the money committees in Congress, simultaneously decreasing the importance both of the authorizing committees, such as Judiciary, and of non-fiscal issues, such as school prayer. The congressional agenda shifted, and the Christian Right's leadership failed to redefine and revamp its agenda to meet the changing conditions. They found themselves locked out of most of the action.

The 101st Congress (1989–1990) continued the inattention to the major social issues. Items such as tuition tax credits were not discussed; school-prayer proposals were no longer taken seriously. There was a great deal of rhetoric over the abortion issue, caused by the Supreme Court's decision in *Webster* v. *Reproductive Health Services* (1989), which allowed some statutory restriction of abortion rights.[39] Despite all of the rhetoric, though, the real action on the abortion issue was not on Capitol Hill, but in a wide variety of mostly conservative states where statutory restrictions were hotly contested.[40] The Christian Right retained a presence on Capitol Hill in the 101st Congress, but mostly in tangential or even trivial ways. As noted in the previous chapter, it was one of many players in the struggle over child-care legislation; it was involved in the debate over the reauthorization of the National Endowment for the Arts, trying to create opposition to the NEA on the grounds that it granted tax dollars for objectionable projects, such as photographs taken by Robert Mapplethorpe.[41] Such participation in the legislative process was exceedingly minor, especially in contrast to the Christian Right's earlier role in bringing major constitutional amendments to the Senate floor for votes. It would be erroneous to suggest that the Christian Right had left Capitol Hill completely by the end of the 1980s; however, it would also be fair to say that its presence was negligible.

The declining attention to the social issues, coupled with changed party control and the recentralization of power, caused Christian-Right leaders to consider other avenues for activism, such as the bureaucracy, the courts, and the states. Once the opportunities on Capitol Hill dried up, it was time to look elsewhere.

Other Branches of Government

If Capitol Hill was no longer the proper focal point at the end of the 1980s, then perhaps an acceptable alternative was the executive branch. A Republican president was safely ensconced in the White House, and the executive branch was open to penetration and infiltration. In the early 1980s, this option was mostly dismissed, because the bureaucracy was not an effective means to institutionalize fledgling interest groups. As activity on the Hill drew to a close, however, it emerged as a viable focus.

One of the more sagacious leaders of the Christian Right recognized that the congressional environment was changing in the mid-1980s, even as he was lobbying the Congress. He offered the possibility of infiltrating the executive branch in the future, saying in a 1984 interview that there had not been "enough appointments in the executive branch," because those "payoffs go to people in line, not to a mass voting bloc." Tim LaHaye, of the American Coalition for Traditional Values, voiced similar sentiment at ACTV's 1984 national meeting in Washington: "Among government employees there should be the same number of Christians as in the population at large."[42] Those comments suggested that the Christian Right's leadership had an emerging interest in executive-branch appointments, which only grew as opportunities on the Hill declined. LaHaye's comment was remarkable for its affirmation of quota-based representation, a position normally associated with liberal Democrats.

It is impossible to examine the extent of the infiltration of the executive branch in the 1980s in anything but the broadest, and unfortunately crudest, of terms. Only highly circumstantial evidence can be brought to bear, coupled with some anonymous comments and specific examples. While such an approach is admittedly not very satisfying, it is the only way to address the Christian Right's infiltration of the executive branch, short of interviewing thousands of bureaucrats about their religious predispositions and political allegiances.

The starting point for determining infiltration of the bureaucracy is noting that there were mechanisms for placing religious conservatives in the executive branch. While it was in existence, LaHaye's ACTV organization performed such a role. Similarly, Morton Blackwell's Leadership Institute worked to place conservatives in the bureaucracy. Blackwell was the White House liaison to religious conservatives during Reagan's first term of office. He left that position to devote full attention to the task of placing conservatives in public jobs. Although less affiliated with the Christian Right than with libertarian and New-Right philosophies, the Heritage Foundation and the Institute for Educational Affairs also sought to place religious conservatives in positions.[43]

The sheer size of the bureaucracy assured that there were many openings. Gary King and Lyn Ragsdale gathered data on the size of the executive branch from 1980 through 1986. What they uncovered was a remarkable degree of consistency in the size of the executive branch, despite Reagan's continual rhetoric about cutting the size of government. In 1980, there were approximately 1.1 million positions in some three dozen independent federal agencies and 1.7 million positions in thirteen cabinet departments; by 1986, there were approximately 1.2 and 1.8 million positions, respectively.[44] The vast majority of those positions were probably irrelevant to policy formulation, staffed with carryovers from the Carter Administration, or essentially irrelevant to the political objectives of the Christian Right. Certainly it would be a mistake to think in terms of thousands of important appointments. By the same token, many of the positions that might be irrelevant to policy formulation at the time might nonetheless provide their holders with the necessary government experience to move into jobs with policy implications. In that sense, even seemingly unimportant clerical positions might eventually prove significant.

The other important dimension of this discussion is the manner in which the Reagan Administration considered ideology when making its appointments. Reagan's five predecessors, on average, filled about 58 percent of 2,386 major appointments (defined as cabinet, subcabinet, policy-level and ambassadorial positions) with people sharing their political-party affiliation. The Reagan Administration was much more partisan. By the end of his first term, Reagan had appointed Republicans to some 82 percent of 524 major positions.[45] That figure was particularly striking because it was fully 17 percent above the next most partisan president (Nixon), with respect to appointments.

The partisan nature of the Reagan administration was particularly evident in certain cabinet departments, where there was a virtual litmus test. According to King and Ragsdale, 100 percent of Justice Department and Commerce Department employees in Reagan's first term of office were registered Republicans. Over one-half of the remaining cabinet departments had a minimum of 90 percent Republican appointments; in fact, the State Department was the only cabinet department with fewer than 70 percent of its appointees sharing Reagan's partisan affiliation.[46] According to Ronald Brownstein, that infiltration of the bureaucracy "proceeded steadily" far into Reagan's second term, particularly in Attorney General Ed Meese's Justice Department and Secretary William Bennett's Education Department.[47] Even the Heritage Foundation's "placement director" for conservatives indicated satisfaction with the breadth of Reagan administration appointments, saying in 1986 that he felt "confident that there are a handful of technically competent conservatives touching every area of government."[48]

How the partisanship of the Reagan administration trickled down to tangible appointments for the Christian Right is not entirely clear. It is known that there were "talent banks" for placing conservatives in the bureaucracy, that there were many opportunities over the course of Reagan's presidency, and that the administration was partisan in its choices. Moreover, the demographic characteristics of appointees fit the broad categories of Christian-Right supporters, with some 92 percent of Reagan's major first-term appointees being white and 82 percent being Republican.[49] Those are very broad categories, of course, and it would be short-sighted to make inferences about the actual number of Christian-Right appointees from those percentages. All that can be projected from those numbers is that the potential for appointments was great.

One 1984 interviewee thoroughly familiar with the "talent banks" did place an actual figure on the number of appointments at that time, saying that on average "about five conservatives a day are being placed in the policy process." That figure over the eight years of the Reagan presidency would have translated into something just short of 3,000 appointees. Although the person who provided that figure had some incentive to inflate it (to make the Christian Right appear more influential), it seems like a plausible figure given the countless opportunities in a sizeable executive branch. It is also plausible simply given the number of Christian-Right sympathizers this author met in the interviewing process who at some point took executive-branch appointments.[50] Perhaps significantly, the person who provided the estimate of five persons per day also indicated that the number of appointments was not so important as the fact that the Reagan White House "involved the Religious Right people in relevant matters to the greatest extent possible." The interviewee saw the placement of five conservatives per day as a rather perfunctory matter.

At the end of the Reagan presidency, there was satisfaction in Christian-

Right circles with the pace and breadth of appointments to the executive branch. One person interviewed in 1989, who sought anonymity, flatly stated: "The Christian Right has infiltrated the bureaucracy. There are many of its followers set into the structure of government, even at the highest levels of the civil service. It will take years to measure the effect of that success." Gary Jarmin was willing to state for the record in a 1989 interview: "Reagan assisted in that process [of bringing in quality people] by allowing the movement to use the White House as a training ground for people like Gary Bauer. We [in the Christian Right] did not get all that we sought from the administration, but we did get the chance to get people experience."[51] One other interviewee, who sought anonymity on this subject, put the matter directly: "Reagan's greatest achievement has been to credential a new generation of leaders. That credentialing, more than enactment of any agenda, has been his greatest triumph." The fact that both liberal and conservative interviewees agreed that religious conservatives received many appointments suggests that in fact they did. The consensus "inside the Beltway," was that the nature of the bureaucracy was vastly different from what it was at the start of the 1980s.

The widespread satisfaction with the Reagan Administration's efforts to place religious conservatives in the bureaucracy, though, did not carry over into the early years of the Bush presidency. In particular, evangelical and fundamentalist leaders were dismayed with the appointment of Health and Human Services Secretary Louis Sullivan (on the grounds that he was "pro-choice" at heart), as well as Secretary of State James Baker and Treasury Secretary Nicholas Brady (because they were too moderate). They were also concerned initially with the nomination of Alfred Sikes to head the Federal Communications Commission, because of his refusal to take a public stand against television and radio indecency.[52] (Sikes eventually won them over by attacking media indecency.) They backed the appointment of Indianapolis attorney John Price, who had spearheaded support for Donald Lynch's 1986 congressional campaign (discussed shortly).

Christian-Right leaders also registered their discontent with the sheer number of appointments in the Bush Administration. The Reverend Adrian Rogers, former president of the Southern Baptist Convention and a long-time fundamentalist involved in the Christian Right, publicly alleged that religious conservatives had been given only 1 percent of all Bush Administration appointments during 1989.[53] He remarked: "We don't want to sound ungrateful, but we also don't want to seem satisfied. We feel used . . .

[because] in this infrastructure, there is not an understanding of who we are."[54] Pat Robertson echoed Rogers's comments, warning Bush's appointments coordinator, Chase Untermeyer, that "if you don't want us to be identified [in the appointments process], we won't be identified next election."[55] Although some appointments met with the Christian Right's approval—most notably Housing and Urban Development Secretary Jack Kemp, whose 1988 presidential campaign had been strongly endorsed by Tim and Beverly LaHaye—religious conservatives generally have not been pleased with Bush's efforts. Of course, the relatively limited number of new appointments overlooks the fact that people were set in many positions during the Reagan years.

Judicial Appointments

The judiciary was also an avenue for activism as the Christian Right's focus shifted away from Capitol Hill. As with the executive branch, there were many openings in the judiciary, many opportunities to "pack the courts" with justices sympathetic to the concerns of religious conservatives. Heading into his last year of office, Ronald Reagan had appointed 44 percent of all of the nation's federal judges.[56] As with the bureaucracy, most of those appointments were white male Republicans, with upwards of 90 percent of 290 district and appellate judges having those characteristics.[57] In contrast to the case of the bureaucracy, though, those racial, gender, and partisan characteristics were fairly consistent with the track record of Reagan's predecessors. By the end of his second term, Reagan had appointed over 50 percent of the nation's federal judges.[58]

The sheer number of appointments to the federal bench excited religious conservatives and alarmed liberals interviewed for this volume. Gary Bauer, of the Family Research Council, offered this assessment: "The remaking of the judiciary during the Reagan years provides another opportunity for conservatives."[59] Colleen Kiko, Minority Counsel for the Civil and Constitutional Rights subcommittee, of the House Judiciary Committee, concurred: "The courts increasingly present an opportunity for social conservatives. With the appointments during the Reagan years, they are now more open to the concerns of social conservatives."[60] Joseph Conn, of Americans United for the Separation of Church and State, viewed the appointments with concern: "With President Reagan having appointed many judges who are less sympathetic to church-state separation, the courts are now fertile territory for the Christian Right and probably will be quite a battleground [in the future]." [61]

The major story with regard to the judiciary, of course, was the appointment of Supreme Court justices in the 1980s. Reagan successfully placed Sandra Day O'Connor, Antonin Scalia, and Anthony Kennedy on the Supreme Court, as well as elevated conservative justice William Rehnquist to the position of Chief Justice. The only major tussle the Reagan Administration lost was its attempt to place Robert Bork on the Supreme Court, a bruising battle that involved widespread political mobilization on both sides. None of those justices who were appointed could be construed as Christian-Right supporters per se, but their appointment resulted in a more conservative Supreme Court by the end of the 1980s. In 1989, the Court handed down two major decisions that pleased religious conservatives: *Webster* v. *Reproductive Health Services,* in which the Court upheld state restrictions on the availability of abortion, and *Wards Cove Packing* v. *Atonio,* in which the Court ruled that statistical underrepresentation of women and minorities was not sufficient proof for a discrimination lawsuit, absent proof of deliberate intent to discriminate.[62] Early in 1990, the Supreme Court upheld the constitutionality of the 1984 "Equal Access Act" that passed the Congress with support from the Christian Right, in *Board of Education of the Westside Community Schools* v. *Mergens.*[63]

Perhaps equally important over the long term is that the Reagan appointments to the federal bench were more inclined to be "strict constructionists," meaning that they interpreted statutes in light of the intentions of the Founding Fathers. Their general approach is one of "judicial restraint," more deferential to the majoritarian political process than are their "judicial activist" brethren. One liberal activist said contemptuously of the Christian Right's support for appointment of "strict constructionists," when he was interviewed in 1984: "They fail to understand that courts making policy is not a new thing. They think that the judicial activism that has occurred [in previous decades] is somehow new. . . . The Religious Right fails to recognize that the Constitution is much more than the Founding Fathers said that it was." Setting aside that normative comment, the significance of more judges sympathetic to the principles of judicial restraint is the likelihood that issues will be turned back to the political process for resolution. Conservatives have labeled that trend the "defederalization" of the judiciary.

In effect, the controversial *Webster* decision "defederalized" the abortion issue, turning it back to the states. It set loose a torrent of intense struggles throughout the country, involving such states as Idaho, Florida, Pennsylvania, and Louisiana. Not only were there more conservative judges sympathetic to the concerns of religious conservatives by the end of the decade, then, but also more opportunities for the Christian Right in the grass-roots, as the "strict constructionists" of the Reagan era remanded controversial social issues back to the majoritarian political process. The Bush administration followed its predecessor's lead in the last year of the 1980s and into the 1990s, appointing 46 judges mostly out of the same "strict constructionist" mode.[64] President Bush's Supreme Court nominations of David Souter in 1990 and Clarence Thomas in 1991 also seemed to fit that pattern.

One certainty is that the Christian Right realizes that opportunities exist in the judiciary. In an earlier chapter, the deliberate legal strategies of Concerned Women for America were examined in some detail; it has been assisted for some years by such organizations as the Christian Legal Society, the National Legal Foundation, and Christian Advocates Serving Evangelism.[65] Colleen Kiko stated in a 1989 interview that, "the major test cases are brought by the Washington conservative groups. . . . The Webster case [for instance] was picked because it was the perfect test case."[66] There is, then, a systematic attempt to exploit the courts, in search of friendly decisions and/or the return of certain issues, where the courts have been hostile, to the political process. On the latter point, Gary Bauer stated optimistically: " A variety of issues which were federalized may become defederalized with a remade judiciary. That would return a number of issues to the states and local communities. Since our side may be closer [than the liberals] to the average person in the grass roots, the defederalization is a heartening development."[67] In the 1990s, look for the Christian Right to be an active litigant, because judges are more sympathetic than at any time in recent memory.

Heading to the Hinterlands

The other avenue for activism that has been pursued, in addition to infiltrating the bureaucracy and plying the legal system, has been to organize followers at the grass roots. One of the difficulties for the

Christian Right in the aftermath of the "highwater" 98th Congress was to keep the movement afloat as its agenda withered and as its national lobbies dissolved or reorganized. The grass roots provided a means to cope with that problem, organizing local citizens around issues of local interest. As Gary Jarmin observed in an earlier chapter, it could be difficult to keep local people focused on national issues, a difficulty that impelled Christian-Right leaders to organize at the grass roots.

In chapter 3, the grass-roots oriented organizations of the Christian-Right were explained in some detail. Among the groups heavily involved in the grass roots in the 1980s were the American Coalition for Traditional Values, with its structure of pastors in three hundred cities; the American Freedom Coalition, which continues to erect "precinct councils"; and Concerned Women for America, with its genesis in women's prayer chapters. When the Reverend Pat Robertson launched his "Christian Coalition" in the opening months of 1990, it too was designed as a grass-roots group. Its executive director remarked: "We believe that the Christian community in many ways missed the boat in the 1980s by focusing almost entirely on the White House and Congress when most of the issues that concern conservative Catholics and evangelicals are primarily determined in the city councils, schools boards, and state legislatures." Although the group is not very ecumenical nor the only one operating in the grass roots, its executive director captures the gist of its focus in saying: "We think the Lord is going to give us this nation back one precinct at a time, one neighborhood at a time, and one state at a time."[68]

Complementing the national organizations led by the "heavy hitters" of the Christian Right are a wealth of exclusively state and local groups. Some of those organizations are intertwined with the national organizations, and some of them are relatively autonomous. Examples would include the Coalition for Traditional Morality in California, which has been active particularly in gay rights issues in that state; "Citizens for Excellence in Education," an organization in San Antonio that has endeavored to carve out a greater role for religion in the public schools; the Christian Civic League, a group operating in Maine that has actively contested abortion and gay rights laws, and whose leader, Jasper Wyman, challenged Majority Leader George Mitchell for his U.S. Senate seat in 1988; and Virginians for Family Values, an organization fighting state-mandated sex education in Virginia schools. The number of such groups is sufficiently large, and their organizational titles sufficiently vague, that it is impossible to chronicle their existence in any systematic fashion. The periodical *Church & State* devoted a special section to the activity of local socially conservative groups at the end of the 1980s,[69] but even that effort could not capture all those that existed, nor could it anticipate those that would continue to surface. Just as it is impossible to document the patchwork of organizations, it is impossible to assess their impact in any systematic fashion. Joseph Conn of Americans United pointed out one advantage the local groups have compared to the national organizations: "Opposition at the grass-roots is less considerable than at the national level. If one minister in a local community can turn his church out to a city council meeting, their voices will be heard. It is not easy to combat that type of influence. . . . [In contrast] the Congress represents the religious diversity of about 250 million people."[70]

Another manifestation of grass-roots work has been the efforts of Christian-Right forces to elect their people to public office. Those efforts occurred throughout the 1980s but really began to take root after the "highwater" 98th Congress (1983–1984) and the organizational transition that followed. In the 1986 election cycle, in particular, religious conservatives vied for control of the Republican party in many states, trying to nominate their candidates for the November general elections. *Congressional Quarterly* noted the phenomenon: "In no modern election year have there been so many primaries in which the split between evangelicals and the GOP establishment has been a central—if often unspoken—issue."[71] Ultimately, Christian-Right candidates contended for an estimated twenty-three House seats that year, in such states as Arizona, Georgia, Indiana, Michigan, Minnesota, Nebraska, North Carolina, Oregon, South Carolina, Tennessee, and Texas.[72]

Perhaps the most interesting of those races was the challenge that the Reverend Don Lynch proffered to Democratic incumbent Phil Sharp in Indiana's second congressional district. He quietly organized hundreds of people in local churches to secure a primary victory, and then challenged the six-term incumbent on particularly the abortion and AIDS issues (calling for an end to abortion and holding open the possibility of quarantining AIDS patients).[73] A Nazarene minister, Lynch did not smoke, drink, or watch television; his son attended school at his church.[74] With a narrowly drawn campaign and the absence of any political credentials, Lynch managed to draw only 37 percent of the vote in the general election, a fairly dismal performance for heavily Republican east-central Indiana. It was appreciably worse than almost all of Sharp's previous opponents. The interesting point, though, is that Lynch even ran for office. His race was symptomatic of the growing interest in grass-roots politics and electioneering by religious conservatives. That budding interest peaked in 1988, with the candidacy of the Reverend Pat Robertson.

Robertson and the Invisible Army

Pat Robertson's run for the presidency was the most visible expression of grass-roots activism. He began his campaign with a grass-roots ploy, saying he would seek the presidency only if three million people signed petitions asking him to run.[75] The petition gimmick helped Robertson assemble an impressive grass-roots mailing list, which was used to raise some $10 million even before Robertson formally announced his presidential candidacy in October 1987.[76] By the time he suspended his campaign, in April 1988, Robertson had raised and spent virtually all of the $27 million permitted under federal campaign law.[77]

It is not necessary to relate the story of the Robertson presidential quest in detail, since it has already been told in several places.[78] Overall, he received about 1.1 million votes in Republican primaries, about 9% of the total votes cast. That showing put him well behind George Bush (68%) and Robert Dole (20%) but ahead of Republican contenders Jack Kemp (2.7%), Pete DuPont (0.4%), and Al Haig (0.2%). Because he fared well in the caucus states, however, Robertson finished second overall in the delegate count, just ahead of Dole.[79]

Where did Robertson draw his support? In geographic terms, most of it came from the Deep South, the Great Plains, and the far West. Table 5-2 reflects that finding, listing Robertson's top five primary and caucus showings.

Robertson's best percentage showing during the primary season came in Oklahoma, where he won 21.1% of the vote. That was followed by South Dakota, and then the Deep South states of South Carolina, Arkansas, and Louisiana. His best percentage caucus showing came in Hawaii, with 81.3% of the vote. It was followed by Alaska and Washington, where Robertson won the caucuses, and then by Minnesota and Arizona. Looking at those results, plus the results from other states not mentioned here, it is evident that Robertson fared quite well nationally, except for the Northeastern and New England states.

Where did Robertson draw his support in demographic terms? ABC

Table 5-2 Robertson's Best Performances in 1988 Republican Presidential Primaries and Caucuses

	Vote won by Robertson (%)	Finish
Primaries		
Oklahoma	21.1	3
South Dakota	19.6	2
South Carolina	19.1	3
Arkansas	18.9	3
Louisiana	18.3	2
Caucuses		
Hawaii	81.3	1
Alaska	46.8	1
Washington	39.0	1
Minnesota	28.2	2
Arizona	25.2	2

conducted exit polls in primary states, and not surprisingly, found that Robertson fared well with people who considered themselves evangelicals or "born again."[80] He drew heavily from people who claimed a religious affiliation, with the notable exception of Jewish voters, who provided him 0% in many different states.[81] In terms of income, age, and education, Robertson drew fairly evenly across all categories, though there was fluctuation by state. The only other demographic findings of interest were that Robertson did much better among females than among males, and surprisingly well among black Republicans. Table 5-3 illustrates those points.

The table shows that out of twenty-three primary states where ABC News conducted exit polls, females voted more for Robertson than males in seventeen states. Only in Texas did males opt for Robertson in greater percentage terms, with the remaining five states divided evenly. Not much can be made of the precise results, since in virtually all cases, the percentage differences are modest and probably not statistically significant. However, the nature of the relationship between gender and support for Robertson is fairly consistent and therefore noteworthy.

Table 5-3 Gender and Racial Differences in Support for Robertson in the 1988 Primary Season

	Voters for Robertson (%)		Voters for Robertson (%)	
	Male	Female	White	Black
Alabama	14	17	15	17
Arkansas	16	22	19	38
Connecticut	3	4	NA	NA
Florida	12	13	13	6
Georgia	18	22	20	38
Illinois	6	7	7	6
Kentucky	14	16	15	40
Louisiana	13	15	14	44
Maryland	6	7	6	26
Massachusetts	3	6	4	11
Mississippi	17	22	20	6
Missouri	11	13	12	0
New Hampshire	10	12	NA	NA
North Carolina	8	8	8	31
Oklahoma	24	24	24	50
Rhode Island	4	5	5	0
South Carolina	17	19	17	38
South Dakota	22	22	21	25
Tennessee	15	17	16	27
Texas	13	12	12	13
Vermont	4	9	6	33
Virginia	12	12	12	25
Wisconsin	6	6	6	0

Source: Compiled by author from *The 1988 Vote* (New York: ABC News, 1989).

The table also shows that Robertson fared quite well among the limited pool of black Republicans. That performance is mildly surprising, because the Christian Right historically has been perceived as threatening the black community, despite the fact that many black Americans consider themselves evangelical Christians.[82] Yet the table shows that Robertson received up to as much as one-half of the black Republican vote in the twenty-one states where the relationship of race to vote was measured. His average in those states was 23 percent, meaning that Robertson won about one in four black Republican votes.

On balance, how successful was the Robertson campaign? If the basis for judgment is the proportion of delegates won, or the number of delegates won in comparison to the amount of money spent, then the Robertson campaign was a dismal failure. Despite some $23 million spent, he won only 103 delegates total, about 4.5% of the total number of delegates available.[83] If the standard for judging his campaign is different, though, then so is the interpretation. All things considered, Robertson might be viewed as having performed quite well in the Republican primary season. He was a minister, virtually without political credentials, making his first bid for public office, against the sitting vice-president and the Senate Republican leader. He finished second in terms of the number of delegates received overall, out of six contenders, and third in percentage of the aggregate vote received. In order to achieve that standing, he won caucuses in Alaska, Hawaii, and Washington, as well as took second in Minnesota and Iowa. Then, too, as W. Craig Bledsoe noted, Robertson's candidacy encouraged some sympathizers to seek congressional seats in 1988.[84] Most of them fared poorly, as had Christian-Right candidates in 1986, but their presence was richly symbolic of grass-roots activity.

Equally significant was the infusion of newcomers to the Republican party. Journalists coined the phrase "invisible army" to describe the legions of committed Robertson supporters who quietly and efficiently organized in precincts across America.[85] By the end of the campaign season, many of those people were in positions of power in the Republican party. Joseph Conn said in an interview that Robertson's placement of religious conservatives in the Republican party was a major feat: "His efforts have been very sophisticated, and those recruits will be able to influence the party platform and its candidates. Once they are in the corridors of power, they will exert an influence they did not when they were on the outside protesting about the way they were treated and lamenting the GOP's lack of concern with their issues."[86] There is another dimension to Robertson's 1988 presidential quest as well. His campaign helped shape the tenor of the Republican party, even though religious conservatives came away with few, if any, victories in 1988.

Political Credentials and Campaign Law

Quite apart from questions of success, the Robertson campaign was notable for its elevation of political expediency over principle. Perhaps because he had less political credentials than his major Republican rivals, Robertson was hard-pressed to justify his candidacy for the nation's highest political office. In the process of doing so, he succumbed to the temptation to overstate his credentials. His words and actions on a wide range of matters were inconsistent with religious underpinnings and reflected a willingness to place political advantage ahead of religious precepts.

A particular source of difficulty was his war record. Robertson portrayed himself as a "combat veteran" of the Korean conflict, a claim that was challenged as far back as 1986 by former U.S. Representative Pete McCloskey, who served with him in Korea. McCloskey asserted that Robertson never really participated in combat, and even suggested that he used the influence of his father, A. Willis Robertson (U.S. Senator from Virginia) to win transfer off a troop ship to supply duty. In October 1986, a year before his formal announcement that he would seek the presidency, Robertson filed a $35-million libel suit. In 1987, Phil Gailey reported that Robertson had dispatched a journalist with ties to the Christian Broadcasting Network to interview McCloskey about the case, without that journalist revealing his connection to Robertson.[87] That action surely constituted the sacrifice of religious principles for secular political gain. After that time, the case became quite muddled. A court date was set for March 1988, on the same day as "Super Tuesday," the biggest primary day of the 1988 campaign season. In January 1988 Robertson's lawyers requested a postponement, but the request was rebuffed by a U.S. district court judge. Robertson then faced appearing in court or campaigning on Super Tuesday, and he opted for the latter, dropping his libel suit against McCloskey.[88] For his part, McCloskey claimed that Robertson was "chickening out of the trial just like he chickened out 37 years ago [in Korea]."[89]

Robertson had other sources of difficulty surrounding his campaign vita. Specifically, he claimed "graduate study" at the University of London, which turned out to be an introductory summer arts course; he also listed membership on a board of directors for a Virginia bank, which turned out to be a local advisory board.[90]

In some respects, Robertson was simply a victim of the brand of media "pack journalism" that was practiced during the 1988 campaign season.[91]

In the atmosphere bred by Democrat Gary Hart's alleged relationship with model Donna Rice, the media scrutinized candidates to an unprecedented degree. It was revealed, for instance, that Robertson must have impregnated his wife of over thirty years some days prior to their marriage, given the dates of the marriage and the birth of their first child.[92] They fudged that fact by celebrating their anniversary on Robertson's birthday rather than on their official wedding day.[92] Such intrusions into the private lives of candidates were unprecedented, and they became a focus of media introspection once the campaign season ended.

In Robertson's case, though, the aforementioned events were not the only problems. Robertson also ran afoul of the law. In an earlier chapter, it was noted that he used the tax-exempt Freedom Council as a springboard for his presidential campaign, eventually dissolving it in the midst of an Internal Revenue Service audit and a confidentiality agreement with Freedom Council employees. The Robertson campaign also contemplated exceeding the legal spending limit in certain primary states, through a ruse of returning money in escrow to contributors so that more could be raised.[93] For years, presidential contenders had overspent legal limits in early primary states such as Iowa and New Hampshire, preferring to pay fines after the campaign season was over. Hence, Robertson's plans were not new. However, they were evidence of a low set of standards once again, of interest in political objectives overriding religious principles. In the same vein, Robertson also chose large lump-sum payments to a few political consultants, in laying the groundwork for his presidential campaign, thereby avoiding disclosure of how millions of dollars were spent.[94] In this case, the campaign was on firm legal footing, but it was exhibiting ethical standards that were at odds with the practices of the other presidential contenders.[95] At best, in the course of seeking the presidency, the Robertson campaign stayed just within the legal standards governing campaign finance; at worst, the campaign knowingly violated the law. In either case, the ethical standards were unbecoming a minister of the Gospel.

Sophistication in the Robertson Camp

If that twist on the secularization theme was pertinent to the Robertson campaign, so also was the theme of sophistication. However, there was something of a dichotomy in that regard. In terms of local organizing and "getting out the vote," the Robertson campaign proved extremely adept. It caught everyone by surprise with a second-place finish in Iowa, where Robertson placed ahead of an incumbent, two-term vice-president. It was also very well organized and successful in such states as Alaska and Washington and presented a strong challenge initially in states such as Michigan and South Carolina. In the "nuts and bolts" of campaign organizing, in other words, the political sophistication of the Robertson campaign was apparent. That sophistication fits this volume's argument that political skill increased over time.

With respect to the national political scene, though, the Robertson campaign was hopelessly inept. Its top leaders, including Robertson, were insensitive to how issues played out in the national press. Gary Bauer noted in an interview: "When people like Pat Robertson run for public office, they should expect to be the issue."[96] Apparently, the Robertson forces did not expect that to be the case, playing "fast and loose" with his campaign vita and finance laws.

Even more telling, though, were all of the rhetorical mistakes that the candidate personally committed. In charges strenuously denied by the Reagan Administration, Robertson claimed during the primary season that his Christian Broadcasting Network had known the whereabouts of American hostages in Lebanon, that the Soviet Union had placed offensive nuclear weapons in Cuba, and that the Bush campaign had knowingly leaked information about Jimmy Swaggart's rendezvous with a prostitute, in order to sabatoge a fellow television evangelist's presidential hopes.[97] All of those comments came on the heels of an earlier accusation that Planned Parenthood was interested in creating a "master race."[98] The unsubstantiated charges came in the period leading up to Super Tuesday, and were probably an attempt by Robertson to energize his supporters throughout the conservative southern states. In the end, though, they helped sound the death knell for the Robertson campaign nationally. The political skills that grew throughout the 1980s were not manifested in Robertson's own statements. It is important to note this exception to a general rise in political sophistication, but important also to remember that it was an exception. In other facets of presidential campaigning, the Robertson campaign was quite effective indeed.

The Consequences of Grass-roots Activism

By the end of the 1980s, the Christian Right had repositioned itself. Its people had gradually infiltrated the bureaucracy, and its organizations were better situated to exploit the legal system. Perhaps most significantly, though, the Christian Right was relocated in the grass roots. Gone were the national direct-mail lobbies such as Christian Voice and Moral Majority; in their place were grass-roots organizations such as Concerned Women for America and the American Freedom Coalition.

The move to the grass roots over time was a sagacious decision by Christian-Right leaders. It placed their movement where it was likely to be most influential, because of the pressure that could be brought to bear on state and local officials. Yet, there were more subtle things at work as well. Decreasing the flow of mail to Capitol Hill took away an opportunity for the opposition to compile and exploit mailing lists. In the early 1980s, Christian-Right leaders enjoined their followers to write their representatives in Congress on a wide range of issues. That "shotgun" approach was only marginally effective in pressuring members of Congress, because it was clearly so contrived;[99] moreover, it provided liberal members with mailing lists that they could exploit to their best advantage. After years of inundating Capitol Hill with mail, Christian-Right leaders gradually understood that it might be more harmful than helpful to the cause. Gary Jarmin remarked in a 1989 interview: "Both postcards and petitions [sent to Capitol Hill] do your opponents a favor by giving them a mailing list."[100] That statement reflected increased sensitivity to the opportunities that liberal politicians had been afforded, as well as increased political skills on the part of Christian-Right elites.

The grass-roots emphasis at the end of the 1980s also served another important purpose: it allowed Christian-Right leaders to deflect common charges leveled against them. In the early 1980s, a persistent theme sounded by the liberal opposition was that the Christian Right's leaders were entirely too intolerant. They cited rhetoric, "moral report cards," and policy positions as proof. The shift to the grass roots stifled some of that criticism and altered the terms of the debate. The question that hung in the early 1980s often was: How tolerant are Christian-Right leaders? The question posed at the end of the decade, though, was more like this one: How much strength does the Christian Right have in the grass roots? Then too, the whole business of encouraging and organizing local citizens to get involved in their communities was something that the opposition could scarcely criticize. It was the essence of democratic government.

The shift to the grass roots reflected better skills and years of accumulated wisdom among Christian-Right leaders. The ensuing chapter shows how those traits carried over into the rhetoric that leaders offered citizens.

6

From Moralism to Liberalism

Many factors contributed to the rise of the Christian Right in the late 1970s, ranging from tussles with the Internal Revenue Service over the tax-exempt status of private religious schools, to dismay with a litany of Supreme Court decisions, to the existence of a television-evangelism structure that allowed elite leaders to recruit mass followers.[1] Perhaps the single most important factor motivating Christian-Right leaders, though, was the decline of traditional values and morality that occurred in the 1960s and early 1970s. Believing the nation was in the throes of moral decline, they sought to redeem it. As one person, who had been involved in the movement from the outset, put it in a 1984 interview: "What began the movement was concern among many of us involved about the slippage of morality that had occurred in our country. It was a series of Supreme Court decisions, especially on abortion, when coupled with the gay-rights movement and the attempt to legitimize homosexuality, that got us started."

The moral indignation of Christian-Right leaders was plainly evident in words they uttered as the movement was coalescing. In January 1980, Reverend Jerry Falwell observed that the feminist and gay-rights movements had eroded the "moral fiber" of the nation.[2] Several weeks later, he added this tidbit: "I'm convinced this country is morally sick, and will not correct itself unless we [conservative Christians] get involved."[3] Falwell was certainly not alone in his assessment. A Christian fundamentalist leader in

Alaska remarked: "We represent morals. We're pro-life, pro-family, pro-morals, and pro-America."[4] The Reverend Tim LaHaye similarly opined: "We believe government has intruded into areas of morals and if we don't speak out on moral issues, the government will conclude by our silence that we won't care how immoral they get."[5] Those quotations constitute but a small sampling of the convictions publicly expressed.

The indignation of the Christian Right's leaders was also apparent in the political agenda they offered to policymakers for consideration. In 1980, Alan Crawford identified abortion, school busing, gay rights, and the content of school textbooks as the major items on the Christian Right's political agenda; in 1981, Erling Jorstad added pornography to that list, and in 1985, this author added tuition tax credits, which were viewed as a way to extract students from a thoroughly secularized public school system.[6] Together, those issues constituted the bulk of the Christian Right's political objectives, and were the focal point of its leaders' efforts in the early and mid-1980s. The common denominator of those issues, of course, was concern with traditional morality.

The organizational names were still further manifestations of the early obsession with morality and traditional values. What else explains the name *Moral* Majority, or the American Coalition for *Traditional Values*? Less obvious manifestations were those organizations with religious titles, such as the National Christian Action Coalition, Christian Voice, and the Religious Roundtable. While their titles lacked overt moral references, those organizations and their leaders nevertheless were consumed with questions of morality. Why else would they have issued "*moral* report cards?" Why else were organizational leaders involved in the "Washington for Jesus" rally of April 1980? It was inspired by the Bible verse found in II Chronicles 7:14, which enjoins: "If my people who are called by my name humble themselves, and pray and seek my face, and turn from their wicked ways, then I will hear from heaven, and will forgive their sin, and heal their land." That verse conveyed the preoccupation with moral redemption so evident in the Christian Right's early years.[7]

Scholars recognized the obsession with traditional values and morality among the movement's leaders. Jorstad provided an early and lucid exposition, in a book organized around the "moralism" of the Christian Right: "The theme brought home in every speech, every sermon, every pamphlet, every request for funds was that of saving America by a return to what the leaders called its traditional morality."[8] Other scholars measured the extent to which concern over eroding moral standards ignited political activism among the movement's mass supporters.[9] Still other scholars employed moral-reform paradigms, such as status politics, to explain the rise of the Christian Right, sparking a debate between those who subscribed to status politics and those who drew on resource-mobilization theories.[10]

The purpose of this chapter, however, is not to reiterate the findings of early studies or to analyze the utility of existing paradigms; rather, it is to demonstrate how the focus on morality stymied the Christian Right's growth and undermined its staying power, and how its leaders gradually replaced that costly moral rhetoric with the language of liberalism.

Morality and Mortality

The primary virtue of casting political issues almost exclusively in moral terms was that it motivated followers. In contemporary lexicon, it raised the spectre of a *jihad*, or holy war, against secular institutions and culture. Issues that might otherwise be viewed as routine, such as tax credits for children who attended private religious schools, took on new significance when they were defined in terms of rescuing innocent souls from a secular and humanistic public-school system. Other issues with an obvious religious dimension, such as school prayer and abortion, became nothing short of crusades. People were strongly motivated by the thought that their work was God's work, and that their religious duties could be performed in concert with their secular responsibilities.

The proclivity of Christian-Right leaders to frame issues and use language with moral overtones, though, was not cost-free. While it motivated followers, it also severely restricted opportunities for growth and expansion. In the early 1980s, Christian-Right leaders were fond of saying that there were thirty to sixty million religious conservatives, just waiting to be tapped for political activism.[11] While independent polling confirmed the gist of those aggregate numbers, it also uncovered a bewildering diversity of theological and political dispositions held by those people.[12] The moralistic overtones of Christian-Right leaders appealed most heavily to a substratum of that population, namely fundamentalists, with their beliefs in Biblical literalism, traditional morality, and individual commitment to Christ. Of course, that fact should not be surprising, since one of the distinguishing features of the "expansionist period" (1979–1984) of the Christian Right was the presence of fundamentalists in leadership positions. It was only natural that they would recruit mostly fundamentalist followers.

Field research conducted by scholars confirmed the early fundamentalist leanings of the Christian Right. Anson Shupe and William Stacey conducted a door-to-door survey of Moral Majority members in randomly selected neighborhoods in Dallas and Fort Worth in 1981 and found that they came "disproportionately from the ranks of fundamentalists." Specifically, fundamentalists were twice as likely to be Moral Majority members as were other Protestants.[13] Wilcox conducted a similar survey of Moral Majority members in Ohio in 1982 and found that 39 percent of respondents considered themselves fundamentalists, compared to only 9 percent who identified themselves as evangelicals. He also discovered that fundamentalists were more likely to select as reasons for their membership "instrumental satisfactions, such as influencing public policy and raising the moral standards of America," than were their evangelical brethren.[14] Clyde Wilcox continued his work in an analysis of 1980 National Election Study data, in which he found that, nationwide, Moral Majority supporters were "heavily fundamentalist."[15] In a somewhat different vein, James L. Guth sampled Southern Baptist ministerial support for Moral Majority and uncovered an analogous situation: "Quite clearly, Moral Majority members are fundamentalists, sympathizers are fundamentalists and conservatives, while opponents are drawn mostly from conservative and moderate ranks."[16] Finally, Kathleen Murphy Beatty and B. Oliver Walter conducted a national survey of ministerial elites in 1983, and discovered that 60 percent of the fundamentalists sampled reacted positively to Moral Majority, compared to only 11 percent of evangelicals.[17] Repeated studies showed, in other words, that Moral Majority was heavily fundamentalist in orientation; while studies of their constituencies do not exist, it is likely that the National Christian Action Coalition and the Religious Roundtable—both led by avowed fundamentalists—were similarly inclined.

The fundamentalist leanings of the Christian Right should not be overstated, because there was some evangelical element in all of the early organizations, particularly so with Christian Voice, which openly appealed to "evangelical Christians" for support. In addition, it was sometimes difficult to disentangle support for fundamentalism and evangelicalism, because some people viewed the former as a subset of the latter.[18] With those caveats in place, though, it is worth pointing out that the fundamentalist/evangelical dichotomy proved a useful analytic device for scholars,[19] and it is worth reiterating that virtually all of the early studies found that fundamentalists were the backbone of the Christian Right's organizations.

The presence of an overwhelmingly fundamentalist constituency, though, attracted by fundamentalist leaders voicing moralistic themes, created an intractable problem. Christian-Right leaders found it difficult to recruit other conservative Christians, such as evangelicals and pentecostals, because of the perceived intolerance and dogmatism of the fundamentalists. Wilcox's interviews with Moral Majority leaders in Ohio during 1982, confirmed that finding; self-identified evangelicals professed tension at monthly meetings, caused by the fundamentalists' "religious intolerance" toward their religious brethren.[20] The fundamentalist contingent, in other words, "frightened off" many potentially strong supporters from the ranks of conservative Protestantism. In later years, some Christian-Right leaders tried to overcome that problem by emphasizing the secular component of their organization and mission. In the early years, though, the problem was rather devastating, not only because of fundamentalists' general reluctance to become involved in politics for theological reasons,[21] but also because there was not a broad base of recruits in the general population. Jeffrey L. Brudney and Gary W. Copeland, employing National Election Study data, estimated that only 5 to 12 percent of the general population subscribed to fundamentalism, depending on the stringency of the definition that was used.[22] That figure translated roughly into a maximum of 30 million potential followers (not all of voting age), with the possibility that the subgroup was less than one-half that size.[23] So long as fundamentalist leaders sought and attracted mostly fundamentalist followers, then, possibilities for growth and expansion were limited. So long as they emphasized moral themes, those leaders attracted fundamentalists.

Data collected and analyzed by scholars highlighted a paradox that moralistic rhetoric and fundamentalist membership brought Christian-Right leaders. Through an analysis of 1977 General Social Survey data, John H. Simpson demonstrated that there was a "sizable plurality of respondents whose views are identical to those espoused by the Moral Majority."[24] Allen D. Hertzke culled similar findings from 1984 National Election Study data, noting that the leaders of the Christian Right had "not only articulated the opinion of their own fundamentalist constituencies, but apparently the sentiment of a large portion of the American public as well."[25] Despite expressing the views of a sizeable segment of the American public, though, early Christian-Right leaders never attracted many followers outside of their "hard-core" fundamentalist constituency. People shared their issue positions but refused to join their groups. Part of the explanation for the lack of success in translating diffuse support into interest-group membership was the higher level of intensity and effort required, which filtered out all but the most dedicated and fervent believers. Another part of the explanation is that the moralistic emphasis of Christian-Right leaders did not appeal as much to non-fundamentalists. Put in colloquial terms, they did not like the "sales pitch" of Christian-Right leaders, and so refused to select their product.

The moralistic element of the Christian Right did more than simply inhibit its growth, though. It also aroused opposition. That opposition came from predictable quarters, such as atheists and agnostics, but it also stemmed from civil libertarians who held a Jeffersonian interpretation of the First Amendment. In a personal letter to the Danbury Baptist Association, written in 1802, Thomas Jefferson provided a metaphor for understanding the words of the First Amendment which pertain to religion. He argued that "religion is a matter which lies solely between a man and his God; that he owes account to none other for his faith or his worship; that the Legislative powers of the Government reach actions only, and not opinions . . . [and therefore] that act of the whole American people which declared that their Legislature should 'make no law respecting an establishment of religion or prohibiting the free exercise thereof' . . . [should] build a wall of separation between Church and State."[26] That interpretation of the so-called "establishment clause" inhibited, if not discouraged, religious intrusion into the affairs of state. For years, civil libertarians voiced that understanding of the First Amendment, a position that was given an immeasurable boost by the Warren Court in the famous school-prayer case.[27] As Christian-Right leaders tried to inject religiously-based, moral values onto the "public square,"[28] they engendered fierce opposition. One person interviewed in 1984 echoed the civil-libertarian position, vis-à-vis the Christian Right:

> The bottom line is that the Christian Right wants to flatten out diversity in this country. They have a very narrow view of people's rights and seek to restrict those rights both in the realm of public policy and in the realm of personal morality. They see the best way of achieving these goals as legislating in various areas, trying to restrict abortion and to mandate school prayer, rather than making those things an option of individual choice.

Opposition came from other sources as well. Politicians objected to the campaign tactics of the early Christian-Right groups, with sympathetic members of Congress even resigning from Christian Voice's advisory board after the issuance of "moral report cards."[29] Ethnic and religious minorities felt threatened by a heavily fundamentalist movement with majoritarian ambitions. Lobbyists for the so-called "mainline" Protestant churches resented claims that conservative political positions were dictated by Scripture. Academics and the education establishment voiced opposition to incorporation of religious expression into the schools. Even some conservatives loathed the Christian Right, on the grounds that its followers were too intolerant and too concerned with other people's morality, which they argued was not a true conservative position.[30] All of those sources of opposition, in one form or another, raised the specter of religious intolerance on the part of the Christian Right, in the tradition of the Crusades, the Puritans, and the attempts to Christianize North American Indians. Some opponents even drew modern comparisons between Christian-Right leaders and Islamic ayatollahs.[31] Joseph Conn mentioned that point, in the context of a discussion of the early moralism of the Christian Right and the costs that it entailed:

> When the Christian Right began, it was out of a genuine moral indignation. The traditionally fervent religious zeal of the fundamentalist churches was enlisted to fight for conservative political principles. . . . Along the way [however], in the transition from moral indignation to political sophistication, the Christian Right lost a lot of people. Critical attention was focused on the movement, comparisons were drawn between Falwell and Islamic ayatollahs, and fundamentalists were caricatured in the popular press. All of that drove some people out of the movement. Those who stayed, however, became more sophisticated.[32]

Conn's statement is useful, in reinforcing both the argument about the early moralism of the Christian Right and the thesis of increased political sophistication over time.

Besides narrowing the potential base of support and arousing opposition, the moralistic overtones of the Christian Right had little staying power. It was shown that moral messages appealed primarily to fundamentalists, evidenced in their willingness to join the early organizations. The point here is that even among fundamentalists, moral messages eventually lost their seductive appeal. Leaders repeatedly challenged people, in Falwell's words, to "return America to moral sanity."[33] That theme could only be peddled successfully for a time. Eventually, supporters became somewhat numb to the message, concluding that it was an unrealistic (if admirable) goal. Moral indignation gave the Christian Right substance, but it could not give it sustenance. The fervor of followers gradually dissipated, and with it, the early organizations of the Christian Right.

Trends in American culture and society sped up the process, hastening the collapse of moralistic appeals. Gallup polls revealed that by one measure, concern with eroding moral standards in the public at large actually peaked about 1975, in the wake of the Watergate scandal. At that time, about 7 percent of the public cited moral decay as the most important problem facing the nation, a figure that ebbed over the next ten years, dropping to as low as 2 percent.[34] Moral themes resonated in the ears of fundamentalists beyond 1975, but the attraction of such themes was dissipating, even as Christian-Right leaders were constructing a social movement around them. Similar trends occurred with respect to specific social issues. After climbing steadily in the wake of the 1973 *Roe* v. *Wade* abortion decision, the percentage of pregnancies that ended in abortion leveled off beginning in about 1980, and even dropped somewhat by the middle of the decade.[35] The crime rate and the divorce rate also peaked in about 1980, thereafter falling through the mid-1980s.[36] Even sexual promiscuity seemed to level off, because of fear over the AIDS virus. Many of the trends that engendered moral outrage, in other words, were in the process of abating and/or reversing themselves in the early 1980s. The importance of moral themes increasingly was lost on many Americans; the emphasis on morality abetted organizational mortality.

Incorporating the Language of the Left

The pitfalls of moralistic overtones became apparent to Christian-Right leaders during the "transition period" (1985–1986). They were aware of the narrow band of followers that they had attracted and of the opposition they had aroused and the ephemeral nature of moral appeals. The collapse of almost all of the direct-mail lobbies during that time confirmed the need for new strategic focal points and for a new means of framing issues to attract followers. In a nutshell, Christian-Right leaders started adopting the language of the political left, dropping the rhetoric of moralism for the language of liberalism.

The variant of liberalism it adopted was a combination of classical and contemporary usage. The classical understanding of liberalism came to the United States from the secular Enlightenment thinkers of the seventeenth century, notably Thomas Hobbes and John Locke.[37] Their work was an ambitious attempt to redefine the relationship of people to their government, an effort to depose the combination of Greek thought and Christian teachings that reigned in the Western world for most of the Middle Ages. Both Hobbes and Locke deduced that people were inherently self-centered and potentially dangerous, and therefore had to live under the auspices of the state, rather than freely roam the "state of nature." Both Hobbes and Locke emphasized the inherent equality of people within a regime, however, and the rights of the individual vis-à-vis the state. In addition, both men stressed freedom of choice for the individual, who was allowed to rise or fall according to his or her intelligence, ambition, and talent. The legacy of Hobbes and Locke was beliefs in equality, freedom, choice, rights, and liberty—thoughts and words that were incorporated into the American regime and inculcated into its people by America's Founding Fathers.[38] Two centuries later, political scientist Donald Devine examined hundreds of public opinion surveys and concluded that the Lockean liberal tradition was alive and well.[39] In their assessment of Devine's work, Harry Holloway and John George noted: "Devine's study offers convincing evidence that the persistence of a Lockean liberal tradition of values as the core of the political culture best accounts for the remarkable stability of the United States."[40]

The contemporary version of liberalism is that which evolved in the post–New Deal era, but particularly in the aftermath of the social upheaval of the 1960s. The language that developed and became the vogue since then is also what the Christian Right has borrowed, albeit selectively. It has rejected contemporary liberalism's celebration of "diversity" and "cultural pluralism," taking them as euphemisms for quotas and disparagement of white, Anglo-Saxon, Protestant culture. Along similar lines, it has dismissed the emphasis on being "nonjudgmental," as a euphemism for moral relativism and for societal-level explanations of offensive individual behavior.[41] The Christian Right has accepted contemporary liberalism's focus on "victimization," though, in an attempt to strengthen its political position within the polity, as will be discussed below.

The assimilation of classical and some contemporary liberal rhetoric, starting about the mid-1980s, reflected increased political sophistication among elite leaders. They consciously incorporated a new way of advancing their political goals, as their direct-mail lobbies were folding and as the appeal of their moralistic rhetoric tapered off, even to the most faithful followers. Gary Jarmin alluded to the transformation of the Christian Right's rhetoric in a 1989 interview: "There has been growing sophistication on the part of the Christian Right that has led it to employ more effective language. The importance of language and symbols is very real, since the side that controls the 'buzzwords' in politics often controls the outcome.... We have become better at defining issues on our own terms."[42] The terms that leaders adopted were liberal in origin, and the evidence for that proposition is everywhere.

The most obvious manifestation of the switch from moralistic to liberal rhetoric was in the names of the Christian-Right organizations. Almost all of the early groups had references to religion and/or morality in their titles: the National Christian Action Coalition, Christian Voice, the Religious Roundtable, Moral Majority. Some of those groups even had divisions reiterating the same theme, such as Moral Majority's political action committee, called the Moral Government Fund, or Christian Voice's electoral wing, called Christians for Reagan. The only exception to the moralistic titles of the early Christian-Right organizations was the Freedom Council of Pat Robertson, perhaps reflecting his greater political saavy about such matters.

In contrast to the early organizations, those promulgated in and around the "transition period" all eschewed moralistic references. Their leaders either opted for more generic titles, such as the Family Research Council, or else adopted the easily recognizable language of liberalism. The Liberty Federation and the American Freedom Coalition fall into that latter category. The only irony here arose in the early 1990s, when Pat Robertson launched the Christian Coalition. That title is probably best explained by Robertson seeking to reinvigorate his "hard-core" religious constituency, in the wake of the television evangelist scandals and his unsuccessful bid for the 1988 presidential nomination, matters that took their toll on his operations.[43] With the exception of Robertson's two groups (the Freedom Council and the Christian Coalition), though, both of which have been out of sync with the rest of the Christian Right, leaders have exchanged moralistic titles for liberal language.

The same transformation has occurred with respect to specific issues. Allen Hertzke, the most astute observer of this trend, pointed out that in the early 1980s Christian-Right groups framed the school-prayer issue in moral terms, arguing to policy-makers that it was beneficial for children to recite prayers.[44] His interview with the legislative director of Moral Majority, in the "transition" year of 1985, uncovered the switch to the language of liberalism: "We pushed school prayer three years in a row, but we framed the issue in terms of how prayer in schools is good. But some people feel that prayer in school is bad. So we learned to frame the issue in terms of 'student's rights,' so it became a constitutional issue. We are prochoice for students having the right to pray in schools."[45] The reformulation of the school-prayer issue was accompanied by a push for "equal access" legislation, a measure that invoked liberal language to permit student religious groups access to the public school systems during non-curricular hours. When the Supreme Court upheld the constitutionality of that legislation in its 1990 *Mergens* decision, Beverly LaHaye drew further upon liberal language, asserting that the Court had ruled against religious "apartheid" and "bigoted discrimination" against student religious groups.[46]

In a more recent study, Hertzke and Scribner demonstrated how New-Right conservatives and religious conservatives framed the issue of child care in terms of "parental choice."[47] Conservative forces sought to defeat, or substantially amend, the 1989 Act for Better Child Care (the "ABC bill") when it was considered in Congress, on the grounds that it provided federal subsidies for parents who put their children in day care rather than stayed home to care for them. By evoking the rhetoric of choice, they endeavored to expand the reach of ABC, to include child-care providers who stayed at home, such as parents and grandparents.[48] That framing of the child-care issue, incidentally, is perfectly consistent with the way that Christian-Right leaders in recent times have tried to frame the tuition tax-credit issue, which is to say that tax credits would allow parents and their children a "choice" of schools to attend. It is also consistent with a theology that stresses individual choice—to commit to Christ, to be "born-again," to live as godly a life as possible. Because of that congruence, the political rhetoric of "choice" may be especially appealing to the religious supporters of the Christian Right.

Although he did not develop it, Hertzke also noted the potential for reformulating the abortion issue. He quoted from a 1985 source, which contained this comment from Reverend Jerry Falwell: "We are reframing the debate [on abortion]. This is no longer a religious issue, but a civil rights issue."[49] Since that time, of course, the anti-abortion movement, which includes supporters of the Christian Right, has proceeded past formulating the issue in terms of civil rights, actually adopting the practices and rhetoric of the civil rights movement.[50] This "Operation Rescue," as it was dubbed, led to mass sit-ins and arrests, prompting Gary Bauer to remark in a 1989 interview: "The conservative Christian movement is still attracting new recruits. The people involved in Operation Rescue serve as a case in point. In some instances, those people went from being apolitical, skipping involvement in campaigns, right to jail because of their convictions."[51] In a more pedestrian sense, of course, anti-abortion forces have lobbied against the procedure on the basis of the "rights of the unborn." They have even utilized the term "choice," to convey the need for pregnant adolescents to have options other than abortion. As with the other issues, abortion has been recast by religious conservatives, to play into the more widely accepted and inclusive language of classical liberalism.

A final example along these lines is school-textbook content. Religious conservatives have tried to frame that issue in terms of "parental rights." A public-relations specialist for Concerned Women for America said in a radio interview that textbook content was an issue of "parental rights," because parents were taxpayers and entitled to have a say in their children's school books. Later in the interview, she invoked civil-libertarian rhetoric, claiming that school-textbook content was also a "free speech" issue, since some people sought deletion of religious and moral references in books. The clever use of liberal and civil-libertarian rhetoric did not end there, either, as she pressed for use of public-school auditoriums for religious services, on the grounds of "equal access" to public facilities.[52]

In a different vein, Christian-Right leaders have adopted the contemporary liberal rhetoric of "victimization." Growing out of the civil-rights and women's-rights movements of the 1960s, as well as the gay-rights movement, victimization posits that there are larger forces that drive aberrant individual behavior. Thus, armed robbery by a ghetto resident might be explained as the by-product of economic or social deprivation. Concrete examples in the early 1990s include a university president who claimed he was "compelled" to make obscene phone calls to women because he was molested as a child, and a mayor of a large city who claimed that his arrest on drug charges was the product of a racist conspiracy.[53] The proliferation of such incidents prompted a nationally syndicated columnist to write about the emergence of a "victim growth industry."[54]

Setting aside normative questions about the emergence of the politics of "victimization," the point is that Christian-Right leaders began adopting the practice in their efforts to gain political advantage. The most celebrated case in point involved the Reverend Pat Robertson in 1988. In an effort to broaden his potential base of support, Robertson resigned from his ministerial affiliations prior to entering the race for the presidency. Subsequently, he enjoined media representatives to portray him as a "Christian businessman," rather than a television evangelist. Despite his pleas, Robertson was continually characterized as a television evangelist, prompting him to lash out that he was the "victim" of mass-media "bigotry."[55] It is questionable whether his attempt to attain victim status was even partly successful; reporters ignored Robertson's pleas, continuing to cast him as a minister and television evangelist.[56] What is evident, though, is that Robertson's effort to recast his image was a clever and calculated ploy to tap the reservoir of positive sentiment for victims of American society.

Along similar lines, Steve Bruce has noted the increasing tendency of Christian-Right leaders to portray themselves as a persecuted minority. Writing in the late 1980s, he said that "as yet this is a rhetoric that only occasionally appears in fundamentalists' complaints about the neglect of their values" but suggested that "the New Christian Right has been the most successful in the public arena when it has presented its own cause as being that of an oppressed and hard-done-by minority."[57] The implication is that the Christian Right will press such rhetoric in the future in order to evoke the sympathy that people have felt for other modern social movements. This "persecution complex" surfaced in March 1991, in a bill sponsored by a Massachusetts state legislator to ban religious satire on the grounds that it victimized Christians and discriminated against their beliefs.[58]

In the process of incorporating classical and contemporary liberal rhetoric, leaders set aside their moralistic overtones so in evidence in the early 1980s. People interviewed in 1989 were queried on the transformation of language in the Christian Right, and all of them acknowledged the sort of changes discussed here. Joseph Conn, of Americans United for the Separation of Church and State, observed:

> When it [the Christian Right] began in the late 1970s, its leaders used narrow religious language and made statements which were inappropriate in the political dialogue of a pluralistic country. For instance, they continually spoke about 'Christianizing' America. . . . Over time, many Christian-Right

> activists came to see that it was pretty threatening rhetoric. Hence, they quit speaking about the need to 'Christianize' America . . . [and] came to see the need for inclusion rather than exclusion in a pluralistic society. . . . The step toward inclusiveness demonstrated a growing political sophistication on their part, a realization that Bible-believing Christians were only one small part of the American landscape.[59]

Gary Bauer, of the Family Research Council, spoke more directly to the demise of moralistic themes, while lamenting the fact that religiosity and morality seemed to be "out of bounds" in contemporary American public discourse:

> Today the [Christian Right] movement realizes that it must employ the language that the American people feel comfortable with. If one does not use the words and phrases that people are used to, one runs the risk of alienating them. It is unfortunate that leaders cannot use the words and phrases that were once part of the national dialogue. In short, there is more sensitivity to language in the movement now. Religion may still motivate people, but there is no virtue in quoting Bible verses to policymakers with different value perspectives. The movement has come to see that fact, realizing that it must address policymakers with words and phrases to which they are attuned.[60]

Michael Schwartz, of the Free Congress Foundation, provided further elaboration of the switch from moralistic to liberal language. In his view, the change seemed to be driven by the exit of fundamentalists: "The Christian Right has fewer 'Bible toters' today. There is less attention to the rhetoric of morality as a result. Today, Christian-Right activists speak of the need for citizens to work for the public good, rather than speak of the need for Christians to clean up a morally decadent country."[61] He added that while "the early [morality] rhetoric was sorely needed and served a purpose" in getting "people to overcome their reservations about politics," it was useless to "cite Scripture in defense of policy positions."[62] Why was it fruitless? According to Schwartz: "It will not convince those who interpret the Bible differently and it will not affect those who have not read the Bible. The Christian Right realizes today that it must appeal to people's reason, not simply cite the Bible in support of its agenda."[63]

Coupled with the evidence regarding organizational titles and policy issues, the quotations from interviews confirm that the Christian Right's rhetoric was very different at the end of the 1980s than it was at the beginning. At least in terms of public discourse, the New Testament had yielded to the *Second Treatise on Civil Government* as the guiding text. The language of St. Paul had been dropped for the phraseology of John Locke. While the change in rhetoric did not necessarily make the Christian Right more secular in essence, it did so in appearance. Recall that such a finding is consistent with the secularization theme posited in the opening chapter.

A Dichotomy

The greater emphasis on liberal, as opposed to moral, rhetoric was manifested among the elite leaders of the Christian Right but not necessarily among the mass followers. Gary Bauer drew that distinction in a 1989 interview: "The heightened sensitivity to language is particularly present at the leadership level. In the 'rank and file,' the task has not yet been sufficiently completed."[64] That last sentence is particularly illuminating, because it conveys the existence of an "education campaign" by Christian-Right leaders regarding rhetoric.

Joseph Conn of Americans United was privy to the campaign waged by elite leaders: "I attended Christian-Right workshops at which group leaders coached people to employ nonsectarian rhetoric in the political arena so that non-fundamentalist Americans would not be frightened off or turned off." Later in the interview, Conn provided a specific example of the educational efforts: "At an American Coalition for Traditional Values workshop I attended in 1986, a California political activist made a presentation advocating the use of less explicitly religious language so as to appear more moderate. He said Christian-Right activists . . . [should drop terms such as] 'Christian values' or 'Biblical values' in order to advance their agenda. He said the movement could become more explicitly religious as it achieved its goals." The apparent disingenuousness of the presentation made Conn "question whether the changes [over time in language] were sincere or a facade."[65]

There is evidence available to support either interpretation. On the one hand, the statement of the workshop director, and the shift from moralistic to liberal rhetoric, might be viewed as a genuine effort to enter the public arena on the same terms as the other players in the game. That interpretation is consistent with much of the scholarly literature on social movements, which posits that movements generally moderate over time, shifting toward points of societal consensus.[66] If so, the words of the workshop director should be understood as nothing other than an artifact of Christian-Right leaders living in two different worlds: a religiously fundamentalist one, and a secular political one. Bruce noted that cleavage: "In church, with their own people, in prayer meetings, they [Christian-Right leaders] remain fundamentalist Protestants. But when pursuing the public agenda of socio-moral issues they operate with a quite different set of criteria."[67] In that light, the apparent disingenuousness of the workshop director was simply a sincere attempt to straddle two very different worlds.

In the event that altered language connotes moderation, an accompanying characteristic may be the evolution of a stronger social conscience. In an earlier volume, this author argued that while pursuing their legislative agenda Christian-Right leaders often neglected the welfare of other citizens.[68] In a 1989 interview, Gary Jarmin argued that situation had changed: "One of the other positive changes in the movement has been the growth of a stronger social conscience. . . . Previously, the Christian Right failed to do enough on the social side. . . . One of the by-products of the years of political activity has been a stronger social conscience."[69] That change would be welcomed by the opposition and would be in keeping with the drift toward social consensus.

An equally plausible position, though, is that the evolution of rhetoric is simply a facade for "the same sectarian goals . . . under a different guise."[70] The scholarly literature on social movements provides support for this explanation as well. Scholars have shown that less committed citizens invariably drop out of a social movement over time, as compared to their more committed counterparts.[71] Assuming that this finding holds for the Christian Right, it is hard to believe that the emphasis on liberal rhetoric is sincere. Why would Christian-Right leaders publicly adopt more moderate, consensus-oriented language, at the very time that their "hard-core" constituency was the one that remained? Would their most fervent and loyal supporters not become disillusioned? It is certainly feasible that leaders educated supporters on the need to *sound* and *appear* more moderate by mouthing liberal language, without a genuine conversion to society's consensus on appropriate language.

Whether the "education campaign" of Christian-Right leaders has been a by-product of moderation or an artifact of conspiracy is impossible to ascertain. It is unfortunate that there is no survey or interview data available that explores the attitudes of people who attended the workshops that Conn described, since it might be possible to uncover the degree of genuine versus superficial commitment to the values of classical liberalism. Such data would allow researchers to assess the effectiveness of the education campaign on the students, and to gauge the sincerity of the teachers. In the absence of that data, scholars are left with the assertions of Christian-Right leaders that the focus on liberal rhetoric is proof of genuine moderation, and the arguments of the opposition that it is a cynical ploy. A plausible argument can be constructed for either position.

Regardless of the motivation of Christian-Right leaders, though, the more significant point is that the changeover in rhetoric may drive fundamental changes in the movement. Most notably, it may drive out the hard-core "moral crusaders" once and for all. As we saw in chapter 2, Ed McAteer of the Religious Roundtable strenuously objected to Paul Weyrich's recent attempt to recast the social agenda in terms of "cultural conservatism," on the grounds that it did not explicitly cite the "Judeo-Christian ethic" as its foundation.[72] Since Weyrich's formulation was more generic than classically liberal in tone, we can well imagine how "hard-core" fundamentalists will respond to the gradual adoption and incorporation of liberal rhetoric. With people like McAteer, there is "no excuse" for moderation, whether it is genuine or merely tactical. Continued use of liberal rhetoric may increase opportunities for Christian-Right leaders to gain recruits in the general public, but in self-fulfilling fashion, it may eviscerate the fundamentalist contingent on board since the late 1970s.

Steve Bruce, though he did not address the evolution of language per se, had an inkling of the tensions within the fundamentalist contingent of the movement as the 1980s drew to a close. He argued that no matter what changes occurred in the movement, they would "not stop fundamentalists [from] dreaming of the righteous empire." He continued on to argue that fundamentalists would never really accept anything short of becoming a true "moral majority."[73] If he is correct, fundamentalists will exit the Christian Right in droves in the early 1990s, as charismatic and pentecostal Christians, such as Pat Robertson, strive to cast religious conservatives as a persecuted minority, as victims of American culture. The potential effect of the switch from moralistic to liberal language, in other words, is considerable. It is a topic that warrants examination by scholars in the future, because at present the effects of the switch are just surfacing.

Moderation and Secularization

The potential effect of the changeover in language, driven by elite leaders, may well proceed past the fundamentalist element of the Christian Right. The shift toward more moderate language might result in a more moderate movement as a whole. One person interviewed in 1989, who requested anonymity, astutely suggested: "The more moderate language used by the Christian Right, with less emphasis on religion and morality, is primarily a tactical move. However, such a tactical move can have important consequences, *even if they are unintended.* More moderation in language might yield a situation where the Christian Right becomes more moderate in practice." Despite his concern about more moderate language being a "facade," Joseph Conn also added that genuine moderation had taken hold in individual cases. He cited Falwell as an example of someone who actually moderated his worldview, not just his tone:

> The moderation of the Christian Right over time is real for some but tactical for others. Proof that the moderation is real can be seen in events like Falwell inviting Senator Ted Kennedy to Liberty University to deliver an address. For years, Kennedy typified the eastern, secular liberalism that fundamentalists detested. To invite him to Liberty is not to say that Falwell or the people there agreed with Kennedy, but it does suggest a moderation on the part of Falwell.[74]

The moderation in that specific case may reflect a broader pattern, and may be a by-product of more use of liberal rhetoric.

Any trend toward moderation as a whole, though, is bound to be uneven and episodic. Even as the language of liberalism took root, leaders still "played to the faithful." Falwell himself, for instance, likened former National Security Council staff member Oliver North to Jesus Christ, on the grounds that both men were "indicted and convicted."[75] He also called Nobel Peace Prize winner, Bishop Desmond Tutu of South Africa, a "phony" if he purported to speak for all black people in that country.[76] Pat Robertson provided his own rhetorical flourishes. Among other things, he implied that Nancy Reagan was willing to jeopardize national security so that her husband might win a Nobel Peace Prize, that Reagan's secretary of state was intent on moving the nation "towards one-world socialist government", and that the White House chief of staff and defense secretary were incompetent.[77] Recall, too, from the previous chapter, that in the days prior to the "Super Tuesday" primary, Robertson claimed that his Christian Broadcasting Network had known of the location of American hostages in the Middle East, that the Bush campaign had leaked information about Jimmy Swaggart's rendezvous with a prostitute, that Planned Parenthood sought a "master race", and that the Soviet Union had placed offensive ballistic missiles in Cuba. Those latter charges were met with ridicule by Reagan-administration officials, and by the Bush campaign, which publicly pressed Robertson to provide documentation.[78]

Those quotations should be understood primarily as a pitch to faithful supporters, but they should also be seen as evidence of sacrificed religious principles—i.e., secularization. Falwell and Robertson tossed out dubious analogies and unsubstantiated charges, as well as engaged in blatant name-calling. Their words and actions were inconsistent with religious precepts and were undertaken in search of financial and/or secular political advantage.

Just as Christian-Right leaders altered their strategic focal point by the end of the 1980s in order to win policy struggles, they transformed their language in order to garner sympathy and win converts. Writing in the late 1980s, Bruce suggested that the decline of the Christian Right was inevitable, and he may well be correct.[79] However, before scholars write the political obituary of the Christian Right, they should understand that some apparent signs of decline were really deliberate attempts at strategic reorientation. Christian-Right leaders adjusted their tactics and their rhetoric to keep their movement as influential as possible. The task they face in the 1990s might not be so much to keep their movement intact as to succeed where they have steered it.

Part III.

The Evolution of the Christian Right

7

Distinctiveness and Political Influence

Envision the relative secularity and religiosity of American society on an axis. On the left endpoint of that axis is total secularity, where religiously motivated rhetoric and conduct is forbidden. A society ordered along those lines mandates church/state separation, forbids religious symbols from being exhibited in public places, and objects to religious leaders injecting their values into the public arena. On the right endpoint is complete religiosity, where secular rhetoric and values are viewed as subversive.[1] A society ordered along those lines (à la Christian Reconstructionism, covered in the next chapter) seeks universal application of Biblical law and traditions to American culture and institutions.

An argument can be constructed that American politics and culture were appreciably closer to the religious than the secular endpoint in the 1980s, based on strong beliefs in God among the citizenry, stable church attendance, daily commitment to prayer, and respect for religious institutions.[2] An equally compelling case, however, can be made for quite the opposite view. After all, Neuhaus has shown how difficult it has been for religious rhetoric to gain access to the public domain.[3] Then, too, the First Amendment has been largely interpreted in Jeffersonian fashion, that a "wall of separation" should exist between church and state. Accordingly, the Supreme Court ruled that a "moment of silence" at the beginning of the school day constituted an impermissible intrusion of religiosity.[4] For their part, civil libertarians tirelessly eradicated religious symbols, forcing the removal of crosses from public places and either the removal of Christmas decorations or their commingling with the secular trappings of the holiday season.[5] Hubert Morken pointed out that the Christian Right's greatest legislative victory in the 1980s—the "equal access" bill that allowed student religious groups to use school facilities during non-curricular hours—barely edged religious values into the domain of public education.[6] Moreover, the educational product delivered in colleges and universities sometimes completely glossed over religious motivations as a basis for individual behavior. College textbooks, for instance, cast the Pilgrims as happy travelers in search of adventure, rather than as religious people escaping persecution.[7] Purveyors of popular culture, such as television, along with elites in the arts, academy, media, and government, further reinforced cultural secularity.[8] Key religious values remained intact, but secular values challenged them and may well have predominated.

Now envision a second axis, conveying the political success that the Christian Right enjoyed in the 1980s, intersecting the first at midpoint in perpendicular fashion. On the top point of that axis is complete and total victory, represented by the election of sympathetic candidates, the passage of legislative objectives, and the exertion of agenda influence. On the bottom point of that axis is utter failure, represented by defeat in elections and legislative struggles, as well as an inability to shape the political agenda. The intersection of perpendicular axes at midpoint yields four quadrants, which are presented schematically in Figure 7-1.

In the first quadrant, the secularity of American society is high, as is the political success of the Christian Right. In the second, religiosity is high, as is political success. The third quadrant is marked by religiosity in society but a politically impotent Christian Right. The fourth quadrant is characterized by secularity once again and a politically ineffectual Christian Right.

For the sake of argument, if not fact, assume that secular values actually dominated religious ones, so that the Christian Right operated in quadrants I and IV during most of the 1980s. The intriguing follow-up question is which of those two quadrants it occupied most frequently. Put in the form of a question: While working within the confines of a heavily secular culture, was the Christian Right politically influential or not? The proper answer to that question largely depends on how success is measured. Some scholars examined the Christian Right's electoral activities and concluded

Figure 7-1 Secularity and Success in the 1980s

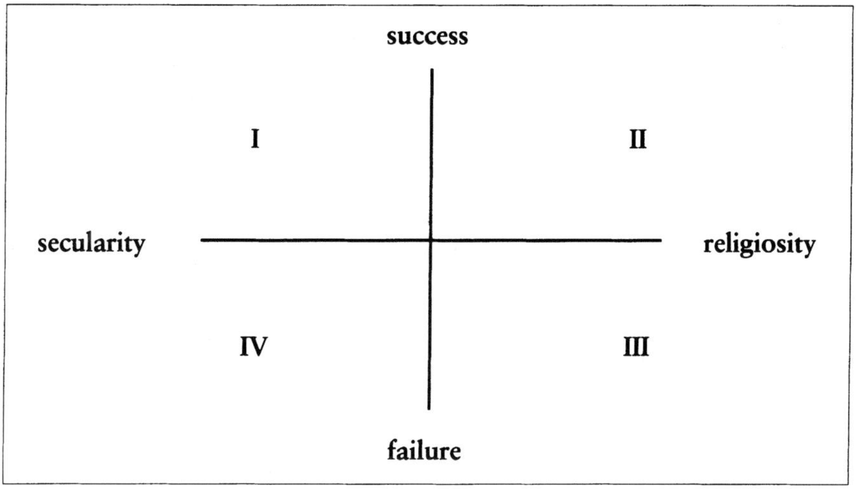

that its influence was minimal at the presidential and congressional levels.[9] Still others viewed the failure of elite leaders to push constitutional amendments through Congress as evidence of political impotence.[10] One person interviewed in 1984 denied that the Christian Right even affected the political agenda, saying flatly: "The Christian Right has not been able to dictate the agenda." People subscribing to such views see the Christian Right operating in quadrant IV during the 1980s, assuming that they accepted the validity of the secularity assessment.

If success is measured in different terms, though, the answer provided about which quadrant the Christian Right operated in is quite different. For instance, while some scholars concluded that the electoral potency of the Christian Right was minimal overall, others pointed out that the impact was substantial in determining Reagan's margin of victory, and in select congressional races.[11] This author noted the considerable influence the Christian Right wielded on the congressional agenda in the early 1980s.[12] Recall too, from an earlier chapter, the hundreds of citations to Christian-Right organizations in such places as the *New York Times,* which convey clout in the broader public arena. Besides, the influence of the Christian Right proceeded past what is quantifiable. The incursion of the Christian Right into the congressional and public agendas removed alternative liberal issues from serious consideration. In that light, the Christian Right operated in quadrant I quite often in the 1980s, demonstrating political influence in the midst of secularity.

Erosion of Distinctiveness

It is reasonable to project that the Christian Right will operate within the confines of a heavily secular culture in the years ahead. There is certainly no reason to believe that anything resembling a "moral majority" is on the horizon, or even that general religiosity will surge in the 1990s.[13] Put schematically, the Christian Right seems destined to act within quadrants I and IV throughout the 1990s and probably well beyond.

Unfortunately for its leaders, the Christian Right will probably be pushed further out of the realm of political influence (quadrant I) as the 1990s unfold. Why is that the case? The Christian Right's ability to affect the national public and legislative agendas will diminish. It will do so because the movement lost much of its distinctiveness as a political force over time, rendering it less able to capture the attention of policymakers and the imagination of the media.

The majority of changes that eradicated the movement's distinctive character already have been covered. Rapid organizational changes gave rise to a greater diversity of groups than existed when several fundamentalist, direct-mail lobbies were the principal players. Though probably not as dramatic, personnel changes brought some evangelical and charismatic Christians into the leadership, most notably Pat Robertson. The Christian Right continued to be led by conservative Protestants, but there was somewhat more theological diversity among the leadership at the end of the 1980s than there was at the beginning of the decade. More obvious, the adoption of the language of liberalism eradicated distinctiveness, by placing the Christian Right in the "rhetorical mainstream." Even the shift from Capitol Hill to the grass roots, as a focal point for activism, played a part. Though controversial, the perception existed that the Christian Right was a product of a conspiratorial coterie of ministerial elites, providing direction from the top down.[14] Grass-roots work signaled a decentralization of leadership and an end to an era of control by a distinctive clique of nationally prominent religious figures. Finally, the secular trappings of the Christian Right removed some of its unique religious character, placing it alongside most contemporary political players.

Two other changes occurred in the Christian Right over time that eradicated its distinctiveness. First, on some issues, its leaders moderated their views. The most celebrated case in point was the shift of the Reverend Jerry Falwell on the abortion issue. Initially, he opposed abortion without exception; over time, he adjusted that view to allow for abortion in certain cases.[15] A less celebrated but no less important example was Christian-Right leaders acceding to "equal access" legislation, when initially they sought nothing short of vocal prayer in public schools.[16] Second, the infusion of evangelical and pentecostal Christians into the leadership structure both spurred and reflected a more diverse mass constituency, as evangelicals and pentecostals joined their fundamentalist brethren.[17] Pat Robertson's entry into presidential politics fueled this change, which gave the Christian-Right movement a somewhat broader theological bent over time. In the context of a secular American culture it still was quite distinctive, but the fact of the matter is that its constituency became less theologically homogeneous over time. Gary Jarmin noted the greater theological diversity, arguing that a healthy by-product of it was increased religious tolerance: "We [in the Christian Right] have brought together evangelical and fundamentalist Christians who have developed a respect for one another and cooperated. I think that is a good thing."[18]

The diminished distinctiveness of the Christian Right cut deeply into its ability to shape the nation's political agenda, because journalists lost their inclination to cover the movement. It was one thing for them to report on a small set of fundamentalist lobbies pushing constitutional amendments on Capitol Hill as "life or death" issues in the early 1980s; it was quite another matter to cover a panoply of organizations, of greater theological diversity and more moderate leadership, whose modus operandi was quietly recruiting people at the local level to participate in politics with the same sort of rhetoric used by everyone else. Where was the story? What was newsworthy about organizing local people to participate in politics? How could coverage of grass-roots work, done by more moderate political actors using secular language and symbols, possibly compare with titanic legislative struggles pitting religious fundamentalists against their "secular humanist" enemies? In point of fact, it could not compare. The novelty and distinctiveness of the Christian Right, traits which Roger Cobb and Charles Elder suggest command attention in politics,[19] wore off during the 1980s and bred a loss of agenda-setting ability.

Once the 1987 television evangelist scandals involving Reverends Jim

Bakker, Jimmy Swaggart, and Oral Roberts in tales of sex and greed ended, journalists surmised that the Christian Right was a spent political force.[20] Certain developments, such as rapid organizational and leadership changes, were then interpreted as confirmation of weakness and decline. With its political obituary written at the national level, it became impossible for the Christian Right to retain, let alone regain, its access and influence over the agenda. In that sense, the death knell of the Christian Right was partly self-executing. It became impossible to exert influence on the agenda when coverage ceased, and coverage ceased because journalists concluded that the movement's ability to affect the public agenda had dissipated. An analogous situation has been shown with respect to House elections, where challengers lose because they cannot raise adequate sums of money, and they cannot raise enough money because political contributors assume they will lose.[21]

Closely related to a decreasing predilection on the part of journalists to cover the Christian Right was an eroding ability to do so. Tormented national reporters, facing deadlines and a rapidly changing world, lacked the time and resources to sift through and document the complexities of organizational and leadership changes in the Christian Right. They also lacked a vantage point, once Christian-Right leaders began focusing their energies and resources on grass-roots activism. Coverage of the Christian Right by the national media became more difficult, and so less desirable and thorough. Quite simply, the national media lost track of, and lost interest in, an evolving Christian Right. Evidence of that assertion is found in Table 7.1, which documents the attention accorded the ten national organizations of the Christian Right over the course of the 1980s, by the "newspaper of record."

The table requires relatively little explication. The major organizations of the Christian Right were covered less and less as the 1980s passed. A total of 179 stories were written about them from 1980 through 1982, and only 14 from 1987 through 1989 (a 92 percent reduction). In fact, except for a slight increase in coverage during what I earlier labeled the "transition period" (1985–1986), the decrease in attention was monotonical in nature. The pattern of coverage is somewhat different if stories on the Christian Right's prominent leaders (Falwell, Robertson, Dobson, Jarmin, Grant, and Tim LaHaye) are incorporated, because of the intense media attention Robertson received surrounding his 1988 presidential bid. Specifically, the pattern is skewed toward heavy coverage in the early and late 1980s

Table 7-1 Popular Attention to the Christian Right, 1980–1989

Year	Number of Citations
1980	53*
1981	85
1982	41
1983	10
1984	9
1985	16
1986	16
1987	6
1988	4
1989	4

*The organizations included are the following: American Coalition for Traditional Values; American Freedom Coalition; Christian Voice; Concerned Women for America; Family Research Council; Freedom Council; Liberty Federation; Moral Majority; National Christian Action Coalition; Religious Roundtable.

Source: Compiled from the indexes of the *New York Times.*

(because of Falwell and Robertson respectively), with relatively little coverage in the middle years. Even so, there were 17 percent more stories on the organizations and prominent leaders of the Christian Right in the first three years of the 1980s than in the last three (255 versus 212 citations).[22] The conclusion one must draw is that the media lost the inclination and the ability to cover an evolving Christian Right. Joseph Conn thought so, saying in a 1989 interview: "Today the news media is not very interested in the dangers posed by the Christian Right. They have written it off as a political force."[23] Along with its lost influence over the public agenda (and partly caused by it), the Christian Right lost clout vis-à-vis the congressional agenda.

There is little reason to believe that the Christian Right will regain its agenda-setting abilities in the 1990s. In fact, the evidence suggests just the opposite. The furor of religious fundamentalists across America has abated somewhat, the distinctiveness of the Christian Right has diminished, and the novelty of its participation in the political arena is past. Equally important, the organizations that exercised influence on the national agenda, such as Moral Majority, are gone. Their replacement organizations are sufficient in number to exert influence, but they are structured to recruit and organize local people to participate in politics. They will wield political power, but not so much in the realm of agenda-setting. It will be problematic to shape the nation's agenda with organizations focused on what Gary Jarmin earlier labeled the "four-S" issues: sewers, sidewalks, streets, and schools.

The Absence of an Ayatollah

The difficulty of shaping the national agenda in the years ahead will be exacerbated by the lack of a clear leader comparable to Jerry Falwell in the early 1980s. Howard Phillips summarized the situation in an interview conducted in 1989, in the week following the formal dismantling of Moral Majority: "There are many people who are capable leaders out there working, but there is no single person in charge. If I may use an Islamic analogy, there is no single ayatollah leading the Christian Right today."[24] That assessment was widely shared in conservative circles, at least if the interviews conducted for this book are an accurate barometer of that opinion. New-Right activist Michael Schwartz opined: "There is no person with the stature of a Jerry Falwell to provide leadership."[25] Christian-Right leader Gary Jarmin concurred, suggesting that: "In a sense, we are back to where we were at the very beginning [of the movement], before the big-name ministers were aboard. There is no one particularly highly visible leader these days; there is no one spokesman for the movement who has been latched onto by the media. The movement is not leaderless by any means, but it is not led by the single 'big' person."[26] Along similar lines, Christian-Right leader Gary Bauer remarked: "The Christian Right is well served [today] by focusing less on individual leaders."[27]

The lack of a high-profile minister is not necessarily an injurious development. It insulates the Christian Right from the fall of any one person, just as a plethora of groups insulates the movement from the demise of any single group. It also allows the issues of religious conservatives to transcend personalities. Gary Bauer was cognizant of that point: "The movement was ill-served when particular personalities were prominent, because they were then the issue. Take the case of Jerry Falwell. Over time, he became the issue. That was unfortunate, because people ceased to focus on the individual issues when they focused on the individual person. It is important not to personalize the Christian Right, lest concern over personalities overshadow concern over issues. . . . Here at the Family Research Council, we will strive to make certain that Dr. [James] Dobson does not become the issue, so that the focus is not lost on the real issues of public policy facing the nation."[28] Finally, the lack of a single leader has the potential of reinvigorating the movement, as individual leaders vie for that role.

Some conservative opinion leaders even saw the decentralization of leadership as preferable to the situation that existed with Falwell in the early 1980s. Gary Jarmin asserted that it was better, because "local leadership has real consequences; national spokesmen only make headlines."[29] That statement was rather ironic, coming from someone who spent a decade in national leadership positions, but it was entirely consistent with the view he had expressed five years earlier.[30] Howard Phillips also welcomed the change, claiming that it was a "sign" that the Christian Right was "beginning to mature as a political movement."[31] Interestingly, Phillips' view runs contrary to the existing literature on social movements, which posits that a leadership "oligarchy" naturally emerges over time.[32] Which view vis-à-vis the Christian Right is correct? It is hard to say, because there seems to be something of an oligarchy in the form of "old timers" such as Robert Grant, Pat Robertson, and Beverly LaHaye, but also some fluidity with the likes of James Dobson and Gary Bauer. The early 1990s do not provide a reliable vantage point to answer the question. In the event that the literature proves wrong, though, scholars are obliged either to explain why no oligarchy emerged in this specific instance or to reconsider their theoretical paradigm.

Not everyone agreed that the lack of a titular leader was beneficial. Michael Schwartz suggested that it was a serious problem: "Decentralization of leadership can be beneficial. However, there is still a need for a national spokesman, a bellwether who can speak for everyone. The Christian Right has a sizeable national constituency and it needs someone who can speak for that constituency. . . . At present, the Christian Right lacks that person. It needs a credible national spokesman, and no one exists."[33] Although no person interviewed described specific problems that stemmed from a relatively decentralized leadership structure, they are easily discernable. When the Christian Right had a national spokesperson in Jerry Falwell it could communicate with supporters in a cost-effective manner. Even if publicity was hostile it nonetheless was free, and "true believers" could easily filter out the negative coverage.[34] The absence of such a visible leader means a loss of cost-effective communication to a national constituency—an especially serious problem for organizations continuously raising money. A related problem is an inability to articulate the sentiments of religious conservatives across America, convey the message that their views are appropriate for the public arena, and thereby efficiently and effectively recruit them into politics.

In the context of the broader theme of this chapter, the absence of a titular leader means a loss of agenda influence. In 1984, the legislative director of a Christian-Right organization said that Jerry Falwell could "call a press conference and get fifty reporters there in a short span of time." By the end of the 1980s, no person could accomplish something comparable for the Christian Right. The Reverend Pat Robertson attracted considerable attention for a time in the late 1980s, but as a presidential candidate who had resigned his ministerial credentials in pursuit of a political party nomination rather than as the figurehead of the Christian Right.

It is unclear whether a titular leader will eventually emerge in the 1990s. It is possible, but there are obstacles to it. For example, there are several different organizations with regular sources of financial support that have their own leaders. It is unlikely that a single person will be anointed leader by the others, which means that Pat Robertson, Gary Bauer, Beverly LaHaye, James Dobson, and Robert Grant may all vie for the honor. None of them transcends all of the current organizations, the way that Falwell did with the fundamentalist, direct-mail lobbies. Keep in mind, too, that Christian-Right leaders are dealing with a fractured conservative movement, torn asunder in the late 1980s by Ronald Reagan's exit from the political stage and the apparent end of the Cold War. It will be difficult for any one individual to emerge as spokesman for the Christian-Right element of the conservative coalition in that context. Conservatism itself is in disarray.

The political situation further contributes to the problem. So long as a moderate Republican is in the White House, such as George Bush, the Christian Right cannot count on the support of the administration for its agenda; neither can it turn toward the Democrats. Christian-Right leaders are stuck biding their time, hoping for a much more sympathetic conservative administration but wondering if they are not better off with a hostile liberal administration for the purposes of organizational maintenance.

With no place to turn, they howl about administration positions and personnel choices but mute their protests sufficiently to retain their ties to the White House.[35] It is hard to envision any single leader emerging from the cacophony of voices.

In addition to those difficulties, it may well be the case that no one among the current crop of leaders has the desire, stature, and/or ability to lead. According to Michael Schwartz, whose candid comments about Christian-Right leaders were partly excerpted earlier, Beverly LaHaye "is very good with her own followers" but lacks "the stature and skills to reach out to a broader constituency"; the Reverend James Dobson "has the stature to lead the Christian Right," but is "very nervous about his present [political] role"; Don Wildmon, who has been involved in monitoring the content of television programming through the American Family Association (located in Tupelo, Mississippi), is "a man of great integrity" but without "the vision and charisma to lead the movement." Schwartz suggested that Gary Bauer had the requisite skills to lead the entire movement, but also added that "[what] the Christian Right is lacking is a new generation of leaders."[36] If that assessment is correct, someone from the current crop (perhaps Bauer) must emerge if anyone is to lead, and that prospect appears dim given the constraints mentioned. The result is a Christian Right with a diminished ability to recruit followers and communicate with them in a cost-effective manner, and with less agenda-setting power.

Relocation of Influence

The inability of the Christian Right to set the political agenda in the 1990s does not mean that it will be bereft of influence. Its political clout simply will be expressed in other ways. In terms of the axes and quadrants evoked in the opening to this chapter, the Christian Right will operate in quadrant I from time to time, the realm of political influence, but in ways other than agenda-setting.

The principal way that the Christian Right will exercise a political impact will be through shaping the Republican party. Elsewhere, this author documented the Christian Right's impact on the 1980 and 1984 Republican platforms, as well as President Reagan's State of the Union speeches.[37] Earlier in this volume, the Christian Right's voter-registration campaigns and takeover of some Republican state party apparatuses were chronicled. All of those components are evidence of influence in the Republican party.

Other scholarship suggests that the Christian Right was exercising electoral and state party influence as the 1980s drew to a close. Lyman A. Kellstedt and his colleagues analyzed National Election Study data and concluded that evangelical Protestants were a key component of President Bush's winning coalition in 1988. Moreover, by examining evangelical membership within the Republican coalition over time, they discovered that the percentage of evangelicals in the electorate who identified with the Republican party (rather than simply voted for it at mostly the presidential level) had increased.[38] Because of salient voter registration campaigns by the likes of Jerry Falwell and Pat Robertson in the 1980s, religious conservatives registered and voted more Republican over time.

On the state party side, Duane Oldfield collected interview data on the impact of the Christian Right in the states of Washington, Michigan, and Virginia during the 1988 campaign season. He showed that bruising battles often occurred between the insurgent Christian-Right forces and "establishment" Republicans but suggested that much of the conflict was the product of the Christian Right's initiation into party politics and of the specific tussle over the presidential nomination in a year when one of the Christian Right's own people (Pat Robertson) was a contender.[39] With those matters behind it, the Christian Right should have a more harmonious relationship with Republican state parties. In that context, Oldfield believes that the Christian Right is positioned to "tip the balance" between the (conservative) Reagan and (liberal) Rockefeller wings, an influence that he believes can be exerted only if the Christian Right adopts a strategy of compromise and conciliation that will "downplay some of the specifically Christian aspects of its appeal."[40] Needless to say, his analysis admirably fits the secularization theme of this volume. It calls upon Christian-Right leaders to convey the trappings of secularism in order to be effective at the state party level.

Given the fact that the Christian Right has lost much of its agenda-setting clout, the move toward electoral and state party participation may accelerate in the 1990s. After all, is that not what is available? Is that not the kind of activism that leaders began positioning their movement for in the late 1980s? In 1984, a liberal interviewee suggested that the Christian Right constituted a "lunatic fringe" that someday might be "mainstreamed" into the Republican Party. In 1989, an interviewee who requested anonymity said the infiltration had occurred: "The Christian Right has clearly exercised an impact on the Republican Party. The movement has influenced its leadership, its platform, and its candidates. The tone and tenor of the Republican Party have changed, in large part because the Christian Right agenda is contained within the current Republican agenda." That quotation verifies the Christian Right's influence in the Republican party and suggests that it lost its particular agenda-setting abilities because its concerns were assimilated. Such co-optation means the movement will exert political influence in the 1990s, but not the same sort of high-profile, agenda-setting clout it demonstrated in the early 1980s.

8

Political Skills and Religious Belief

It would be an overstatement to say the Christian Right had a chameleonic character in the 1980s, but not to assert that it experienced a dramatic transformation. After all, the organizations that ignited religious conservatives expended themselves, and were replaced by new groups. Leaders concluded that their agenda should be plied elsewhere than Capitol Hill and acted on that premise. They also substituted liberal for moralistic language en route.

Flowing out of those changes were a host of others. Many new people ascended to leadership positions, displacing the more sectarian fundamentalist ministers of the early 1980s. That trend prompted Gary Jarmin to observe: "I think what you see [in 1989] is a change in leadership and organization. There is no one or two people who are thought to embody and speak for the entire Christian movement."[1] Another change was that leaders solicited new sources of financial support for their organizations, such as the Unification Church, after operating funds became scarce. A third change was that pentecostal and evangelical Christians joined the movement in larger numbers, at both the elite and mass levels, to accompany and/or replace their fundamentalist brethren. Michael Schwartz, of the Free Congress Foundation, mentioned the political reticence of pentecostals and evangelicals initially and then asserted: "The clear tendency, though, is for greater pentecostal and evangelical involvement in the Christian Right. The fundamentalists were the first ones out of the starting gate. The others are catching up."[2]

Issues were another area of change. Gary Jarmin drew upon the great charter of the liberal tradition to make that point: "When the [Christian Right] movement began, there was a Magna Carta of sorts, which had a list of issues that all of the groups made their priorities, such as school prayer, abortion, and pornography. Today, there are a variety of groups working on a variety of issues. There are no set 'big' issues, as there was at one time."[3] Howard Phillips concurred, though he approached the same point from a different direction: "There are many people working hard for the values of the Christian Right out in the grass roots. Most of those people are awaiting a galvanizing issue. In the absence of that issue, the work will go on quietly."[4] The lack of a 'Magna Carta' of important issues, coupled with some of the other changes previously mentioned, bred still further changes, such as a loss of influence over the public and congressional agendas and a loss of access to the White House. When all of those changes are taken together, the transformation of the Christian Right in the 1980s was remarkable indeed.

Accompanying the panoply of changes in the Christian Right was a noticeable rise in levels of political sophistication and skill. In addition to manifestations of increased sophistication already mentioned—such as the infusion of more astute leaders, the shift in strategic focal points, and the use of more moderate language—there was also more sensitivity to the link between public policy and private life. In the early 1980s, Robert Wuthnow correctly observed that religious conservatives had gradually recognized the tie between "private morality and the collective good."[5] Accordingly, they embarked on a crusade to put "morality back into politics." By the end of the 1980s, religious conservatives were beyond that stage of thinking, recognizing not only that morality and politics were linked but also that specific public policies had monumental effects on private life itself. They grew to understand that the tax code could be used to structure familial relations, such as giving spouses incentives to work or remain home with children. They realized that state-sponsored sex-education programs, taught outside the context of religion and marital monogamy, might encourage some young people to experiment, because they were provided the clinical skills and sometimes even a prophylactic. Laurie Tryfiates of Concerned Women for America noted the increased understanding of the effect of public policies on private lives: "People have come to see more and more how public policy affects the family—for example, entitlement programs, which encourage government dependency and create disincentives for dependence on family support systems. There is greater awareness of the consequences of public policy for private life."[6] Elite leaders surely perceived the impact of governmental policies upon family life better than their mass supporters, though Tryfiates's comment suggests the existence of an "education campaign" by leaders that probably resulted in a more sophisticated constituency as well.

Another manifestation of increased sophistication was the willingness of Christian-Right leaders to work together and with other groups sharing common objectives. The movement's leaders lost some of their inclination to "take no prisoners," gradually realizing that other cell mates might be effective conspirators in their bid to liberate society from its secular wardens. Gary Bauer explained that this change was under way in the waning days of Moral Majority's existence: "The emphasis on coalitions was more and more evident in the Moral Majority over time. In recent years, it was not unusual to see the Moral Majority meeting with Catholic groups, Jewish groups, or something like the Knights of Columbus in pursuit of common goals."[7] (It was also not unusual to see ties to Mormon leaders.[8]) Bauer also stated, though, that "the Moral Majority and some of the other Christian-Right groups may not have been coalition-minded enough. One piece of evidence of growing sophistication within the movement is the [greater] tendency toward coalition politics. The fact that people are willing to bridge differences and form coalitions suggests more sophistication."[9] Bauer's point is buttressed by examples cited in previous chapters, such as Concerned Women for America fighting for the nomination of Robert Bork to the Supreme Court, in tandem with a host of conservative groups.

Bauer proceeded with a final example of increased political sophistication, this time focusing on the proclivity of leaders to accept something short of total victory. He cited the tussle over the 1984 school-prayer constitutional amendment as evidence that a more conciliatory attitude was emerging: "Back in 1984, when the school-prayer issue was very visible, emotions within the Christian Right were very high. Another bit of evidence of increased sophistication was the Christian Right's decision, at that time, that it could live with equal-access legislation in lieu of a prayer amendment. Their willingness to accept something a little less than they sought was proof that changes were under way."[10] In the same vein, Colleen Kiko of the House Judiciary Subcommittee on Civil and Constitutional Rights noted that anti-abortion groups, like those of the Christian Right "have become more sophisticated . . . [in the sense that] they see the need and utility of slowly chipping away at the 1973 abortion decision."[11] Above and beyond the obvious manifestations of increased political skill, then, were more subtle developments, such as a better understanding of the effects of public policy on personal lives, a greater willingness to work with like-minded groups, and a more accepting attitude toward what was possible.

Virtually all of those changes are in keeping with pluralist understandings of American politics.[12] Pluralist thinkers have argued that the genius of the American system of government is its ability to force moderation and assimilation of divergent viewpoints. Robert Dahl put it this way: "Probably this strange hybrid, the normal American political system, is not for export to others. But so long as the social prerequisites of democracy are substantially intact in this country, it appears to be a relatively efficient system for reinforcing agreement, encouraging moderation, and maintaining social peace in a restless and immoderate people operating a gigantic, powerful, diversified, and incredibly complex society."[13] The Christian Right's assimilation into a pluralist system conveys a much higher level of political sophistication than it exhibited in the early 1980s. If it may be presented so starkly, the institutionalization of several groups working on a variety of issues, and acting on the principles of coalition-building and compromise, is a quantum leap in sophistication from the early discussions by fundamentalist ministers of "putting God back in government."

By the same token, the growth of political sophistication proceeded unevenly. In fact, there were notable exceptions to the process, such as Jerry Falwell and Pat Robertson flinging misleading and harsh language, and leaders' failure to discern that their agenda was eroding over time. Then too, the timing of Christian-Right leaders was not always the best, such as Tim and Beverly LaHaye moving to the nation's capital just as the significant struggles there petered out, or the emphasis on moralism in the early 1980s even as concern with it was ebbing in the general populace. The Christian Right's overall political sophistication increased, to be sure, but it did so incrementally and unevenly. That same pattern will probably be exhibited for years to come.

The Rise or Fall of Religious Belief?

In addition to increased sophistication, another major change in the Christian Right during the 1980s was its higher degree of secularization.[14]

Some of its organizations assumed the trappings of secularism, with their redefined organizational titles and missions. The American Freedom Coalition even went so far as to openly acknowledge its secular character. Gary Jarmin of the coalition remarked in a 1989 interview that "we need to separate church and state formally in order to protect both. Otherwise, we risk in particular, secularizing the church."[15] What a remarkable shift in sentiment from talk of putting "God back in government!" In a different vein, several of the Christian Right's leaders engaged in rhetorical flourishes that were inconsistent with religious teachings. Still others took the money of the Reverend Moon, whose religious teachings were antithetical to their beliefs. In short, the leaders of the Christian Right assimilated the trappings of secularism, as well as periodically sacrificed religious principles in pursuit of secular political objectives. Keep in mind, however, that just as the sophistication theme required circumscription because it did not apply evenly to all organizations and their leaders, so also does the secularization theme.

It is unclear whether the secularization that occurred over the course of the 1980s is enduring. It might be an artifact of the Reagan years, when the Christian Right was part and parcel of the electoral and governing coalition. Joseph Conn noted the problem the Christian Right faced with Ronald Reagan in the White House: "It could scarcely protest about liberals and secular humanists running the government, when its man was head of the government. Similarly, it was difficult to run against the Washington establishment, when it became part of the power structure."[16] With Reagan as president, Christian-Right leaders were coalition partners. It was natural for them to mimic some of the language and adopt some of the norms of their secular political allies. Their assumption of secular trappings and their sacrifice of religious principles, then, might be heavily restricted to the years of the Reagan presidency.

Other evidence that the secularization of the Christian Right may be limited to that time frame is found in the emergence of Christian Reconstructionism. It emphasizes the utility of the first five books of the Old Testament for ordering contemporary American society, a goal that Bruce Barron and Anson Shupe have noted proceeds well beyond the Christian Right in scope yet has certain affinities related to "recapturing" institutions from secular forces.[17] It is unnecessary to discuss Reconstructionism at length in this context; scholars have analyzed the movement elsewhere.[18] The only point that necessitates mention is that the penetration of the Christian Right by Reconstructionists may halt, or even reverse, the process of secularization described. It is too early to tell.[19]

While the notion that the secularization of the Christian Right is only temporary has appeal, though, it is also probably wrong. Scholars have shown that the mass constituency of the Christian Right was secularized with respect to its voting behavior in the 1980s;[20] previous chapters of this volume contain numerous examples of secularized elite behavior. It will not be easy to undo those effects, to abruptly change the character of the Christian Right. One person, who unfortunately requested anonymity, observed in a 1989 interview: "There is an identifiable pattern in evangelical Protestantism. It is that as people get more involved [in politics], they also become less motivated by purely religious concerns. It is a natural pattern. Once involved, they develop other motivations beside religious ones." The interviewee continued on to say: "In my view, that is what is happening today with the Christian Right. It has become part of the Republican establishment, shedding some of its religious motivation along the way." In his study of state Republican parties, in the wake of Robertson's 1988 presidential bid, Duane Oldfield found support for that proposition. He discovered that once they became active in politics, Robertson supporters often "were bitten by the political bug" and "found that they enjoyed operating within the secular discourse of the political world."[21] In other words, they grew fond of politics for its own sake, rather than as part of any religious crusade.

In that light, it is difficult to conceive of a reversion to pervasive religious underpinnings in the Christian Right. Its mass constituency and elite leadership have edged toward secular norms and behavior; in all probability, that general drift will be reinforced by trends already under way, and thereby become a self-fulfilling prophecy. New people will be drawn to the movement on those terms; those people currently involved, who find the revamping of the Christian Right along those lines completely unacceptable, will either drop out of it or head off to start a *new* "New Christian Right." The words of Charles Colson, implicated in the Watergate scandal of the 1970s before he became an evangelist, may be prophetic: "Our well-intentioned attempts to influence government can become so entangled with a particular political agenda that it becomes our focus; our goal becomes maintaining political access. When that happens the gospel is held hostage to a political agenda, and *we become part of the very system we were seeking to change* [emphasis added]."[22] More than a return to religious moralism or an infusion of Reconstructionist theology, that prospect seems likely in the years ahead. The Christian Right will be a more secular and sophisticated player as it presses its vision for America.

Notes

1. The Metamorphosis

1. Interview with Gary Jarmin, June 8, 1989.

2. For related work, see Matthew C. Moen, "The Political Transformation of the Christian Right," paper delivered at the Annual Meeting of the American Political Science Association, San Francisco, September 1990, and "The Christian Right in the United States," in *The Religious Challenge to the State,* ed. Matthew C. Moen and Lowell S. Gustafson (Philadelphia: Temple University Press, 1992), 75–101.

3. See Matthew C. Moen, *The Christian Right and Congress* (Tuscaloosa: University of Alabama Press, 1989), 55, 153–56.

4. For a fine discussion of the Christian Right's theological underpinnings, see Jeffrey K. Hadden and Anson Shupe, *Televangelism: Power and Politics on God's Frontier* (New York: Henry Holt, 1988), 99–100; Gabriel Fackre, *The Religious Right and Christian Faith* (Grand Rapids, Mich.: William B. Eerdman's, 1982).

5. John H. Simpson, "Moral Issues and Status Politics," in *The New Christian Right,* ed. Robert C. Liebman and Robert Wuthnow (New York: Aldine, 1983), 198.

6. Kenneth D. Wald, *Religion and Politics in the United States* (New York: St. Martin's, 1987), 182.

7. Interview with Gary Jarmin, June 8, 1989.

8. Interview with Laurie Tryfiates, June 9, 1989.

9. Interview with Joseph Conn, June 14, 1989.

10. Interview with Gary Bauer, June 14, 1989.

11. Based on examination of brochures and newsletters received from those

organizations during visits to their Washington, D.C., offices on July 17 and July 27, 1984; see Erling Jorstad, The *Politics of Moralism* (Minneapolis: Augsburg, 1981), 8–10.

12. The figure is a projection of Moral Majority membership estimates. See "Religious Right Goes for Bigger Game," *U.S. News & World Report,* November 17, 1980, 42.

13. Wald, *Religion and Politics in the United States,* 195.

14. Interview with Gary Jarmin, June 8, 1989.

15. Excellent overviews include: James Davison Hunter, "Operationalizing Evangelicalism: A Review, Critique and Proposal," *Sociological Analysis* 42 (1982): 363–72; Clyde Wilcox, "Fundamentalists and Politics: An Analysis of the Effects of Differing Operational Definitions," *Journal of Politics* 48 (1986): 1041–51. For our purposes, *evangelicals* are identified by belief in traditional morality, mission work, and individual commitment to Christ; *fundamentalists* are identified by those beliefs plus a literal interpretation of the Bible. *Pentecostals* embrace some or all of the views of evangelicals and fundamentalists and also stress gifts from the Holy Spirit, such as speaking in tongues. *Charismatics* are essentially pentecostals from traditionally "mainline" denominations, such as Methodists.

16. Wald, *Religion and Politics in the United States,* 195.

17. Albert J. Menendez, "Religious Lobbies," *Liberty* 77 (March/April 1982): 5.

18. Kenneth L. Woodward and Eleanor Clift, "Playing Politics at Church," *Newsweek,* July 9, 1984, 52.

19. Rob Gurwitt, "1986 Elections Generate GOP Power Struggle," *Congressional Quarterly Weekly Report,* April 12, 1986, 803.

20. Ibid., 802.

21. Interview with Joseph Conn, June 14, 1989.

22. Moen, *The Christian Right and Congress,* 141–47.

23. Ibid., 1.

24. Daniel Hofrenning, "The Agenda Setting Strategies of Religious Interest Groups and Institutions," 10, 13, paper delivered at the Annual Meeting of the American Political Science Association, Atlanta, September 1989.

25. Interview with Gary Jarmin, June 8, 1989.

26. On electoral clout, see Steven D. Johnson and Joseph B. Tamney, "The Christian Right and the 1980 Presidential Election," *Journal For the Scientific Study of Religion,* 21 (1982): 123–31; Arthur H. Miller and Martin P. Wattenberg, "Politics from the Pulpit," *Public Opinion Quarterly* 48 (1984): 301–17; Jerome H. Himmelstein and James A. McRae, Jr., "Social Conservatism, New Republicanism, and the 1980 Election," *Public Opinion Quarterly* 48 (1984): 592–605; Jeffrey L. Brudney and Gary W. Copeland, "Evangelicals as a Political Force: Reagan and the 1980 Religious Vote," *Social Science Quarterly* 65 (1984): 1072–79; Emmett H.

Buell, Jr., and Lee Sigelman, "An Army That Meets Every Sunday? Popular Support for the Moral Majority in 1980," *Social Science Quarterly* 66 (1985): 426–34; Lee Sigelman, Clyde Wilcox, and Emmett H. Buell, Jr., "An Unchanging Minority: Popular Support for the Moral Majority, 1980 and 1984," *Social Science Quarterly* 68 (1987): 876–84; Corwin Smidt, "Born Again Politics," in *Religion and Politics in the South,* ed. Tod A. Baker, Robert P. Steed, and Laurence W. Moreland (New York: Praeger, 1983), 27–56; Clyde Wilcox, "Popular Support for the Moral Majority in 1980: A Second Look," *Social Science Quarterly* 68 (1987): 157–66; Ted G. Jelen, "The Effects of Religious Separatism on White Protestants in the 1984 Presidential Election," *Sociological Analysis* 48 (1987): 30–45; Corwin Smidt, "Evangelicals and the 1984 Election," *American Politics Quarterly* 15 (1987): 419–44; Jeffrey L. Brudney and Gary W. Copeland, "Ronald Reagan and the Religious Vote," paper delivered at the Annual Meeting of the American Political Science Association, Washington, D.C., September 1988; on its lobbying efforts, see Moen, *The Christian Right and Congress;* Allen D. Hertzke, *Representing God in Washington* (Knoxville: University of Tennessee Press, 1988); on its political action committees, see James L. Guth and John C. Green, "Faith and Politics: Religion and Ideology Among Political Contributors," *American Politics Quarterly* 14 (1986): 186–200; James L. Guth and John C. Green, "The Moralizing Minority: Christian Right Support Among Political Contributors," *Social Science Quarterly* 68 (1987): 598–610; Margaret Ann Latus, "Ideological PACs and Political Action," in *The New Christian Right,* ed. Robert C. Liebman and Robert Wuthnow (New York: Aldine, 1983), 75–99; on its influence with the Reagan administration, see Matthew C. Moen, "Ronald Reagan and the Social Issues," *Social Science Journal* 27 (1990): 199–207; Richard G. Hutcheson, Jr., *God in the White House* (New York: Macmillan, 1988), 153–78; on its attempts to recruit candidates, see Gurwitt, "1986 Elections Generate GOP Power Struggle," 802–07.

27. On the closing of Moral Majority, see Laura Sessions Stepp, "Falwell Says Moral Majority to be Dissolved," *Washington Post,* June 12, 1989, 11.

28. David Shribman, "Going Mainstream: Religious Right Drops High-Profile Tactics, Works on Local Level," *Wall Street Journal,* September 26, 1989, 18.

2. The Kaleidoscopic Structure

1. Leslie Bennetts, "National Anti-Liberal Crusade Zeroing in on McGovern in South Dakota," *New York Times,* June 2, 1980, 11.

2. William H. Riker, "Heresthetic and Rhetoric in the Spatial Model," 8, paper presented at the APSA/Spoor Dialogues on Political Leadership, Dartmouth College, July 21, 1988.

3. "The Gurus of the New Right Maintain a Web of Relationships" (July

1980): 60. Document distributed by McGovern campaign committee, Sioux Falls, S. Dak.

4. Richard Viguerie, *The New Right* (Falls Church, Va.: Viguerie, 1981), 78.

5. Interview with Gary Jarmin, June 8, 1989.

6. Bill Keller, "Evangelical Conservatives Move from Pews to Polls, But Can They Sway Congress?" *Congressional Quarterly Weekly Report,* September 6, 1980, 2629.

7. Viguerie, *The New Right,* 9.

8. Erling Jorstad, *The Politics of Moralism* (Minneapolis: Augsburg, 1981), 94.

9. Daniel Golden, "Who, What Will Follow Reagan?" *Boston Globe,* April 12, 1987, 22; "Back to Basics," *Washington Times,* September 26, 1989, 6.

10. Interview with Joseph Conn, June 14, 1989.

11. Jeffrey K. Hadden and Charles E. Swann, *Prime Time Preachers* (Reading, Mass.: Addison-Wesley, 1981), 139; James Endersby, "The Cross and the Flag," 3–5, paper delivered at the Annual Meeting of the Southwestern Political Science Association, Fort Worth, Texas, March 1984.

12. Matthew C. Moen, *The Christian Right and Congress* (Tuscaloosa: The University of Alabama Press, 1989), 125–29.

13. "Christian Voice: Preserving a Free Society," 8, undated pamphlet available from Christian Voice, 214 Massachusetts Avenue, N.E., Washington, D.C. 20002.

14. Ibid., 7.

15. Interview with Gary Jarmin, June 8, 1989.

16. Based on visit to Christian Voice on June 6, 1989, to gather current materials from the group for an interview with Gary Jarmin two days later.

17. Interview with Gary Jarmin, June 8, 1989.

18. Associated Press, "Moral Majority to Disband," 22, June 12, 1989, *Bangor Daily News.*

19. Dr. George H. Gallup, *The Gallup Poll 1980* (Wilmington, Del.: Scholarly Resources, Inc., 1981), 263; Dr. George H. Gallup, *The Gallup Poll 1981* (Wilmington, Del.: Scholarly Resources, Inc., 1982), 22.

20. For assessments of the Moral Majority constituency, see Jeffrey K. Hadden et. al., "Why Jerry Falwell Killed the Moral Majority," in *The God Pumpers,* ed. Marshall Fishwick and Ray B. Browne (Bowling Green, Ohio: Bowling Green State University Popular Press, 1987), 106; Robert C. Liebman, "Mobilizing the Moral Majority," in *The New Christian Right,* ed. Robert C. Liebman and Robert Wuthnow (New York: Aldine, 1983), 54–55.

21. See Peter Steinfels, "Moral Majority to Dissolve; Says Mission Accomplished," *New York Times,* June 12, 1989, 14; Moen, *The Christian Right and Congress,* 141–47.

22. Moen, *The Christian Right and Congress,* 156–58.

23. Jeffrey K. Hadden and Anson Shupe, *Televangelism: Power and Politics on God's Frontier* (New York: Henry Holt, 1988), 172.

24. Knight-Ridder Newspapers, "Falwell Quitting as President of Moral Majority," 16, November 4, 1987, *Bangor Daily News.*

25. Larry Witham, "Falwell Bids Adieu to Moral Majority," *Washington Times,* August 29, 1989, B2.

26. Mark Miller, "Goodbye to All That," *Newsweek,* November 16, 1987, 10; "Falwell Quitting as President of Moral Majority," November 4, 1987.

27. Laura Sessions Stepp, "Falwell Says Moral Majority to be Dissolved," *Washington Post,* June 12, 1989, 11.

28. In its early years, new Moral Majority members were mailed an eight-page pamphlet, "What is the Moral Majority Inc.?" in which the "moral sanity" objective was mentioned.

29. Interview with Howard Phillips, June 16, 1989.

30. Gallup, *The Gallup Poll 1980,* 263. The percentages do not total 40% because the polling organization screened out the "uninformed public" on the contingency question.

31. Gallup, *The Gallup Poll 1981,* 22.

32. Emmett H. Buell, Jr., and Lee Sigelman, "An Army That Meets Every Sunday? Popular Support for the Moral Majority in 1980," *Social Science Quarterly* 66 (1985): 433.

33. Clyde Wilcox, "Popular Support for the Moral Majority in 1980: A Second Look," *Social Science Quarterly* 68 (1987): 166.

34. Lee Sigelman, Clyde Wilcox, and Emmett H. Buell, Jr., "An Unchanging Minority: Popular Support for the Moral Majority, 1980 and 1984," *Social Science Quarterly* 68 (1987): 883.

35. James L. Guth and John C. Green, "The Moralizing Minority: Christian Right Support Among Political Contributors," *Social Science Quarterly* 68 (1987): 606.

36. Anson Shupe and William Stacey, "The Moral Majority Constituency," in *The New Christian Right,* ed. Robert C. Liebman and Robert Wuthnow (New York: Aldine, 1983), 114.

37. Interview with Gary Bauer, June 14, 1989.

38. Interview with Michael Schwartz, October 16, 1989.

39. Based on a visit to the Moral Majority office on June 6, 1987, five days prior to Falwell's announcement.

40. Interview with Howard Phillips, June 16, 1989.

41. Based on repeated phone calls made throughout 1984.

42. Moen, *The Christian Right and Congress,* 175.

43. Popular periodicals reflected the sudden rise of the Christian Right. See

James Mann, "Old Time Religion on the Offensive," *U.S. News & World Report,* April 7, 1980, 40–42; Allan Mayer, "A Tide of Born Again," *Newsweek,* September 15, 1980, 28.

44. John E. Mueller, "Presidential Popularity from Truman to Johnson," *American Political Science Review,* 64 (1970): 18–34.

45. "To The Churches in 20th Century America," 3, undated pamphlet distributed by Christian Voice.

46. An excellent recent treatment of the political abstinence of conservative Protestants is Lyman A. Kellstedt and Mark A. Noll, "Religion, Voting for President, and Party Identification, 1948–1984," in *Religion and American Politics,* ed. Mark A. Noll (New York: Oxford University Press, 1970), 370–76.

47. Murray Edelman, *The Symbolic Uses of Politics* (Urbana: University of Illinois Press, 1964), 39–40.

48. Matthew C. Moen, "The Political Agenda of Ronald Reagan," *Presidential Studies Quarterly* 18 (1988): 777; Moen, *The Christian Right and Congress,* 32–41, 142–44.

49. For nine months in 1984, I was on the Moral Majority mailing list. During that time, I received direct-mail solicitations that stacked up about four inches high.

50. Interview with Howard Phillips, June 16, 1989.

51. Interview with Gary Jarmin, June 8, 1989.

52. Viguerie, *The New Right,* 9; Jorstad, *The Politics of Moralism,* 92–96.

53. See two undated pamphlets: Christian Voice's "Calling the Church to Prayer, Repentence, National Restoration and Action," and Moral Majority's "What is the Moral Majority, Inc.?"

54. Roger Cobb and Charles Elder, *Participation in American Politics,* 2d ed. (Baltimore: Johns Hopkins University Press, 1983), 151–57; Kay Lehman Schlozman and John T. Tierney, *Organized Interests and American Democracy* (New York: Harper & Row, 1986), 396.

55. Hadden and Swann, *Prime Time Preachers,* 139.

56. Moen, *The Christian Right and Congress,* 156–57.

57. See Jane J. Mansbridge, *Why We Lost the ERA* (Chicago: University of Chicago Press, 1986).

58. Barney Glaser and Anselm Strauss, *The Discovery of Grounded Theory: Strategies for Qualitative Research* (New York: Aldine, 1967), 5–6.

59. Cobb and Elder, *Participation in American Politics,* 28.

60. For a discussion of such matters, see Clyde Wilcox, "The Christian Right in Twentieth Century America," *The Review of Politics* 23 (1988): 659–81.

61. R. Douglas Arnold, "Overtilled and Undertilled Fields in American Politics," *Political Science Quarterly* 97 (1982): 97–98.

62. Barbara Sinclair, "Agenda, Policy, and Alignment Change From Coolidge to Reagan," in *Congress Reconsidered,* ed. Lawrence C. Dodd and Bruce I.

Oppenheimer, 3d ed. (Washington, D.C.: CQ Press, 1985), 291–314; Hadden and Swann, *Prime Time Preachers,* 69–124.

3. The Reconstitution Continues

1. Mary McGrory, "Falwell By Any Other Name," *Washington Post,* January 7, 1986, 2.
2. Jeffrey K. Hadden and Anson Shupe, *Televangelism: Power and Politics on God's Frontier* (New York: Henry Holt, 1988), 173.
3. See James F. Clarity and Warren Weaver, Jr., "Articles and Morals," *New York Times,* January 3, 1986, 10; Robert Pear, "Falwell Forming Group to Look at Broad Issues," *New York Times,* January 4, 1986, 5; "Name That Majority," *New York Times,* January 8, 1986, 22.
4. Based on examination of the *New York Times* indexes. The two 1987 articles are "Falwell Political Funds Shifted to Religious Arms," August 23, 1987, 27, and Stephen Farber, "Bringing Mandela to Television," September 19, 1987, 54.
5. Based on examination of the *New York Times* indexes, 1980–1982.
6. "Falwell Political Funds Shifted to Religious Arms," 27.
7. Ibid.
8. Farber, "Bringing Mandela to Television," 54.
9. Based on examination of the directories. Interestingly, the Moral Majority was listed in Atlanta's directory, but a telephone call to that number reached an answering service, which gave out a Washington, D.C., number that did not ring through despite repeated attempts.
10. Interview with Gary Jarmin, June 8, 1989.
11. Eileen Ogintz, "Evangelists Seek Political Clout," *Chicago Tribune,* January 13, 1980, 5.
12. For descriptions of the rally, see Sara Diamond, *Spiritual Warfare* (Boston: South End Press, 1988), 61; Jeffrey K. Hadden and Charles E. Swann, *Prime Time Preachers* (Reading, Mass.: Addison-Wesley, 1981), 129.
13. Interview with Howard Phillips, June 16, 1989.
14. See Hadden and Swann, *Prime Time Preachers,* 127–30; Erling Jorstad, *The Politics of Moralism* (Minneapolis: Augsburg, 1981), 92–96.
15. Jorstad, *The Politics of Moralism,* 95.
16. Hadden and Shupe, *Televangelism,* 249.
17. Interview with Howard Phillips, June 16, 1989.
18. Diamond, *Spiritual Warfare,* 74.
19. Interview with Gary Jarmin, June 8, 1989.
20. Charles Babcock, "Robertson: Blending Charity and Politics," *Washington Post,* November 2, 1987, 1.

21. Diamond, *Spiritual Warfare,* 74.

22. Jeff Gerth, "Tax Data of Pat Robertson Groups are Questioned," *New York Times,* December 10, 1986, 18.

23. Jeff Gerth, "Robertson and Confidentiality," *New York Times,* March 19, 1987, 24.

24. Ibid.

25. Ibid. CBN University has since changed its name to Regent University.

26. Hadden and Shupe, *Televangelism,* 254–55.

27. Ibid.

28. Diamond, *Spiritual Warfare,* 74.

29. Gerth, "Robertson and Confidentiality," 24.

30. See Jean McNair, "Robertson Lays Off 470, Blames TV Ministry Scandals," *Boston Globe,* June 6, 1987, 1; Associated Press, "CBN Revamps The 700 Club," 7, September 5, 1987, *Bangor Daily News;* Wayne King, "Robertson, Returning to Brooklyn Home, Enters Race," *New York Times,* October 2, 1987, 16.

31. Diamond, *Spiritual Warfare,* 66.

32. Beth Spring, "Some Christian Leaders Want Further Political Activism," *Christianity Today,* November 9, 1984, 46. That conclusion was disputed by a 1984 interviewee, who said that the talent bank was already in operation at that time.

33. "ACTV: Who We Are and What We Stand For," undated pamphlet distributed by ACTV during 1984. It was obtained during a visit to its headquarters on July 27, 1984, at 122 C Street, NW, Washington, D.C.

34. Ibid.

35. Diamond, *Spiritual Warfare,* 66.

36. Matthew C. Moen, *The Christian Right and Congress* (Tuscaloosa: The University of Alabama Press, 1989), 51.

37. Spring, "Some Christian Leaders Want Further Political Activism," 46.

38. Ibid.

39. Ibid.

40. "Tim LaHaye Will Move to Washington to Promote Christian Political Activity," *Christianity Today,* December 14, 1984, 37.

41. "Leaders of the Christian Right Announce Their Next Step," *Christianity Today,* December 13, 1985, 65.

42. Carolyn Weaver, "Unholy Alliance," *Mother Jones* (January 1986): 14+.

43. Ibid., 14–15.

44. Beth Spring, "Magazine Says Tim LaHaye Received Help From Unification Church," *Christianity Today,* January 17, 1986, 40–41.

45. On the image problems of the Unification Church in the United States, see Anson Shupe, "Sun Myung Moon's American Disappointment," *The Christian Century,* August 22–29, 1990, 764–66.

46. Larry Witham, "LeHaye [sic] Continues Ministry on Local Level," *Washington Times,* October 20, 1989, F5.

47. Associated Press, "Moral Majority to Disband," 22, June 12, 1989, *Bangor Daily News.*

48. Moen, *The Christian Right and Congress,* 163–64.

49. Interview with Gary Jarmin, June 8, 1989.

50. Irving L. Janis, *Victims of Groupthink* (Boston: Houghton Mifflin, 1972).

51. John B. Judis, "Rev. Moon's Rising Political Influence," *U.S. News & World Report,* March 27, 1989, 27.

52. Ibid.; interview with Gary Jarmin, June 8, 1989.

53. Kim Lawton, "Unification Church Ties Haunt New Coalition," *Christianity Today,* February 5, 1988, 46.

54. Judis, "Rev. Moon's Rising Political Influence," 28.

55. William Bole, "Making Hay on a New Hero," *Christianity Today,* September 16, 1988, 49.

56. The booklet is entitled, "A Promise for Their Future." It was obtained from AFC headquarters, 1001 Pennsylvania Avenue, NW, Suite 850, Washington, D.C. 20004.

57. That inference is drawn from the fact that many of the AFC's enthusiastic supporters are unaware of the ties to the Reverend Moon and that many of Christian Voice's state directors were recruited into those positions by the AFC. See Lawton, "Unification Church Ties Haunt New Coalition," 46; Eleanor Clift and Mark Miller, "Rev. Moon's Political Moves," *Newsweek,* February 15, 1988, 31.

58. Clift and Miller, "Rev. Moon's Political Moves," 31.

59. Jorstad, *The Politics of Moralism,* 8–10.

60. Allan Bloom, *The Closing of the American Mind* (New York: Simon & Schuster, 1987).

61. Lawton, "Unification Church Ties Haunt New Coalition," 46.

62. "A Promise For Their Future," AFC promotional booklet, 2.

63. Bole, "Making Hay on a New Hero," 49; Lawton, "Unification Church Ties Haunt New Coalition," 46.

64. Hadden and Swann, *Prime Time Preachers,* 47–67.

65. "A Promise For Their Future," AFC promotional booklet, 3–4, 8; "What is the Moral Majority Inc.?," undated Moral Majority pamphlet, 1–3.

66. "A Promise For Their Future," AFC promotional booklet, 2.

67. Interview with Gary Jarmin, June 8, 1989.

68. "Economic Justice Task Force," AFC brochure, available from Gerald Leighton, 1304 Princeton Place, Rockville, Maryland 20850.

69. Ibid.

70. "Environmental Task Force," AFC brochure, available from Merrill Sikorski, 94549 Sterling Highway, Suite 5, Souldotna, Alaska 99669.

71. "National Education Task Force," AFC brochure, available from Wendy Flint, 9612 North East 91st Avenue, Vancouver, Washington 98662.

72. "Religious Freedom Task Force," AFC brochure, available from Donald Sills, 325 Pennsylvania Avenue, SE, Washington, D.C. 20003.

73. Diamond, *Spiritual Warfare,* 69–70.

74. "A Pageant For Religious Freedom: Let Freedom Ring," promotional poster distributed throughout Washington, D.C., in July 1984.

75. Diamond, *Spiritual Warfare,* 69.

76. "World Freedom Task Force," AFC brochure, available from Steven Trevino, 501 Capitol Court, NE, Suite 100, Washington, D.C. 20002.

77. Interview with Gary Jarmin, June 8, 1989.

78. Ibid.

79. David Mayhew, *Congress: The Electoral Connection* (New Haven: Yale University Press, 1974).

80. Interview with Gary Jarmin, June 8, 1989.

81. Clift and Miller, "Rev. Moon's Political Moves," 31; Lawton, "Unification Church Ties Haunt New Coalition," 46–47; and Judis, "Rev. Moon's Rising Political Influence," 27–32.

82. Bole, "Making Hay on a New Hero," 49.

83. Judis, "Rev. Moon's Rising Political Influence," 28; Gary Jarmin, "What Bush's Victory Means to America," *American Freedom Journal* (December 1988/January 1989): 3.

84. Interview with Joseph Conn, June 14, 1989.

85. Interview with Gary Jarmin, June 8, 1989.

86. The *Washington Times,* a daily newspaper owned by the Unification Church through a holding company, One Up Enterprises, has sustained losses estimated at $2 million annually since 1982. It has remained in business with assistance from the Reverend Moon, which demonstrates both his proclivity and ability to prop up organizations when he deems them useful. See "The Unification Church and the Subjugation of America," *Capital Research Center* (November 1988): 1–4. The publication may be obtained from 1612 K Street, NW, Suite 704, Washington, D.C. 20006.

87. Michael Isikoff, "Moon Group Financing Anti-Communist Lobby," *Washington Post,* September 14, 1984, 1.

88. One manifestation of that support is acceptance of "Earth Day." See Barnaby Feder, "The Business of Earth Day," *New York Times,* November 12, 1989, F4.

89. For a discussion of the problem, see Cal Thomas, "Faith, Credibility and the Real Thing," *Washington Times,* October 12, 1989, F1. Thomas was Moral Majority's communications director in the early 1980s.

90. Interview with Joseph Conn, June 14, 1989.

91. Ibid.

92. Interview with Laurie Tryfiates, June 9, 1989.

93. "Come Help Save America!" undated pamphlet distributed by Concerned Women for America, 370 L'Enfant Promenade, SW, Suite 800, Washington, D.C., 20024.

94. Nadine Brozan, "Politics and Prayer: Women on a Crusade," *New York Times,* June 15, 1987, 18.

95. Interview with Laurie Tryfiates, June 9, 1989.

96. Brozan, "Politics and Prayer," 18.

97. See "Come Help Save America!," undated CWA pamphlet.

98. Allen D. Hertzke, *Representing God in Washington* (Knoxville: University of Tennessee Press, 1988), 34.

99. On child care, feminist groups generally favor federally subsidized daycare centers, while CWA favors tax credits for young children, so that parents who stay at home with their children also receive assistance. In the 101st Congress (1989–1990), CWA rallied behind H.R. 2008, the "Holloway/Schulze Toddler Tax Credit," even drafting a "position report" to that effect.

100. Interview with Michael Schwartz, October 16, 1989.

101. Moen, *The Christian Right and Congress.*

102. Russell Chandler, "Religious Right Makes Political Arena Its Major Battleground," *Los Angeles Times,* March 29, 1986, 7.

103. Hertzke, *Representing God in Washington,* 52–53.

104. Interview with Laurie Tryfiates, June 9, 1989.

105. Diamond, *Spiritual Warfare,* 109.

106. Interview with Laurie Tryfiates, June 9, 1989.

107. Ibid.

108. "Come Help Save America!," undated CWA pamphlet.

109. Interview with Laurie Tryfiates, June 9, 1989.

110. Moen, *The Christian Right and Congress,* 147–63.

111. Brozan, "Politics and Prayer," 18.

112. Position papers on child care and tax credits were authored by the legal affairs division, formally called the Education and Legal Defense Foundation.

113. Informal conversations about the lobbying operations were similarly rebuffed.

114. Chandler, "Religious Right Makes Political Arena Its Major Battleground," 7.

115. Brozan, "Politics and Prayer," 18.

116. From an undated sheet entitled "News," which lists the various divisions of CWA and describes them, available from CWA headquarters.

117. The textbook cases were *Smith* v. *Board of Commissioners of Mobile County,* 655 F. Sup. 939 (1987); *Mozert* v. *Hawkins County,* 765 F. 2d 78 (1985).

The special-education case was *Witters* v. *Washington Department of Services for the Blind* 106 S. Ct. 748 (1986), which was argued before the Supreme Court in November 1985, with a decision handed down January 27, 1986. Argued by CWA attorney Michael Ferris, the Court ruled 9–0 in favor of CWA's position.

118. For example, see Ezra Bowen, "A Courtroom Clash Over Textbooks," *Time,* October 27, 1986, 94.

119. Beth Tuttle, Carol Blum, Matthew Freeman, and Mary Conway, "Who's Who in the Family Forum," June 29, 1988, 3. Document obtained from People for the American Way, 2000 M Street, NW, Suite 400, Washington, D.C. 20036.

120. Brozan, "Politics and Prayer," 18.

121. Ibid.

122. "News," undated CWA information sheet.

123. "Dr. and Mrs. LaHaye Dedicate School of Liberty in Costa Rica," *Friends of Refugees Report* (Winter 1989): 3.

124. Chandler, "Religious Right Makes Political Arena Its Major Battleground," 7.

125. Hertzke, *Representing God in Washington,* 177.

126. Brozan, "Politics and Prayer," 18.

127. Chandler, "Religious Right Makes Political Arena Its Major Battleground," 7.

128. Tuttle et al., "Who's Who in the Family Forum?," 3.

129. Brozan, "Politics and Prayer," 18.

130. Interview with Gary Jarmin, June 8, 1989.

131. John Elvin, "Fly a Kite," *Washington Times,* February 15, 1990, 5.

132. Matthew Scully, "Right Wing and a Prayer—Still Alive and Kicking," *Washington Times,* November 8, 1989, E1.

133. Interview with Howard Phillips, June 16, 1989.

134. Stepp, "Falwell Says Moral Majority to be Dissolved," 11.

135. On the Bundy interview, see Jon Nordheimer, "Bundy is Put to Death in Florida After Admitting Trail of Killings," *New York Times,* January 25, 1989, 1; on the Morgan interview, see Don Kowet, "The Friends of Elizabeth Morgan," *Washington Times,* October 17, 1989, E10.

136. Scully, "Right Wing and a Prayer," 2.

137. Interview with Gary Bauer, June 14, 1989.

138. Interview with Michael Schwartz, October 16, 1989.

139. See Matthew C. Moen, "The Resurrection of the Christian Right," *Church & State* (February 1990): 19–20; John Elvin, "Ain't Dead Yet," *Washington Times,* February 13, 1990, 6; and Elvin, "Fly a Kite," 5.

140. Elvin, "Fly a Kite," 5.

141. Interview with Gary Bauer, June 14, 1989.

142. Ibid.

143. Interview with Gary Jarmin, June 8, 1989.

144. Scully, "Right Wing and a Prayer," 2.

145. Interview with Gary Bauer, June 14, 1989.

146. Joyce Price, "Family Group Sees 1990s as Perilous," *Washington Times,* December 15, 1989, 5.

147. Ibid.

148. Ibid.

149. Allen D. Hertzke and Mary K. Scribner, "The Politics of Federal Day Care," 16, paper delivered at the Annual Meeting of the American Political Science Association, Atlanta, September 1989.

150. Interview with Gary Bauer, June 14, 1989.

151. This goal was stated by Pat Robertson in Eileen Ogintz, "Evangelists Seek Political Clout," *Chicago Tribune,* January 13, 1980, 5.

152. Scully, "Right Wing and a Prayer," 2.

153. John Elvin, "A Real Concern," *Washington Times,* August 23, 1990, 5.

4. Continuity and Change

1. Interview with Joseph Conn, June 14, 1989.

2. See Matthew C. Moen, "The Christian Right in the United States," in *The Religious Challenge to the State,* ed. Matthew C. Moen and Lowell S. Gustafson (Philadelphia: Temple University Press, 1992), 82–85.

3. Jack L. Walker, "The Origins and Maintenance of Interest Groups in America," *American Political Science Review* 77 (1983): 397.

4. Jeffrey M. Berry, *The Interest Group Society.* 2d ed. (Boston: Scott, Foresman, 1989), 18–31; Theodore J. Lowi, *The End of Liberalism.* 2d ed. (New York: W. W. Norton, 1979), 44.

5. For information on the organizations formed by New-Right leaders, see Richard Viguerie, *The New Right* (Falls Church, Va.: Viguerie, 1981).

6. Cited in Viguerie, *The New Right,* 79.

7. Ibid., 78.

8. Ibid., 55.

9. William Billings, *The Christian's Political Action Manual* (Washington, D.C.: NCAC, 1980).

10. Interview with Gary Jarmin, June 8, 1989.

11. Interview with Joseph Conn, June 14, 1989.

12. Interview with Howard Phillips, June 16, 1989.

13. Kenneth D. Wald, *Religion and Politics in the United States* (New York: St. Martin's, 1987), 190.

14. Robert Zwier, "The New Christian Right and the 1980 Elections," in *New Christian Politics,* ed. David G. Bromley and Anson Shupe (Macon, Ga.: Mercer University Press, 1984), 175.

15. Interview with Gary Jarmin, June 8, 1989.

16. Interview with Joseph Conn, June 14, 1989.

17. For example, Thomas J. McIntyre, *The Fear Brokers* (Boston: Beacon Press, 1979).

18. Moral Majority fundraising letter, September 28, 1984; Viguerie, *The New Right,* 132.

19. For an excellent discussion, see J. Steven Ott, *The Organizational Culture Perspective* (Pacific Grove, Calif.: Brooks/Cole, 1989), 1–19.

20. Steve Bruce, *The Rise and Fall of the New Christian Right* (New York: Oxford University Press, 1988), 132.

21. In the fashion of "grounded theory," the author let the data determine the cut-off point of three years. See Barney Glaser and Anselm Strauss, *The Discovery of Grounded Theory: Strategies for Qualitative Research* (New York: Aldine, 1967).

22. Interview with Gary Jarmin, June 8, 1989.

23. Interview with Howard Phillips, June 16, 1989.

24. Matthew C. Moen, *The Christian Right and Congress* (Tuscaloosa: The University of Alabama Press, 1989), 26–28.

25. Ibid., 10–11, 26–27.

26. Louise Lorentzen, "Evangelical Life Style Concerns Expressed in Political Action," *Sociological Analysis* 41 (1980): 144–54; Pamela Johnston Conover, "The Mobilization of the New Right," *Western Political Quarterly* 36 (1984): 632–49.

27. Roger Cobb and Charles Elder, *Participation in American Politics.* 2d ed. (Baltimore: Johns Hopkins University Press, 1983), 126–27.

28. Moen, *The Christian Right and Congress,* 54–55.

29. Matthew C. Moen, "Ronald Reagan and the Social Issues," *Social Science Journal* 27 (1990): 199–207.

30. Interview with Howard Phillips, June 16, 1989.

31. Dick Kirschten, "Reagan Looks to Religious Leaders for Continuing Support in 1984," *National Journal,* August 20, 1983, 1731.

32. Ronald Reagan, "Remarks at the Annual Convention of Concerned Women for America," in *Public Papers of the President* 2 (Washington, D.C.: Government Printing Office, 1989), 1079–82.

33. A particularly complete address on the subject was delivered by President Reagan on September 9, 1985. See "South Africa Sanctions," *Congressional Quarterly Almanac* 41 (Washington, D.C.: Congressional Quarterly, 1986), 28–30D.

34. See Alan Cowell, "Botha Sees South African Churchmen and Falwell,"

New York Times, August 20, 1985, 6; Robert Pear, "Falwell Denounces Tutu as Phony," *New York Times,* August 22, 1985, 10; "Jackson Attacks Falwell Trip," *New York Times,* August 22, 1985, 10; "Falwell Gives Qualified Apology for Calling Bishop Tutu a Phony," *New York Times,* August 24, 1985, 4.

35. Stephen Farber, "Bringing Mandela to Television," *New York Times,* September 19, 1986, 54.

36. People for the American Way issued an "editorial memorandum" following Falwell's South African visit, entitled, "Jerry Falwell: From Advocate of Segregation to Apologist For Apartheid," September 1985.

37. Clyde Wilcox, "Lingering Support for the Christian Right," 12. Paper presented at the Annual Meeting of the Midwest Political Science Association, Chicago, April 1990. For a somewhat different interpretation, see Moen, "Ronald Reagan and the Social Issues," 199–207.

38. Rob Hutcheson, "Arts Endowment Warned to Stop Funding Dirty Pictures," *Washington Times,* June 14, 1989, 5; Allen D. Hertzke and Mary K. Scribner, "The Politics of Federal Day Care," 6–8. Paper presented at the Annual Meeting of the American Political Science Association, Atlanta, September 1989.

39. Interview with Michael Schwartz, October 16, 1989.

40. John Kingdon, *Agendas, Alternatives and Public Policies* (Boston: Little, Brown & Co., 1984), 147.

41. For a summary of the Heritage Foundation's agenda for the 1990s, see Donald Lambro, "Conservative Charts Domestic Path for Movement," *Washington Times,* April 6, 1990, 7.

42. "North Says Criminal Charges Against Him Are an Honor," *New York Times,* May 3, 1988, B7.

43. "Come Help Save America!," undated pamphlet obtained from Concerned Women for America.

44. See Henry Mohr, "End Ollie's Persecution Now, Mr. President," and Dan Fefferman, "The First Annual National AFC Board of Governors Meeting," *American Freedom Journal* (December 1988/January 1989): 5–7.

45. Moen, *The Christian Right and Congress,* 141–47.

46. Jerrold Footlick, "What Happened to the Family?" *Newsweek,* (Winter/Spring 1990), 14–34. This article was in a special edition of the weekly newsmagazine, entitled "The 21st Century Family."

47. The term is borrowed from: Richard John Neuhaus, *The Naked Public Square,* 2d ed. (Grand Rapids, Mich.: William B. Eerdman's, 1984).

48. Sara Diamond, *Spiritual Warfare* (Boston: South End Press, 1989), 59–60.

5. Farewell to Capitol Hill

1. Kenneth Briggs, "Evangelical Preachers Gather to Polish Their Politics," *New York Times,* August 21, 1990, B9.

2. Matthew C. Moen, *The Christian Right and Congress* (Tuscaloosa: The University of Alabama Press, 1989); also see Matthew C. Moen, "The Christian Right in the United States," in *The Religious Challenge to the State,* ed. Matthew C. Moen and Lowell S. Gustafson (Philadelphia: Temple University Press, 1992), 85–89.

3. Norman J. Ornstein, Thomas E. Mann, and Michael J. Malbin, *Vital Statistics on Congress* (Washington, D.C.: CQ Press, 1987), 142–46.

4. Leroy Rieselbach, *Congressional Reform* (Washington, D.C.: CQ Press, 1986), 69.

5. Ornstein et al., *Vital Statistics on Congress,* 72–73.

6. Ibid., 77–78.

7. For example: Mark Green, *Who Runs Congress?* 4th ed. (New York: Dell, 1984).

8. Ornstein et al., *Vital Statistics on Congress,* 104.

9. Moral Majority's political action committee raised only $22,089 before it was dismantled. See Bill Keller, "Evangelical Conservatives Move from Pews to Polls, But Can They Sway Congress?" *Congressional Quarterly Weekly Report,* September 6, 1980, 2628.

10. Moen, *The Christian Right and Congress,* 84.

11. R. Kenneth Godwin, *One Billion Dollars of Influence* (Chatham, N.J.: Chatham House, 1988), 19–24.

12. Ibid., 23.

13. See Jeffrey L. Brudney and Gary W. Copeland, "Evangelicals as a Political Force," *Social Science Quarterly* 65 (1984): 1071–1079; Steven D. Johnson and Joseph B. Tamney, "The Christian Right and the 1980 Presidential Election," *Journal for the Scientific Study of Religion* 21 (1982): 123–31: Emmett H. Buell, Jr., and Lee Sigelman, "An Army That Meets Every Sunday? Popular Support for the Moral Majority in 1980," *Social Science Quarterly* 66 (1985): 426–34.

14. Senate Subcommittee on Separation of Powers, *Hearings on the Human Life Bill,* 97th Cong., 1st Sess., S. 158.

15. Moen, *The Christian Right and Congress,* 67.

16. Richard Strout, "Church-State Skirmishes in Sight?" *Christian Science Monitor,* November 10, 1980, 3.

17. "Religious Right Goes for Bigger Game," *U.S. News & World Report,* November 17, 1980, 42.

18. James Roberts, "The Christian Right: New Force in American Politics," *Human Events,* November 8, 1980, 10.

19. "Partisan Voting Averages Increased in 97th Congress," *Congressional Quarterly Almanac* 37 (Washington, D.C.: Congressional Quarterly, 1982), 32–33C. The average was calculated from the party unity scores provided for individual members.

20. Melinda Gipson, "Hatfield Hits Fear Tactics in Fundraising," *Washington Star,* May 2, 1981, 8; Jim Castelli, "Senator Offers Plan to Battle Religious Right," *Washington Star,* June 20, 1981, 6.

21. "President Reagan's Inaugural Address," *Congressional Quarterly Weekly Report,* January 24, 1981, 186–88.

22. Dick Kirschten, "Putting the Social Issues on Hold: Can Reagan Get Away With It?" *National Journal,* October 10, 1981, 1810.

23. The following account is taken from Moen, *The Christian Right and Congress,* 93–110.

24. Allen D. Hertzke, *Representing God in Washington* (Knoxville: University of Tennessee Press, 1988), 193.

25. For an overview of the litigation spawned by the Equal Access Act, see Hubert Morken, "Public Secondary Education: Equal Access and the Clash Over Student Religious Expression." Paper delivered at the Annual Meeting of the American Political Science Association, Atlanta, September 1989.

26. Ibid., 36.

27. Moen, *The Christian Right and Congress,* 111–24.

28. Ibid., 142–44.

29. Ibid., 124.

30. Roger Cobb and Charles Elder, *Participation in American Politics,* 2d ed. (Baltimore: Johns Hopkins University Press, 1983), 158.

31. Interview with Colleen Kiko, June 7, 1989.

32. Moen, *The Christian Right and Congress,* 151–58.

33. There were hearings in the 99th Congress on related topics, such as family planning and educational vouchers, but not on constitutional amendments or comparable statutory proposals.

34. Nadine Cohodas, "Senate Rejects Bill to Permit School Prayer," *Congressional Quarterly Weekly Report,* September 14, 1985, 1842.

35. Moen, *The Christian Right and Congress,* 162.

36. The percentage was calculated using figures from Matthew C. Moen, "Ronald Reagan and the Social Issues," *Social Science Journal* 27 (1990): 201.

37. Richard Ostling, "TV's Unholy Row," *Time,* April 6, 1987, 60–67; Wayne King, "Swaggart Says He Has Sinned; Will Step Down," *New York Times,* February 22, 1988, 1.

38. Lawrence Dodd and Bruce Oppenheimer, "The New Congress: Fluidity and Oscillation," in *Congress Reconsidered,* ed. Lawrence Dodd and Bruce Oppenheimer, 4th ed. (Washington, D.C.: CQ Press, 1989), 443–49.

39. 106 L.Ed.2d 410 (1989).

40. For an overview of the situation in all fifty states, see Eloise Salholz, "Voting in Curbs and Confusion," *Newsweek,* July 17, 1989, 16–20; "Status of Abortion Laws," *Congressional Quarterly Weekly Report,* July 8, 1989, 1699.

41. Allen D. Hertzke and Mary K. Scribner, "The Politics of Federal Day Care." Paper delivered at the Annual Meeting of the American Political Science Association, Atlanta, September 1989; Joyce Price, "NEA Chief Wavers on Mapplethorpe," *Washington Times,* April 27, 1990, 1.

42. Beth Spring, "Some Christian Leaders Want Further Political Activism," *Christianity Today,* November 9, 1984, 46.

43. Jeffrey L. Pasley, "Paper Pushers," *The New Republic,* December 1, 1986, 24–25.

44. Gary King and Lyn Ragsdale, *The Elusive Executive* (Washington, D.C.: CQ Press, 1988), 228–29.

45. Ibid., 225. The figures were calculated from data provided by King and Ragsdale. Their data, in turn, came from Roger M. Brown, "Party and Bureaucracy: From Kennedy to Reagan," *Political Science Quarterly,* 97 (1982): 283.

46. King and Ragsdale, *The Elusive Executive,* 234.

47. Ronald Brownstein, "Credentialing the Right," *National Journal,* July 19, 1986, 1764.

48. Ibid.

49. King and Ragsdale, *The Elusive Executive,* 225, 236.

50. Included in this category would be Stephen Markman and Tom Bovard of the Senate Judiciary Committee, who pushed the social issues from their committee positions before moving to the Justice Department in Reagan's second term; Laura Clay, a legislative assistant for New-Right Senator Don Nickles (R-Okla.), who moved over to Health and Human Services in Reagan's second term. The cases of Bob Billings and Gary Bauer, both of whom served in the Department of Education, have been mentioned earlier in this volume.

51. Interview with Gary Jarmin, June 8, 1989.

52. Larry Witham, "FCC Chief Welcomes Participation of Nation's Religious Broadcasters," *Washington Times,* February 2, 1990, B5.

53. Kim Lawton, "Evangelicals Still Not Sure About Bush," *Christianity Today,* January 15, 1990, 44.

54. Ibid.

55. Ibid.

56. Martin Tolchin, "Reagan's Power to Name Judiciary Going Lame," *New York Times.* Reprinted in *Maine Sunday Telegram,* December 6, 1987, 20.

57. Harold W. Stanley and Richard G. Niemi, *Vital Statistics on American Politics* (Washington, D.C.: CQ Press, 1988), 240–41.

58. Neil A. Lewis, "Bush Picking the Kind of Judges Reagan Favored," *New York Times,* April 10, 1990, 1.

59. Interview with Gary Bauer, June 14, 1989.

60. Interview with Colleen Kiko, June 7, 1989.

61. Interview with Joseph Conn, June 14, 1989.

62. See respectively, 106 L.Ed.2d. 410 (1989); 109 S.Ct. 2115 (1989).

63. 110 S.Ct. 2356 (1990).

64. Lewis, "Bush Picking the Kind of Judges Reagan Favored," 1.

65. "Doing the Right Thing: Other Legal Aid Groups," *Church & State* (May 1990): 11.

66. Interview with Colleen Kiko, June 7, 1989.

67. Interview with Gary Bauer, June 14, 1989.

68. "Robertson Group Vows to Fight for Sectarian Sex Ed," *Church & State* (June 1990): 14.

69. Rob Boston, "States of Confusion," *Church & State* (October 1990): 8–10; see also: Hubert Morken, "Religious Lobbying at the State Level: Case Studies in a Continuing Role for the New Religious Right," paper presented at the Annual Meeting of the American Political Science Association, San Francisco, September, 1990.

70. Interview with Joseph Conn, June 14, 1989.

71. Rob Gurwitt," 1986 Elections Generate GOP Power Struggle," *Congressional Quarterly Weekly Report,* April 12, 1986, 803.

72. Gurwitt, "1986 Elections Generate GOP Power Struggle," 803.

73. Marsha Blakemore, "Religious Right's Zeal Worries Republican Mainstream," *Tampa Tribune,* August 4, 1986, 4.

74. Ibid.

75. Jeffrey K. Hadden and Anson Shupe, *Televangelism: Power and Politics on God's Frontier* (New York: Henry Holt, 1988), 254.

76. Howard Fineman, "The Pat Robertson Effect," *Newsweek,* September 28, 1987, 29.

77. David E. Rosenbaum, "Robertson Ends Active Campaigning," *New York Times,* April 7, 1988, D23.

78. Hadden and Shupe, *Televangelism;* Sara Diamond, *Spiritual Warfare* (Boston: South End Press, 1989); Lisa Langenbach, "Evangelical Elites and Political Action: The Pat Robertson Presidential Candidacy," paper delivered at the Annual Meeting of the American Political Science Association, Washington, D.C., September, 1988.

79. Peter Jennings and David Brinkley, *The 1988 Vote* (New York: Capital Cities/ABC, 1989), 305–6.

80. Ibid., 325–67.

81. Ibid.

82. Philip Secret, James Johnson, and Susan Welch, "Racial Differences in Attitudes Toward the Supreme Court's Decision on Prayer in the Public Schools," *Social Science Quarterly,* 67 (1986): 878–79.

83. Jennings and Brinkley, *The 1988 Vote,* 305.

84. W. Craig Bledsoe, "Post Moral Majority Politics," 9–11. Paper delivered at Annual Meeting of the American Political Science Association, San Francisco, September 1990.

85. Tamar Jacoby, "Is It Time to Take Pat Seriously: The Invisible Army," *Time,* January 4, 1988, 21.

86. Interview with Joseph Conn, June 14, 1989.

87. Phil Gailey, "Robertson Used Journalist to Get Data for Libel Suit on War Record," *New York Times,* April 2, 1987, 25.

88. Associated Press, "Robertson Allowed to Drop Suit for Libel," 5, March 5, 1988, *Bangor Daily News.*

89. Ibid.

90. Knight-Ridder Newspapers, "Robertson Blasts Journalists for Exposing Family Skeleton," 17, October 9, 1987, *Bangor Daily News.*

91. The term is from Timothy Crouse, *The Boys on The Bus* (New York: Ballantine, 1972).

92. Wayne King, "Wild Oats, Robertson Says of Late Marriage," *New York Times,* October 9, 1987, 22.

93. Steven Waldman, "A Case of Creeping Irrelevance," *Newsweek,* March 14, 1988, 20.

94. Richard Berke, "Consultants Get Robertson Funds," *New York Times,* January 20, 1988, 18.

95. Ibid.

96. Interview with Gary Bauer, June 14, 1989.

97. Larry Martz, "Day of the Preachers," *Newsweek,* March 7, 1988, 44.

98. Associated Press, "Robertson Charges Planned Parenthood Wants Master Race," 14, February 3, 1988, *Bangor Daily News.*

99. Moen, *The Christian Right and Congress,* 154.

100. Interview with Gary Jarmin, June 8, 1989.

6. From Moralism to Liberalism

1. See Jerome L. Himmelstein, "The New Right," in *The New Christian Right,* ed. Robert C. Liebman and Robert Wuthnow (New York: Aldine, 1983), 13–30; Matthew C. Moen, *The Christian Right and Congress* (Tuscaloosa: The University of Alabama Press, 1989), 9–31; Jeffrey K. Hadden and Charles E. Swann, *Prime Time Preachers* (Reading, Mass.: Addison-Wesley, 1981).

2. Eileen Ogintz, "Evangelists Seek Political Clout," *Chicago Tribune,* January 13, 1980, 5.

3. George Vecsey, "Militant Television Preachers Try to Weld Fundamentalist Christians' Political Power," *New York Times,* January 21, 1980, 2.

4. Kathy Sawyer and Robert Keiser, "Evangelicals Flock to GOP Standard Feeling They Have a Friend in Reagan," *Washington Post,* July 10, 1980, 5.

5. Joan Sweeney, "Evangelicals Seeking to Establish Political Force," *Los Angeles Times,* May 19, 1980, 21.

6. Alan Crawford, *Thunder on the Right* (New York: Pantheon, 1980), 144; Erling Jorstad, *The Politics of Moralism* (Minneapolis: Augsburg, 1981), 76; Matthew C. Moen, "The New Christian Right and the Legislative Agenda: 1981–84," 14–15. Paper delivered at the Annual Meeting of the Southwestern Political Science Association, Houston, March 1985.

7. The Reverend Stan Hastey, of the Baptist Joint Committee on Public Affairs, called the verse found in II Chronicles the "controlling text" of the Christian Right in its early days. See Moen, *The Christian Right and Congress,* 38.

8. Jorstad, *The Politics of Moralism,* 8.

9. Anson Shupe and William Stacey, "The Moral Majority Constituency," in *The New Christian Right,* ed. Robert C. Liebman and Robert Wuthnow (New York: Aldine, 1983), 103–16.

10. Ibid., 114; Louise Lorentzen, "Evangelical Life Style Concerns Expressed in Political Action," *Sociological Analysis* 41 (1980): 144–54. For criticisms of status politics applications to the Christian Right, see: John H. Simpson, "Moral Issues and Status Politics," in *The New Christian Right,* ed. Robert C. Liebman and Robert Wuthnow (New York: Aldine, 1983), 187–205; Matthew C. Moen, "Status Politics and the Political Agenda of the Christian Right," *Sociological Quarterly* 29 (1988): 429–37; James L. Guth and John C. Green, "The Moralizing Minority: Christian Right Support Among Political Contributors," *Social Science Quarterly* 68 (1987): 598–610; Helen Moore and Hugh Whitt, "Multiple Dimensions of the Moral Majority Platform," *Sociological Quarterly* 27 (1986): 423–39. On resource mobilization theories, see Margaret Ann Latus, "Ideological PACs and Political Action," in *The New Christian Right,* ed. Robert C. Liebman and Robert Wuthnow (New York: Aldine, 1983), 75–99, and Steve Bruce, *The Rise and Fall of the New Christian Right* (New York: Oxford University Press, 1988), 21–24.

11. "Religious Right Talks Politics," *Guardian,* September 3, 1980, 4; James Mann and Sarah Peterson, "Preachers in Politics," *U.S. News & World Report,* September 15, 1980, 24–26.

12. E. J. Dionne, Jr., "Evangelical Vote is a Major Target," *New York Times,* June 29, 1980, G18.

13. Shupe and Stacey, "The Moral Majority Constituency," 106, 114.

14. Clyde Wilcox, "Evangelicals and Fundamentalists in the New Christian Right," *Journal for the Scientific Study of Religion* 25 (1986): 356, 360.

15. Clyde Wilcox, "Popular Support for the Moral Majority in 1980: A Second Look," *Social Science Quarterly* 68 (1987): 163.

16. James L. Guth, "Southern Baptist Clergy: Vanguard of the Christian

Right?" in *The New Christian Right,* ed. Robert C. Liebman and Robert Wuthnow (New York: Aldine, 1983), 120.

17. Kathleen Murphy Beatty and B. Oliver Walter, "Fundamentalists, Evangelicals, and Politics," *American Politics Quarterly* 16 (1988): 51–52.

18. Ibid., 47; Robert Booth Fowler, *Religion and Politics in America* (Metuchen, N.J.: Scarecrow, 1985).

19. In addition to the studies already noted, see Clyde Wilcox, "Fundamentalists and Politics: An Analysis of the Effects of Differing Operational Definitions," *Journal of Politics* 48 (1986): 1041–51; Lyman A. Kellstedt, "The Meaning and Measurement of Evangelicalism," in *Religion and Political Behavior in the United States,* ed. Ted G. Jelen (New York: Praeger, 1989), 3–21; Corwin Smidt, "Identifying Evangelical Respondents," in *Religion and Political Behavior in the United States,* ed. Ted G. Jelen (New York: Praeger, 1989), 23–43, and "Evangelicals Versus Fundamentalists: An Analysis of the Political Characteristics and Importance of Two Major Religious Movements Within American Politics." Paper delivered at the Annual Meeting of the Midwest Political Science Association, Chicago, April 1983; A. James Reichley, *Religion in American Public Life* (Washington, D.C.: Brookings Institution, 1985), 311–27.

20. Wilcox, "Evangelicals and Fundamentalists in the New Christian Right," 356.

21. Jeffrey K. Hadden and Anson Shupe, T*elevangelism: Power & Politics on God's Frontier* (New York: Henry Holt, 1988), 74–95.

22. Jeffrey L. Brudney and Gary W. Copeland, "Evangelicals as a Political Force," *Social Science Quarterly* 65 (1984): 1074.

23. Ibid., 1078.

24. Simpson, "Moral Issues and Status Politics," 190.

25. Allen D. Hertzke, *Representing God in Washington* (Knoxville: University of Tennessee Press, 1988), 121.

26. Joel B. Grossman and Richard S. Wells, *Constitutional Law and Judicial Policymaking.* 2d ed. (New York: John Wiley & Sons, 1980), 1276.

27. *Engel* v. *Vitale* 82 S.Ct. 1261 (1962).

28. Richard John Neuhaus, *The Naked Public Square.* 2d ed. (Grand Rapids, Mich.: William B. Eerdman's, 1984).

29. James L. Guth, "The Politics of the Christian Right," in *Interest Group Politics,* ed. Allan J. Cigler and Burdett A. Loomis (Washington, D.C.: CQ Press, 1983), 75.

30. Alan Crawford, *Thunder on the Right* (New York: Pantheon, 1980), 144–64.

31. "Christian Right Equated With Iran's Mullahs," *Washington Star,* September 24, 1980, 4.

32. Interview with Joseph Conn, June 14, 1989.

33. "What is the Moral Majority, Inc.?" 2. Undated pamphlet distributed by Moral Majority to its new members in the early 1980s.

34. Compiled from *Gallup Opinion Polls* (Wilmington, Del.: Scholarly Resources, 1975–1982). The specific polls were reported on April 3, 1975; February 1, 1976; April 10, 1977; March 12, 1978; March 22, 1979; August 3, 1980; March 8, 1981; February 7, 1982; May 8, 1983; July 15, 1984; February 28, 1985.

35. Harold W. Stanley and Richard G. Niemi, *Vital Statistics on American Politics* (Washington, D.C.: CQ Press, 1988), 31.

36. Ibid., 337; *The World Almanac,* 1986 (New York: Newspaper Enterprise Association, 1985), 779.

37. Thomas Hobbes, *Leviathan* (Indianapolis: Bobbs-Merrill, 1958); John Locke, *Two Treatises of Government* (New York: Cambridge, 1960). The *Leviathan* was first published in 1651, and the second of Locke's two treatises was written around the Glorious Revolution of 1688.

38. The most notable exegesis of the political thought and legacy of Hobbes and Locke is Leo Strauss, *Natural Right and History* (Chicago: University of Chicago Press, 1953).

39. Donald J. Devine, *The Political Culture of the United States* (Boston: Little, Brown & Co., 1972).

40. Harry Holloway and John George, *Public Opinion* (New York: St. Martin's, 1979), 38.

41. Thomas Sowell, "Buzzword Brain Drain," *Washington Times,* July 31, 1990, G3.

42 . Interview with Gary Jarmin, June 8, 1989.

43. Jean McNair, "Robertson Lays Off 470, Blames TV Ministry Scandals," *Boston Globe,* June 6, 1987, 1; Hadden and Shupe, *Televangelism,* 267.

44. Hertzke, *Representing God in Washington,* 195.

45. Ibid.

46. Dawn Weyrich, "Prayer Allowed After School," *Washington Times,* June 5, 1990, 11.

47. Allen D. Hertzke and Mary K. Scribner, "The Politics of Federal Day Care," 30. Paper delivered at the Annual Meeting of the American Political Science Association, Atlanta, September 1989.

48. Ibid., 15–17.

49. Hertzke, *Representing God in Washington,* 196.

50. Garry Wills, "Save the Babies," *Time,* May 1, 1989, 26–28.

51. Interview with Gary Bauer, June 14, 1989.

52. National radio broadcast entitled, "Focus on Issues," August 17, 1989, on KSOO radio, Sioux Falls, S. Dak.

53. Wesley Pruden, "A Growing Trade in Victimhood," *Washington Times,* June 15, 1990, 4.

54. Mike Royko, "Victim Growth Industry," *Washington Times,* June 12, 1990, F3.

55. Wayne King, "Robertson Plans an Ad Campaign to Enhance TV Minister's Image," *New York Times,* September 7, 1987, 7; Associated Press, "Pat Robertson Shuns TV Evangelist Label," 18, February 11, 1988, *Bangor Daily News.*

56. For example; Larry Martz, "Day of the Preachers," *Newsweek,* March 7, 1988, 44–46.

57. Steve Bruce, *The Rise and Fall of the New Christian Right* (New York: Oxford University Press, 1988), 172.

58. "Bill Would Ban Religious Satire," *Washington Times,* March 22, 1991, B5.

59. Interview with Joseph Conn, June 14, 1989.

60. Interview with Gary Bauer, June 14, 1989.

61. Interview with Michael Schwartz, October 16, 1989.

62. Ibid.

63. Ibid.

64. Interview with Gary Bauer, June 14, 1989.

65. Interview with Joseph Conn, June 14, 1989.

66. Robert Michels, *Political Parties* (Glencoe, Ill.: Free Press, 1915); for an application of the social movement literature to the Christian Right, see Michael Lienesch, "Christian Conservatism as a Political Movement," *Political Science Quarterly* 97 (1982): 403–25.

67. Bruce, *The Rise and Fall of the New Christian Right,* 191.

68. Moen, *The Christian Right and Congress,* 123–24.

69. Interview with Gary Jarmin, June 8, 1989.

70. Interview with Joseph Conn, June 14, 1989.

71. Mayer Zald and Roberta Ash, "Social Movement Organizations: Growth, Decay, and Change," *Social Forces* 44 (1966): 327–41.

72. Kathy Palen, "Southern Baptist Rejects Cultural Conservatism," *Baptist Press,* January 26, 1989.

73. Bruce, *The Rise and Fall of the New Christian Right,* 181.

74. Interview with Joseph Conn, June 14, 1989.

75. "North Says Criminal Charges Against Him are an Honor," *New York Times,* May 3, 1988, B7.

76. Robert Pear, "Falwell Denounces Tutu as a Phony," *New York Times,* August 22, 1985, 10.

77. Peter Brown, "Robertson's Attack on Reagan Breaks the 11th Commandment," Scripps-Howard wire story, October 19, 1987.

78. Martz, "Day of the Preachers," 44.

79. Bruce, *The Rise and Fall of the New Christian Right,* 172.

7. Distinctiveness and Political Influence

1. For a comparative perspective on the relative religiosity of regimes, see *Religious Resurgence and Politics in the Contemporary World,* ed. Emile Sahliyeh (Albany: State University of New York Press, 1990); *The Religious Challenge to the State,* ed. Matthew C. Moen and Lowell S. Gustafson (Philadelphia: Temple University Press, 1992).

2. Two excellent discussions of the vitality of religion in the 1980s are George H. Gallup, Jr., "Religion in America 1984," *The Gallup Report* 22 (March 1984): 7–16, and Kenneth D. Wald, *Religion and Politics in the United States* (New York: St. Martin's, 1987), 6–15.

3. Richard John Neuhaus, *The Naked Public Square,* 2d ed. (Grand Rapids, Mich.: William B. Eerdman's, 1984), 37.

4. *Wallace* v. *Jaffree,* 105 S.Ct. 2479 (1985).

5. Seth Rosenfeld, "Coalition Files Suit to Remove Cross From Public Park," *San Francisco Examiner.* Reprinted in the *Washington Times,* July 2, 1990, 6; *Lynch* v. *Donnelly* 465 U.S. 471 (1984).

6. Hubert Morken, "Public Secondary Education: Equal Access and the Clash Over Student Religious Expression," 36. Paper delivered at the Annual Meeting of the American Political Science Association, Atlanta, September 1989.

7. For example, David V. Edwards, *The American Political Experience,* 3d ed. (Englewood Cliffs, N.J.: Prentice-Hall, 1985), 14.

8. An interesting discussion of Pat Robertson's response to perceived secularity may be found in Allen D. Hertzke, "Populist Echoes of Discontent," 21–25. Paper delivered at the Annual Meeting of the American Political Science Association, San Francisco, September 1990.

9. Paul Abramson, John Aldrich, and David Rhode, *Change and Continuity in the 1980 Election* (Washington, D.C.: CQ Press, 1982), 101; Seymour Martin Lipset and Earl Rabb, "The Election and the Evangelicals," *Commentary* (March 1981), 25–31.

10. Steve Bruce, *The Rise and Fall of the New Christian Right* (New York: Oxford University Press, 1988), 93–94.

11. Arthur H. Miller and Martin P. Wattenberg, "Politics From the Pulpit," *Public Opinion Quarterly* 48 (1984): 301–17; Lee Sigelman, Clyde Wilcox, and Emmett H. Buell, Jr., "An Unchanging Minority: Popular Support for the Moral Majority, 1980 and 1984," *Social Science Quarterly* 68 (1987): 876–84; Jeffrey L. Brudney and Gary W. Copeland, "Evangelicals as a Political Force," *Social Science Quarterly* 65 (1984): 1072–79.

12. Matthew C. Moen, *The Christian Right and Congress* (Tuscaloosa: The University of Alabama Press, 1989), 142–44.

13. Philip Hammond, "Another Great Awakening?" in *The New Christian Right,* ed. Robert C. Liebman and Robert Wuthnow (New York: Aldine, 1983), 219–20.

14. For example, Jeffrey K. Hadden and Charles Swann, *Prime Time Preachers* (Reading, Mass.: Addison-Wesley, 1981).

15. Moen, *The Christian Right and Congress,* 154–55.

16. Ibid., 126.

17. There are no firm numbers available on the proportion of fundamentalists, evangelicals, and pentecostals in particular Christian-Right organizations. Scholars have posited that the mix has changed, though, and have conducted voting studies delineating differences among the subgroups of conservative Protestants. See Corwin Smidt, "Religion and the 1988 Elections." Precis of a roundtable discussion at the Annual Meeting of the American Political Science Association, Washington, D.C., September 1988; Lyman A. Kellstedt and Mark A. Noll, "Religion, Voting for President, and Party Identification, 1948–1964," in *Religion and American Politics,* ed. Mark Noll (New York: Oxford University Press, 1990), 355–79; Lyman Kellstedt, Paul Kellstedt, and Corwin Smidt, "Evangelical and Mainline Protestants in the 1988 Presidential Election." Paper delivered at the Annual Meeting of the American Political Science Association, San Francisco, September 1990.

18. Interview with Gary Jarmin, June 8, 1989.

19. Roger Cobb and Charles Elder, *Participation in American Politics.* 2d ed. (Baltimore: Johns Hopkins University Press, 1983), 46.

20. Michael D'Antonio, "Fierce in the '80s, Fallen in the '90s, the Religious Right Forgets Politics," *Los Angeles Times,* February 4, 1990, M3.

21. Gary Jacobson, *Money in Congressional Elections* (New Haven: Yale University Press, 1980).

22. Calculated from the indexes of *The New York Times.*

23. Interview with Joseph Conn, June 14, 1989.

24. Interview with Howard Phillips, June 16, 1989.

25. Interview with Michael Schwartz, October 16, 1989.

26. Interview with Gary Jarmin, June 8, 1989.

27. Interview with Gary Bauer, June 14, 1989.

28. Ibid.

29. Interview with Gary Jarmin, June 8, 1989.

30. Moen, *The Christian Right and Congress,* 155.

31. Interview with Howard Phillips, June 16, 1989.

32. See Mayer Zald and Roberta Ash, "Social Movement Organizations: Growth, Decay, and Change," *Social Forces* 44 (1966): 327–41.

33. Interview with Michael Schwartz, October 16, 1989.

34. The filtering out of information is called "selective perception." See Thomas Patterson and Robert McClure, *The Unseeing Eye* (New York: G. P. Putnams' Sons, 1976), 63–68.

35. See Chris Harvey, "GOP Right is Angry—but not Mutinous," *Washington Times,* July 30, 1990, 3; Frank Murray and George Archibald, "Bush Link to Right is Fired," *Washington Times,* August 2, 1990, 1.

36. Interview with Michael Schwartz, October 16, 1989.

37. Moen, *The Christian Right and Congress,* 146–47, and "Ronald Reagan and the Social Issues," *Social Science Journal* 27 (1990): 199–207.

38. Kellstedt, Kellstedt, and Smidt, "Evangelical and Mainline Protestants in the 1988 Presidential Election," 22.

39. Duane Oldfield, "The Christian Right and State Republican Parties," 13, 23. Paper delivered at the Annual Meeting of the American Political Science Association, San Francisco, September 1990.

40. Ibid., 28, 31.

8. Political Skills and Religious Belief

1. Interview with Gary Jarmin, June 8, 1989.

2. Interview with Michael Schwartz, October 16, 1989.

3. Interview with Gary Jarmin, June 8, 1989.

4. Interview with Howard Phillips, June 16, 1989.

5. Robert Wuthnow, "The Political Rebirth of American Evangelicals," in *The New Christian Right,* ed. Robert C. Liebman and Robert Wuthnow (New York: Aldine, 1983), 177.

6. Interview with Laurie Tryfiates, June 9, 1989.

7. Interview with Gary Bauer, June 14, 1989.

8. Anson Shupe and John Heinerman, "Mormonism and the New Christian Right: An Emerging Coalition?" *Review of Religious Research* 27 (December 1985): 146–57.

9. Interview with Gary Bauer, June 14, 1989.

10. Ibid.

11. Interview with Colleen Kiko, June 7, 1989.

12. Michael Lienesch, "Christian Conservatism as a Political Movement," *Political Science Quarterly* 97 (1982): 421–23.

13. Robert A. Dahl, *A Preface to Democratic Theory* (Chicago: University of Chicago Press, 1956), 151.

14. For a related treatment, see Matthew C. Moen, "The Christian Right in the United States," in *The Religious Challenge to the State,* ed. Matthew C. Moen and Lowell S. Gustafson (Philadelphia: Temple University Press, 1992), 92–96.

15. Interview with Gary Jarmin, June 8, 1989.

16. Interview with Joseph Conn, June 14, 1989.

17. Bruce Barron and Anson Shupe, "Determined to Attain Dominion: Rea-

sons for the Growing Popularity of Christian Reconstructionism," 2. Paper delivered at the Annual Meeting of the Society for the Scientific Study of Religion, Virginia Beach, Virginia, November 1990.

18. For example, Anson Shupe, "The Christian Reconstructionists," *The Christian Century,* October 4, 1989, 880–82.

19. For a discussion of Reconstructionist influence in the Christian Right, see Barron and Shupe, "Determined to Attain Dominion: Reasons for the Growing Popularity of Christian Reconstructionism," 20–35.

20. Jeffrey L. Brudney and Gary W. Copeland, "Ronald Reagan and the Religious Vote," 19. Paper delivered at the Annual Meeting of the American Political Science Association, Washington, D.C., September 1988.

21. Duane Oldfield, "The Christian Right and State Republican Parties," 23. Paper delivered at the Annual Meeting of the American Political Science Association, San Francisco, September 1990.

22. Beth Spring, "Some Christian Leaders Want Further Political Activism," *Christianity Today,* November 9, 1984, 47.

Bibliography

Abramson, Paul, John Aldrich, and David Rhode. *Change and Continuity in the 1980 Election.* Washington, D.C.: CQ Press, 1982.

Arnold, R. Douglas. "Overtilled and Undertilled Fields in American Politics." *Political Science Quarterly* 97 (1982): 91–103.

Associated Press. "CBN Revamps the 700 Club." *Bangor Daily News* (September 5, 1987), 7.

———. "Moral Majority to Disband." *Bangor Daily News* (June 12, 1989): 22.

———. "Pat Robertson Shuns TV Evangelist Label." *Bangor Daily News* (February 11, 1988): 18.

———. "Robertson Allowed to Drop Suit for Libel." *Bangor Daily News* (March 5, 1988): 5.

———. Robertson Charges Planned Parenthood Wants Master Race." *Bangor Daily News* (February 3, 1988): 14.

Babcock, Charles. "Robertson: Blending Charity and Politics." *Washington Post* (November 2, 1987): 1.

"Back to Basics." *Washington Times* (September 26, 1989): 6.

Barron, Bruce, and Anson Shupe. "Determined to Attain Dominion: Reasons for the Growing Popularity of Christian Reconstructionism." Paper delivered at the Annual Meeting of the Society for the Scientific Study of Religion, Virginia Beach, Virginia, November 1990.

Beatty, Kathleen Murphy, and B. Oliver Walter. "Fundamentalists, Evangelicals, and Politics." *American Politics Quarterly* 16 (1988): 43–59.

Bennetts, Leslie. "National Anti-Liberal Crusade Zeroing in on McGovern in South Dakota." *New York Times* (June 2, 1980): 11.

Berke, Richard. "Consultants Get Robertson Funds." *New York Times* (January 20, 1988): 18.

Berry, Jeffrey M. *The Interest Group Society.* 2nd ed. Boston: Scott, Foresman, 1989.

Billings, Bill. *The Christian's Political Action Manual.* Washington, D.C.: National Christian Action Coalition, 1980.

"Bill Would Ban Religious Satire." *Washington Times* (March 22, 1991): B5.

Blakemore, Marsha. "Religious Right's Zeal Worries Republican Mainstream." *Tampa Tribune* (August 4, 1986): 4.

Bledsoe, W. Craig. "Post Moral Majority Politics." Paper delivered at the Annual Meeting of the American Political Science Association, San Francisco, California, September 1990.

Bloom, Allan. *The Closing of the American Mind.* New York: Simon & Shuster, 1987.

Bole, William. "Making Hay on a New Hero." *Christianity Today* (September 16, 1988): 49.

Boston, Rob. "States of Confusion." *Church & State* 42 (June 1990): 8–10.

Bowen, Ezra. "A Courtroom Clash Over Textbooks." *Time* (October 27, 1986): 94.

Briggs, Kenneth. "Evangelical Preachers Gather to Polish Their Politics." *New York Times* (August 21, 1980): B9.

Brown, Peter. "Robertson's Attack on Reagan Breaks the 11th Commandment." Scripps-Howard wire-story, October 19, 1987.

Brown, Roger M. "Party and Bureaucracy: From Kennedy to Reagan." *Political Science Quarterly* 97 (1982): 279–94.

Brownstein, Ronald. "Credentialing the Right." *National Journal* (July 19, 1986): 1764–69.

Brozan, Nadine. "Politics and Prayer: Women on a Crusade." *New York Times* (June 15, 1987): 18.

Bruce, Steve. *The Rise and Fall of the New Christian Right.* New York: Oxford University Press, 1988.

Brudney, Jeffrey L., and Gary W. Copeland. "Evangelicals as a Political Force." *Social Science Quarterly* 65 (1984): 1072–79.

Brudney, Jeffrey L., and Gary W. Copeland. "Ronald Reagan and the Religious Vote." Paper delivered at the Annual Meeting of the American Political Science Association, Washington, D.C., September 1988.

Buell, Emmett H., Jr., and Lee Sigelman. "An Army That Meets Every Sunday? Popular Support for the Moral Majority in 1980." *Social Science Quarterly* 66 (1985): 426–34.

Castelli, Jim. "Senator Offers Plan to Battle Religious Right." *Washington Star* (June 20, 1981): 6.

Chandler, Russell. "Religious Right Makes Political Arena Its Major Battleground." *Los Angeles Times* (March 29, 1986): 7.

"Christian Right Equated With Iran's Mullahs." *Washington Star* (September 24, 1980): 4.

Clarity, James F., and Warren Weaver, Jr. "Articles and Morals." *New York Times* (January 3, 1986): 10.

Clift, Eleanor, and Mark Miller. "Rev. Moon's Political Moves." *Newsweek* (February 15, 1988): 31.

Cobb, Roger, and Charles Elder. *Participation in American Politics.* 2nd ed. Baltimore: Johns Hopkins University Press, 1983.

Cohodas, Nadine. "Senate Rejects Bill to Permit School Prayer." *Congressional Quarterly Weekly Report* (September 14, 1985): 1842.

Conover, Pamela Johnston. "The Mobilization of the New Right." *Western Political Quarterly* 36 (1984): 632–49.

Cowell, Alan. "Botha Sees South African Churchmen and Falwell." *New York Times* (August 20, 1985): 6.

Crawford, Alan. *Thunder on the Right.* New York: Pantheon Books, 1980.

Crouse, Timothy. *The Boys on the Bus.* New York: Ballantine, 1972.

Dahl, Robert A. *A Preface to Democratic Theory.* Chicago: University of Chicago Press, 1956.

D'Antonio, Michael. "Fierce in the '80s, Fallen in the '90s: The Religious Right Forgets Politics." *Los Angeles Times* (February 4, 1990): M3.

Devine, Donald J. *The Political Culture of the United States.* Boston: Little, Brown & Co., 1972.

Diamond, Sara. *Spiritual Warfare.* Boston: South End Press, 1988.

Dionne, E. J., Jr. "Evangelical Vote is a Major Target." *New York Times* (June 29, 1980): G18.

Dodd, Lawrence, and Bruce Oppenheimer. "The New Congress: Fluidity and Oscillation." In *Congress Reconsidered,* 4th ed., edited by Lawrence Dodd and Bruce Oppenheimer, 443–49. Washington, D.C.: CQ Press, 1989.

"Doing the Right Thing: Other Legal Aid Groups." *Church & State* (May 1990): 11.

"Dr. and Mrs. LaHaye Dedicate School of Liberty in Costa Rica." *Friends of Refugees Report* (Winter 1989): 3.

Edelman, Murray. *The Symbolic Uses of Politics.* Urbana: University of Illinois Press, 1964.

Edwards, David V. *The American Political Experience.* 3rd ed. Englewood Cliffs, N.J.: Prentice-Hall, 1985.

Elvin, John. "Ain't Dead Yet." *Washington Times* (February 13, 1990): 6.

———. "Fly a Kite." *Washington Times* (February 15, 1990): 5.

———. "A Real Concern." *Washington Times* (August 23, 1990): 5.

Endersby, James. "The Cross and the Flag." Paper delivered at Annual Meeting of the Southwestern Political Science Association, Fort Worth, Texas, March 1984.

Fackre, Gabriel. *The Religious Right and Christian Faith.* Grand Rapids, Mich.: William B. Eerdman's, 1982.

"Falwell Gives Qualified Apology for Calling Bishop Tutu a Phony." *New York Times* (August 24, 1985): 4.

"Falwell Political Funds Shifted to Religious Arms." *New York Times* (August 23, 1987): 27.

Farber, Stephen. "Bringing Mandela to Television." *New York Times* (September 19, 1987): 54.

Feder, Barnaby. "The Business of Earth Day." *New York Times* (November 12, 1989): F4.

Fefferman, Dan. "The First Annual National AFC Board of Governors Meeting." *American Freedom Journal* (December 1988/January 1989): 5–7.

Fineman, Howard. "The Pat Robertson Effect." *Newsweek* (September 28, 1987): 29.

Footlick, Jerrold. "What Happened to the Family?" *Newsweek* (Winter/Spring 1990): 14–34.

Fowler, Robert Booth. *Religion and Politics in America.* Metuchen, N.J.: Scarecrow, 1985.

Gailey, Phil. "Robertson Used Journalist to Get Data for Libel Suit on War Record." *New York Times* (April 2, 1987): 25.

Gallup, George H. *The Gallup Poll: 1980 & 1981.* Wilmington, Del.: Scholarly Resources, 1981–1982.

———. "Religion in America 1984." *The Gallup Report* 22 (March 1984): 1–20.

Gerth, Jeff. "Robertson and Confidentiality." *New York Times* (March 19, 1987): 24.

———. "Tax Data of Pat Robertson Groups are Questioned." *New York Times* (December 10, 1986): 18.

Gipson, Melinda. "Hatfield Hits Fear Tactics in Fundraising." *Washington Star* (May 2, 1981): 8.

Glaser, Barney, and Anselm Strauss. *The Discovery of Grounded Theory: Strategies for Qualitative Research.* New York: Aldine, 1967.

Godwin, R. Kenneth. *One Billion Dollars of Influence.* Chatham, N.J.: Chatham House, 1988.

Golden, Daniel. "Who, What Will Follow Reagan?" *Boston Globe* (April 12, 1987): 22.

Green, Mark. *Who Runs Congress?* 4th ed. New York: Dell Publishing, 1984.

Grossman, Joel B., and Richard S. Wells. *Constitutional Law & Judicial Policymaking.* 2nd ed. New York: John Wiley & Sons, 1980.

Gurwitt, Rob. "1986 Elections Generate GOP Power Struggle." *Congressional Quarterly Weekly Report* (April 12, 1986): 802–7.

Guth, James L. "The Politics of the Christian Right." In *Interest Group Politics,* edited by Allan J. Cigler and Burdett A. Loomis, 60–83. Washington, D.C.: CQ Press, 1983.

———. "Southern Baptist Clergy: Vanguard of the Christian Right?" In *The New Christian Right,* edited by Robert C. Liebman and Robert Wuthnow, 117–30. New York: Aldine, 1983.

Guth, James L., and John C. Green. "Faith and Politics: Religion and Ideology Among Political Contributors." *American Politics Quarterly* 14 (1986): 186–200.

———. "The Moralizing Minority: Christian Right Support Among Political Contributors." *Social Science Quarterly* 68 (1987): 598–610.

Hadden, Jeffrey K., and Anson Shupe. *Televangelism: Power & Politics on God's Frontier.* New York: Henry Holt, 1988.

Hadden, Jeffrey K., Anson Shupe, James Hawdon, and Kenneth Martin. "Why Jerry Falwell Killed the Moral Majority." In *The God Pumpers,* edited by Marshall Fishwick and Ray B. Browne, 101–15. Bowling Green, Ohio: Bowling Green State University Popular Press, 1987.

Hadden, Jeffrey K., and Charles E. Swann. *Prime Time Preachers.* Reading, Mass.: Addison-Wesley, 1981.

Hammond, Philip. "Another Great Awakening?" In *The New Christian Right,* edited by Robert C. Liebman and Robert Wuthnow, 207–23. New York: Aldine, 1983.

Harvey, Chris. "GOP Right is Angry—but not Mutinous." *Washington Times* (July 30, 1990): 3.

Hertzke, Allen D. "Populist Echoes of Discontent." Paper delivered at the Annual Meeting of the American Political Science Association, San Francisco, California, September 1990.

———. *Representing God in Washington.* Knoxville: University of Tennessee Press, 1988.

Hertzke, Allen D., and Mary K. Scribner. "The Politics of Federal Day Care." Paper delivered at Annual Meeting of the American Political Science Association, Atlanta, Georgia, September 1989.

Himmelstein, Jerome L. "The New Right." In *The New Christian Right,* edited by Robert C. Liebman and Robert Wuthnow, 13–30. New York: Aldine, 1983.

Himmelstein, Jerome L., and James A. McRae, Jr. "Social Conservatism, New Republicanism and the 1980 Election." *Public Opinion Quarterly* 48 (1984): 592–605.

Hobbes, Thomas. *Leviathan.* Indianapolis: Bobbs-Merrill, 1958.

Hofrenning, Daniel. "The Agenda Setting Strategies of Religious Interest Groups." Paper delivered at the Annual Meeting of the American Political Science Association, Atlanta, Georgia, September 1989.

Holloway, Harry, and John George. *Public Opinion.* New York: St. Martin's, 1979.

Hunter, James Davidson. "Operationalizing Evangelicalism: A Review, Critique & Proposal." *Sociological Analysis* 65 (1982): 363–72.

Hutcheson, Richard G., Jr. *God in the White House.* New York: Macmillan, 1988.

Hutcheson, Rob. "Arts Endowment Warned to Stop Funding Dirty Pictures." *Washington Times* (June 14, 1989): 5.

Isikoff, Michael. "Moon Group Financing Anti-Communist Lobby." *Washington Post* (September 14, 1984): 1.

"Jackson Attacks Falwell Trip." *New York Times (*August 22, 1985): 10.

Jacobson, Gary. *Money in Congressional Elections.* New Haven, Conn.: Yale University Press, 1980.

Jacoby, Tamar. "Is it Time to Take Pat Seriously: The Invisible Army." *Time* (January 4, 1988): 21.

Janis, Irving L. *Victims of Groupthink.* Boston: Houghton Mifflin, 1972.

Jarmin, Gary. "What Bush's Victory Means to America." *American Freedom Journal* (December 1988/January 1989): 1–3.

Jelen, Ted G. "The Effects of Religious Separatism on White Protestants in the 1984 Presidential Election." *Sociological Analysis* 48 (1987): 30–45.

Jennings, Peter, and David Brinkley. *The 1988 Vote.* New York: Capital Cities/ABC News, 1989.

Johnson, Steven D., and Joseph B. Tamney. "The Christian Right and the 1980 Presidential Election." *Journal for the Scientific Study of Religion* 21 (1982): 123–31.

Jorstad, Erling. *The Politics of Moralism.* Minneapolis: Augsburg, 1981.

Judis, John B. "Rev. Moon's Rising Political Influence." *U.S. News & World Report* (March 27, 1989): 27.

Keller, Bill. "Evangelical Conservatives Move From Pews to Polls, But Can They Sway Congress?" *Congressional Quarterly Weekly Report* (September 6, 1980): 2627–34.

Kellstedt, Lyman A. "The Meaning and Measurement of Evangelicalism." In *Religion and Political Behavior in the United States,* edited by Ted. G. Jelen, 3–21. New York: Praeger, 1989.

Kellstedt, Lyman A., and Mark A. Noll. "Religion, Voting for President, and Party Identification, 1948–1984." In *Religion and American Politics,* edited by Mark A. Noll, 355–79. New York: Oxford University Press, 1990.

Kellstedt, Lyman A., Paul Kellstedt, and Corwin Smidt. "Evangelical and Mainline Protestants in the 1988 Presidential Election." Paper delivered at the Annual Meeting of the Political Science Association, San Francisco, California, September 1990.

King, Gary, and Lyn Ragsdale. *The Elusive Executive.* Washington, D.C.: CQ Press, 1988.

King, Wayne. "Robertson Plans an Ad Campaign to Enhance TV Minister's Image." *New York Times* (September 7, 1987): 7.

———. "Robertson, Returning to Brooklyn Home, Enters Race." *New York Times* (October 2, 1987): 16.

———. "Swaggart Says He Has Sinned; Will Step Down." *New York Times* (February 22, 1988): 1.

———. "Wild Oats, Robertson Says of Late Marriage." *New York Times* (October 9, 1987): 22.

Kingdon, John. *Agendas, Alternatives and Public Policies.* Boston: Little, Brown & Co., 1984.

Kirschten, Dick. "Putting the Social Issues on Hold: Can Reagan Get Away With It?" *National Journal* (October 10, 1981): 1810–15.

———. "Reagan Looks to Religious Leaders for Continuing Support in 1984." *National Journal* (August 20, 1983): 1727–31.

Knight-Ridder Newspapers. "Falwell Quitting as President of Moral Majority." *Bangor Daily News* (November 4, 1987): 16.

———. "Robertson Blasts Journalists for Exposing Family Skeleton." *Bangor Daily News* (October 9, 1987): 17.

Kowet, Don. "The Friends of Elizabeth Morgan." *Washington Times* (October 17, 1989): E10.

Lambro, Donald. "Conservative Charts Domestic Path for Movement." *Washington Times* (April 6, 1990): 7.

Langenbach, Lisa. "Evangelical Elites and Political Action: The Pat Robertson Presidential Candidacy." Paper delivered at Annual Meeting of the American Political Science Association, Washington, D.C., September 1988.

Latus, Margaret Ann. "Ideological PACs and Political Action." In *The New Christian Right,* edited by Robert C. Liebman and Robert Wuthnow, 75–99. New York: Aldine, 1983.

Lawton, Kim. "Evangelicals Still Not Sure About Bush." *Christianity Today* (January 15, 1990): 44.

———. "Unification Church Ties Haunt New Coalition." *Christianity Today* (February 5, 1988): 46.

"Leaders of the Christian Right Announce Their Next Step." *Christianity Today* (December 13, 1985): 65.

Lewis, Neil A. "Bush Picking the Kind of Judges Reagan Favored." *New York Times* (April 10, 1990): 1.

Liebman, Robert C. "Mobilizing the Moral Majority." In *The New Christian Right,* edited by Robert C. Liebman and Robert Wuthnow, 49–73. New York: Aldine, 1983.

Lienesch, Michael. "Christian Conservatism as a Political Movement." *Political Science Quarterly* 97 (1982): 403–25.

Lipset, Seymour Martin, and Earl Rabb. "The Election and the Evangelicals." *Commentary* (March 1981): 25–31.

Locke, John. *Two Treatises of Government.* New York: Cambridge, 1960.

Lorentzen, Louise. "Evangelical Life Style Concerns Expressed in Political Action." *Sociological Analysis* 41 (1980): 144–54.

Lowi, Theodore J. *The End of Liberalism.* 2nd ed. New York: W. W. Norton, 1979.

McGrory, Mary. "Falwell by any Other Name." *Washington Post* (January 7, 1986): 2.

McIntyre, Thomas J. *The Fear Brokers.* Boston: Beacon Press, 1979.

McNair, Jean. "Robertson Lays off 470, Blames TV Ministry Scandals." *Boston Globe* (6 June 1987): 1.

Mann, James. "Old Time Religion on the Offensive." *U.S. News & World Report* (April 7, 1980): 40–42.

Mann, James, and Sarah Peterson. "Preachers in Politics." *U.S. News & World Report* (September 15, 1980): 24–26.

Mansbridge, Jane J. *Why We Lost the ERA.* Chicago: University of Chicago Press, 1986.

Martz, Larry. "Day of the Preachers." *Newsweek* (March 7, 1988): 44–46.

Mayer, Allan. "A Tide of Born Again." *Newsweek* (September 15, 1980): 28ff.

Mayhew, David. *Congress: The Electoral Connection.* New Haven, Conn.: Yale University Press, 1974.

Menendez, Albert J. "Religious Lobbies." *Liberty* 77 (March/April 1982): 2ff.

Michels, Robert. *Political Parties.* Glencoe, Ill.: Free Press, 1915.

Miller, Arthur H., and Martin P. Wattenberg. "Politics From the Pulpit." *Public Opinion Quarterly* 48 (1984): 301–17.

Miller, Mark. "Goodbye to All That." *Newsweek* (November 16, 1987): 10.

Moen, Matthew C. *The Christian Right and Congress.* Tuscaloosa: University of Alabama Press, 1989.

———. "The Christian Right in the United States." In *The Religious Challenge to the State,* edited by Matthew C. Moen and Lowell S. Gustafson. Philadelphia: Temple University Press, 1992.

———. "The New Christian Right and the Legislative Agenda: 1981–1984." Paper delivered at Annual Meeting of the Southwestern Political Science Association, Houston, March 1985.

———. "The Political Agenda of Ronald Reagan." *Presidential Studies Quarterly* XVIII (1988): 775–85.

———. "The Political Transformation of the Christian Right." Paper delivered at Annual Meeting of the American Political Science Association, San Francisco, California, September 1990.

———. "The Resurrection of the Christian Right." *Church & State* (February 1990): 19–20.

———. "Ronald Reagan and the Social Issues." *Social Science Journal* 27 (1990): 199–207.

———. "Status Politics and the Political Agenda of the Christian Right." *Sociological Quarterly* 29 (1988): 23–31.

Mohr, Henry. "End Ollie's Persecution Now, Mr. President." *American Freedom Journal* (December 1988/January 1989): 5–7.

Moore, Helen, and Hugh Whitt. "Multiple Dimensions of the Moral Majority Platform." *Sociological Quarterly* 27 (1986): 423–39.

Morken, Hubert. "Public Secondary Education: Equal Access and the Clash Over Student Religious Expression." Paper delivered at Annual Meeting of the American Political Science Association, Atlanta, Georgia, September 1989.

———. "Religious Lobbying at the State Level: Case Studies in a Continuing Role for the New Religious Right." Paper delivered at Annual Meeting of the American Political Science Association, San Francisco, California, September 1990.

Mueller, John E. "Presidential Popularity from Truman to Johnson." *American Political Science Review* 64 (1970): 18–34.

Murray, Frank, and George Archibald. "Bush Link to Right is Fired." *Washington Times* (August 2, 1990): 1.

"Name That Majority." *New York Times* (January 8, 1986): 22.

Neuhaus, Richard John. *The Naked Public Square.* 2nd ed. Grand Rapids, Mich.: William B. Eerdman's, 1984.

Nordheimer, Jon. "Bundy is Put to Death in Florida After Admitting Trail of Killings." *New York Times* (January 25, 1989): 1.

"North Says Criminal Charges Against Him Are an Honor." *New York Times* (May 3, 1988): B7.

Ogintz, Eileen. "Evangelists Seek Political Clout." *Chicago Tribune* (January 13, 1980): 5.

Oldfield, Duane. "The Christian Right and State Republican Parties." Paper delivered at Annual Meeting of the American Political Science Association, San Francisco, California, September 1990.

Ornstein, Norman J., Thomas E. Mann, and Michael J. Malbin. *Vital Statistics on Congress.* Washington, D.C.: CQ Press, 1987.

Ostling, Richard N. "TV's Unholy Row." *Time* (April 6, 1987): 60–67.

Ott, J. Steven. *The Organizational Culture Perspective.* Pacific Grove, Calif.: Brooks/Cole, 1989.

Palen, Kathy. "Southern Baptist Rejects Cultural Conservatism." *Baptist Press* news release, January 26, 1989.

"Partisan Voting Averages Increased in 97th Congress." *Congressional Quarterly Almanac* 37 (Washington, D.C.: Congressional Quarterly, 1982): 32–33c.

Pasley, Jeffrey L. "Paper Pushers." *New Republic* (December 1, 1986): 24–25.

Patterson, Thomas, and Robert McClure. *The Unseeing Eye*. New York: G. P. Putnum's Sons, 1976.

Pear, Robert. "Falwell Denounces Tutu as a Phony." *New York Times* (August 22, 1985): 10.

———. "Falwell Forming Group to Look at Broad Issues." *New York Times* (January 4, 1986): 5.

"President Reagan's Inaugural Address." *Congressional Quarterly Weekly Report* (January 24, 1981): 186–88.

Price, Joyce. "Family Group Sees 1990s as Perilous." *Washington Times* (December 15, 1989): 5.

———. "NEA Chief Wavers on Mapplethorpe." *Washington Times* (April 27, 1990): 1.

Pruden, Wesley. "A Growing Trade in Victimhood." *Washington Times* (June 15, 1990): 4.

Reagan, Ronald. "Remarks at the Annual Convention of Concerned Women for America." *Public Papers of the President* 2 (Washington, D.C.: Government Printing Office, 1989), 1079–82.

Reichley, A. James. *Religion in American Public Life*. Washington, D.C.: Brookings Institution, 1985.

"Religious Right Goes for Bigger Game." *U.S. News & World Report* (November 17, 1980): 42.

"Religious Right Talks Politics." *Guardian* (September 3, 1980): 4.

Rieselbach, Leroy. *Congressional Reform*. Washington, D.C.: CQ Press, 1986.

Riker, William H. "Heresthetic and Rhetoric in the Spatial Model." Paper presented at APSA/Spoor Dialogues on Political Leadership, Dartmouth College, July 21, 1988.

Roberts, James. "The Christian Right: New Force in American Politics." *Human Events* (November 8, 1980): 10.

"Robertson Group Vows to Fight for Sectarian Sex Ed." *Church & State* (June 1990): 14.

Rosenbaum, David E. "Robertson Ends Active Campaigning." *New York Times* (April 7, 1988): D23.

Rosenfeld, Seth. "Coalition Files Suit to Remove Cross From Public Park." *San Francisco Examiner*. Reprinted in *Washington Times* (July 2, 1990): 6.

Royko, Mike. "Victim Growth Industry." *Washington Times* (June 12, 1990): F3.

Sahliyeh, Emile, ed. *Religious Resurgence and Politics in the Contemporary World*. Albany: State University of New York Press, 1990.

Salholz, Eloise. "Voting in Curbs and Confusion." *Newsweek* (July 17, 1989): 16–20.

Sawyer, Kathy, and Robert Keiser. "Evangelicals Flock to GOP Standard Feeling They Have a Friend in Reagan." *Washington Post* (July 10, 1980): 5.

Schlozman, Kay Lehman, and John T. Tierney. *Organized Interests and American Democracy*. New York: Harper & Row, 1986.

Scully, Matthew. "Right Wing and a Prayer—Still Alive and Kicking." *Washington Times* (November 8, 1989): E1.

Secret, Philip, James Johnson, and Susan Welch. "Racial Differences in Attitudes Toward the Supreme Court's Decision on Prayer in the Public Schools." *Social Science Quarterly* 67 (1986): 877–86.

Shribman, David. "Going Mainstream: Religious Right Drops High-Profile Tactics, Works on Local Level." *Wall Street Journal* (September 26, 1989): 18.

Shupe, Anson. "The Christian Reconstructionists." *The Christian Century* (October 4, 1989): 880–82.

———. "Sun Myung Moon's American Disappointment." *The Christian Century* (August 22–29, 1990): 764–66.

Shupe, Anson, and John Heinerman. "Mormonism and the New Christian Right: An Emerging Coalition?" *Review of Religious Research* 27 (December 1985): 146–57.

Shupe, Anson, and William Stacey. "The Moral Majority Constituency." In *The New Christian Right,* edited by Robert C. Liebman and Robert Wuthnow, 103–16. New York: Aldine, 1983.

Sigelman, Lee, Clyde Wilcox, and Emmett H. Buell, Jr. "An Unchanging Minority: Popular Support for the Moral Majority, 1980 and 1984." *Social Science Quarterly* 68 (1987): 876–84.

Simpson, John H. "Moral Issues and Status Politics." In *The New Christian Right,* edited by Robert C. Liebman and Robert Wuthnow, 187–205. New York: Aldine, 1983.

Sinclair, Barbara. "Agenda, Policy, and Alignment Changes From Coolidge to Reagan." In *Congress Reconsidered,* 3rd ed., edited by Lawrence Dodd and Bruce Oppenheimer, 291–314. Washington, D.C.: CQ Press, 1985.

Smidt, Corwin. "Born Again Politics." In *Religion and Politics in the South,* edited by Tod A. Baker, Robert P. Steed, and Laurence W. Moreland, 27–56. New York: Praeger, 1983.

———. "Evangelicals and the 1984 Election." *American Politics Quarterly* 15 (1987): 419–44.

———. "Evangelicals Versus Fundamentalists: An Analysis of the Political Characteristics and Importance of Two Major Religious Movements Within American Politics." Paper delivered at Annual Meeting of the Midwest Political Science Association, Chicago, Illinois, April 1983.

———. "Identifying Evangelical Respondents." In *Religion and Political Behavior in the United States,* edited by Ted G. Jelen, 23–43. New York: Praeger, 1989.

———. "Religion and the 1988 Elections." Precis of roundtable discussion at Annual Meeting of The American Political Science Association, Washington, D.C., September 1988.

"South Africa Sanctions." *Congressional Quarterly Almanac* 41 (Washington, D.C.: Congressional Quarterly, 1986): 28–30D.

Sowell, Thomas. "Buzzword Brain Drain." *Washington Times* (July 31, 1990): G3.

Spring, Beth. "Magazine Says Tim LaHaye Received Help From Unification Church." *Christianity Today* (January 17, 1986): 40–41.

———. "Some Christian Leaders Want Further Political Activism." *Christianity Today* (November 9, 1984): 46.

Stanley, Harold W., and Richard G. Niemi. *Vital Statistics on Congress.* Washington, D.C.: CQ Press, 1988.

"Status of Abortion Laws." *Congressional Quarterly Weekly Report* (July 8, 1989): 1699.

Steinfels, Peter. "Moral Majority to Dissolve; Says Mission Accomplished." *New York Times* (June 12, 1989): 14.

Stepp, Laura Sessions. "Falwell Says Moral Majority to be Dissolved." *Washington Post* (June 12, 1989): 11.

Strauss, Leo. *Natural Right and History.* Chicago: University of Chicago Press, 1953.

Strout, Richard. "Church-State Skirmishes in Sight?" *Christian Science Monitor* (November 10, 1980): 3.

Sweeney, Joan. "Evangelicals Seeking to Establish Political Force." *Los Angeles Times* (May 19, 1980): 21.

Thomas, Cal. "Faith, Credibility, and the Real Thing." *Washington Times* (October 12, 1989): F1.

"Tim LaHaye Will Move to Washington to Promote Christian Political Activity." *Christianity Today* (December 14, 1984): 37.

Tolchin, Martin. "Reagan's Power to Name Judiciary Going Lame." *New York Times.* Reprinted in the *Maine Sunday Telegram* (December 6, 1987): 20.

Tuttle, Beth, Carol Blum, Matthew Freeman, and Mary Conway. "Who's Who in the Family Forum?" (June 29, 1988). Document produced by People for the American Way.

"Unification Church and the Subjugation of America." *Capital Research Center* (November 1988): 1–4.

U.S. Congress, Senate Committee on the Judiciary, Subcommittee on Separation of Powers. *Hearings on the Human Life Bill* (S. 158). 97th Cong., 1st sess., 1981.

Vecsey, George. "Militant Television Preachers Try to Weld Fundamentalist Christians' Political Power." *New York Times* (January 21, 1980): A21.

Viguerie, Richard. *The New Right.* Falls Church, Va.: Viguerie, 1981.

Wald, Kenneth D. *Religion and Politics in the United States.* New York: St. Martin's, 1987.

Waldman, Steven. "A Case of Creeping Irrelevance." *Newsweek* (March 14, 1988): 20.

Walker, Jack L. "The Origins and Maintenance of Interest Groups in America." *American Political Science Review* 77 (1983): 390–406.

Weaver, Carolyn. "Unholy Alliance." *Mother Jones* (January 1986): 14ff.

Weyrich, Dawn. "Prayer Allowed After School." *Washington Times* (June 5, 1990): 11.

Wilcox, Clyde. "The Christian Right in Twentieth Century America." *The Review of Politics* 23 (1988): 659–81.

———. "Evangelicals and Fundamentalists in the New Christian Right." *Journal for the Scientific Study of Religion* 25 (1986): 355–63.

———. "Fundamentalists and Politics: An Analysis of the Effects of Differing Operational Definitions." *Journal of Politics* 48 (1986): 1041–51.

———. "Lingering Support for the Christian Right." Paper delivered at Annual Meeting of the Midwest Political Science Association, Chicago, April 1990.

———. "Popular Support for the Moral Majority in 1980: A Second Look." *Social Science Quarterly* 68 (1987): 157–66.

Wills, Garry. "Save the Babies." *Time* (May 1, 1989): 26–28.

Witham, Larry. "Falwell Bids Adieu to Moral Majority." *Washington Times* (August 29, 1989): B2.

———. "FCC Chief Welcomes Participation of Nation's Religious Broadcasters." *Washington Times* (February 2, 1990): B5.

———. "LeHaye (sic) Continues Ministry on Local Level." *Washington Times* (October 20, 1989): F5.

Woodward, Kenneth L., and Eleanor Clift. "Playing Politics at Church." *Newsweek* (July 9, 1984): 52.

Wuthnow, Robert. "The Political Rebirth of American Evangelicals." In *The New Christian Right,* edited by Robert C. Liebman and Robert Wuthnow, 167–85. New York: Aldine, 1983.

Zald, Mayer, and Roberta Ash. "Social Movement Organizations: Growth, Decay, and Change." *Social Forces* 44 (1966): 327–41.

Zwier, Robert. "The New Christian Right and the 1980 Elections." In *New Christian Politics,* edited by David G. Bromley and Anson Shupe, 172–94. Macon, Ga.: Mercer University Press, 1984.

Index

About the Author

Matthew C. Moen is Associate Professor of Political Science at the University of Maine. He received his bachelor's degree from Augustana College and his doctorate through the Carl Albert Center at the University of Oklahoma. His other publications include *The Christian Right and Congress* (1989), *The Religious Challenge to the State* (1992), and numerous journal articles.